TO HELL AND BACK

Other Books by the Author

Beyond Death's Door
(Bantam Books, Thomas Nelson Publishers)

Before Death Comes
(Thomas Nelson Publishers)

Life Wish
(Thomas Nelson Publishers)

TO HELL AND BACK

LIFE AFTER DEATH – STARTLING NEW EVIDENCE

AUTHOR OF *BEYOND DEATH'S DOOR*

MAURICE S. RAWLINGS, M.D.

Publishers Since 1798

Thomas Nelson Publishers
Nashville

Published in Nashville, Tennessee, by Thomas Nelson, Inc., Publishers, and distributed in Canada by Word Communications, Ltd., Richmond, British Columbia, and in the United Kingdom by Word (UK), Ltd., Milton Keynes, England.

Unless otherwise noted, Scripture quotations are from the NEW KING JAMES VERSION of the Bible. Copyright © 1979, 1980, 1982, Thomas Nelson, Inc., Publishers.

Scripture quotations noted TLB are from *The Living Bible* (Wheaton, Illinois: Tyndale House Publishers, 1971) and are used by permission.

Scripture quotations noted NIV are taken from the HOLY BIBLE, NEW INTERNATIONAL VERSION®. Copyright © 1973, 1978, 1984 by International Bible Society. Used by permission of Zondervan Bible Publishing House. All rights reserved.

The "NIV" and "New International Version" trademarks are registered in the United States Patent and Trademark Office by International Bible Society. Use of either trademark requires the permission of International Bible Society.

Scripture quotations noted KJV are from The Holy Bible, KING JAMES VERSION.

Scripture quotations noted RSV are from the REVISED STANDARD VERSION of the Bible. Copyright © 1946, 1952, 1971, 1973 by the Division of Christian Education of the National Council of Churches of Christ in the U.S.A. Used by permission.

Scripture quotations noted NASB are from THE NEW AMERICAN STANDARD BIBLE, Copyright © 1960, 1962, 1963, 1968, 1971, 1972, 1973, 1975, 1977 by The Lockman Foundation and are used by permission.

Library of Congress Cataloging-in-Publication Data

Rawlings, Maurice.
    To hell and back : life after death—startling new evidence / Maurice S. Rawlings.
      p.   cm.
    Includes bibliographical references.
    ISBN 0-8407-6758-7 (pbk.)
    1. Near-death experiences—Religious aspects—Christianity. 2. Hell—Christianity. I. Title.
    BT836.2.R   1993
    236′.1—dc20   93-5186
                                                                 CIP

Printed in the United States of America
1 2 3 4 5 6 7 — 99 98 97 96 95 94 93

DEDICATION

To the courage of a friend, Mary Schum Cosby,
who declined recommended abortion, knowing that
carrying her only child near term could spread an
early cancer of the breast.

CONTENTS

ACKNOWLEDGMENTS

My gratitude extends to many people and many libraries, especially to the little packed closet of author John Weldon who, with John Ankerberg of TV fame, and authors Dave Hunt and Tal Brooke, contributed much to the background information. Additional theological expertise emerged from Reverends Ed Byrd, Matthew McGowan, and Ben Haden, assisted by thoughts from Spencer McCallie, Jr., and Kay Arthur of Precept Ministries.

Instigation, prodding, and tireless encouragement came from author and publisher David Manuel as we pattered bare feet far, far out into the ebb tide of Cape Cod's sunset, pondering my literary deficiencies. Meanwhile, Jim Cole corrected my peculiar talent for jamming computers, and Tat Anderson, editor of our local newspaper, kindly counseled me "to never leave it dry—always tell a story."

My special thanks to Demetria Kalodimos, of WSMV-TV out of Nashville, who first televised "A Glimpse of Glory." This book is a continuation of that story as well as a sequel to *Beyond Death's Door* written several years ago. Enthusiastic support came from David Mainse, of Canada's immense Crossroads TV Productions out of Burlington, and encouragement from Thomas Nelson's editors who saw a message in the manuscript.

Correcting my typing errors were two granddaughters, Evie Rawlings and Joy Rawlings, while my tolerant wife waited patiently in the wings.

PREFACE

He said, "Everyone knows he went to hell!"

I said, "But the preacher says he's on his way to heaven!"

Funerals are strange things, but death is stranger still. Wouldn't it be an honor to have just a momentary glimpse into the mysterious life beyond? At first thought an impossibility, but perhaps not so impossible in the days of modern resuscitation, where eight to eleven million Americans have already reported near-death experiences, the majority strangely visualizing a veritable glimpse of glory.[1]

The typical description involves a beautiful light at the end of a very dark tunnel. Many Christians were convinced that the figure of light they encountered was Jesus because they saw him on a cross, the exuberant experience forever changing their lives. Some others perceived a possible heaven conforming to their own particular faith. Remarkably, others saw the same tunnel and the apparent light turn into a horrible ring of fire, the light becoming inexplicably evil, convincing them that they had been to hell and back, an unheralded failure, the ultimate bane of existence.

Of the numerous authors investigating near-death experiences, almost none of them report negative or unpleasant cases. Instead, they insist that all cases are positive and glorious, thus promoting the confident assumption that heaven's gates are open wide for everyone who dies regardless of religion or belief.

The resulting conclusions of these authors seem clear. No longer do these investigators consider death as oblivion or the end of it all. And none of them seem to believe in a place called hell. Because they see only the "good" experiences for the next life—that all near-death experiences report a common glimpse of glory—the birth of a new religion and philosophy has emerged. Some of them call it the "Omega Point," since near-death observations in their experiences indicate that heaven is a free ride for everyone who dies, and this becomes the glorious counselling now given at the bedside of many dying patients.

Some conclude that the popular reincarnation faiths proclaimed by various Shirley MacLainers are not sustained by the persistent and repeated appearance of glory awaiting one and all, suggesting that karma and repeated rebirths (where everyone is essentially given chance after chance until they finally get it right) are no longer supported by the evidence, since the evidence indicates that they "got it right" the first time.

The purpose of this book is simply to expose the negative cases, those secreted, embarrassing cases found primarily during resuscitative procedures, during the heat of the battle for survival, the time when nothing is concealed, the time when the psychologists and psychiatrists who write most of the books on the subject are absent from the scene.

If negative cases can be readily demonstrated, cases disturbing enough to permanently change lives, then a place like hell would seem reasonable. And if hell is possible, then it may not be safe to die. And if it may not be safe to die, then we better look further into the negative reports of those who found glimpses *other* than glory beyond death's door before we make our own decisions.

To accomplish this, we shall travel through the familiar "out-of-the-body experiences" (OBEs) and beyond the numerous "near-death experiences" (NDEs), examining those cases where extreme circumstances may literally have scared the hell out of the individual involved, without any loss of consciousness or heartbeat at all. We will focus primarily upon "flatliners" who were medically retrieved from actual clinical death and describe the glimpses they experienced after prolonged periods of absent heartbeat, absent breathing, and absent vital functions. These are the cases that report more than a glimpse—usually a full sequence of analytical events—many of them occurring in very unpleasant environments.

We shall also emphasize the "Bell Curve" invariance of typical population studies, the curve consistently exhibiting positive events on one end and negative events on the other, neither to the exclusion of the other. We will progressively explore both positive and negative events in dream states (most of us have experienced nightmares, for instance) and proceed to display the same bipolar distribution in drug states, altered states of consciousness, deathbed experiences, and, not surprisingly, in many near-death experiences, particularly in the resuscitated events where the brush with death nears a biological permanency.

If negative events repeatedly occur in all of the above circumstances, then why aren't they reported? I am sure you will find the various reasons quite interesting.

*I have opened a door to you
that no one can shut.*

—Revelation 3:8 (TLB)

1

GLIMPSES
INTO THE
AFTERLIFE

The face was bloated and blue when the dead body arrived, eyes bulging, tongue protruding between swollen lips. Way too late for Heimlich maneuvers or CPR. I found an unchewed piece of steak in the windpipe. Probably suffocation from an obstructed airway, but an unwitnessed departure of life at age thirty-four always requires an autopsy. We called the pathologist and cut the body open.

What is this death we see every day? The old cliche applies, I suppose—the body dies when the spirit leaves it. But what really happens at death? One moment we're animated and moving about. The next moment nothing, and the animation's gone. But gone where? I've never seen a spirit hanging around a dead body, have you? Yet all the ministers give us this ashes-to-ashes routine about how the victim's spirit has moved on to see his heavenly glory, but they never seem to mention hell. Have you ever heard of a hell-funeral?

For years I have pronounced bodies dead, never quite believing this spirit business. Until one day, when modern methods were developed to retrieve some of these patients from clinical death, along came these weird reports about some returnees who excitedly proclaimed "a glimpse of glory." None of the cases volunteered a glimpse of hell—unless someone was there to record it.

NEARLY A GLIMPSE

Was I personally afraid of dying? Simply put, yes, I was.

I came very close one night, flying back in the bitter cold, unaware of the hidden dangers we carried. Correcting the gyro compass and throttling the motors into harmony, I looked over to Charlie. "In a few minutes you won't be able to tell what's up and what's down," I yelled over the noise. "No moon or stars for guidance since the cloud cover settled in after we left Indianapolis."

I looked for ground lights. "Hold on a minute and we'll take a look below."

The right wing of the sleek, twin-engined Aztec immediately banked vertically to the ground, paralleling the freeway lights which linked the vast city below. It was unusually beautiful in the dwindling twilight. Car beams shimmered like streams of upside-down stars, winking in a huge winding arc, swallowed by an icy void as the wing came up.

Banging the instrument panel finally got the old gasoline heater started, something we had been trying to do ever since the sun submerged in a distant lake of clouds about an hour ago. Fortunately no ignition explosion occurred this time. Only the background rattle of old cowl flaps.

> **Resuscitation is something that affords a . . . peek into one's own future —perhaps a glimpse of glory, a glimpse of hell, or no glimpse at all.**

Like a frozen hell, the bitter cold had eerily found its way into the pink haze of the cockpit, the black void crouching outside like the shroud of a living enemy.

"You see those lights down there, Charlie?" I said after righting the Aztec. "Well, that's exactly where you'd want to land if I had the heart attack you proposed." I grinned, easing long legs off the rudder pedals. "But I think the next airport would really be a better choice."

"And just what would you suggest I do if that happens?" Charlie McDonald demanded, his face set off from the darkness by the halo of red panel lights. Charlie looked to be about forty, his dark suit and tie all rumpled under the harness straps. The profile appeared sharp, the chin soft, the hair black, and the rest of him lost in shadow. Charlie was one of three heart specialists in our group of nine physicians at the Diagnostic Center in Chattanooga, Tennessee. He and I were returning from a meeting in Indianapolis.

Throttling back the motors reduced the noise level. "It's simple," I said. "Flight control would give you a compass heading to the nearest airport. About thirty miles out, pull both throttles back and lift the nose to reduce air speed to about 100 miles per hour. After that, adjust the throttle to regulate altitude and descent, and use your feet on the rudders to keep the nose pointed at the runway."

Charlie lifted his hands in exasperation. "But suppose you're out of it? Suppose you're clinically dead? How do you propose I do all this with one hand on the wheel while resuscitating you with the other?"

"Oh," I said peering over the windshield, "just land down there on the freeway with one hand while you hit me on the chest with the other to keep the heart contracting. You can wait to do proper CPR on the ground." I smiled confidently, and wondered if he could see my expression in the dim light.

Charlie finally relaxed and began to smile, so I said, "Mouth-to-mouth breathing might be a little much in the air—they say bad breath can separate the best of friends." Charlie looked absolutely disgusted, holding his head in his hands for a long while, as I spent time thinking back on events from earlier that morning.

Jogging before daylight, I did have trouble keeping up with Charlie. For the prior two days I was becoming easily winded and fatigued. That in itself should have been some kind of warning, because these symptoms were common predecessors of heart attack. Two days later, the bottom dropped out.

Although I was quite aware that heart attacks and hardened arteries kill more people than all other diseases put together, I assumed it would never happen to me. Charlie proved to be right about the heart attack—and what a mess it would have made in the plane.

But, as we shall see, resuscitation is something that affords a new life and often a peek into one's own future—perhaps a glimpse of glory, a glimpse of hell, or no glimpse at all. By reversing the death process, resuscitation can become a window to the soul, a mirror to one's own destiny, and sometimes offer an opportunity to modify the outcome (see the Appendix for CPR information).

HOW THE GLIMPSE OCCURRED

Two days later, the evening of October 18, 1980, there was a peculiar heaviness in my chest, an inexplicable weight, more like indigestion than anything else. It compressed the breastbone, occasionally radiating to the jaws and upper arms, intermittent at first, then relentless.

Foolishly, I took some bicarb of soda for "chest gas" and drove myself to the hospital, not remembering that 50 percent of heart attack victims never make it to the hospital alive.

By the time I reached the hospital, my heartbeat was skipping, I was sweating and clammy with the overwhelming and ruthless pain. Quickly, the nurse placed me onto a stretcher, flicked a nitroglycerine pill under my tongue, and raced me into the coronary care unit where an EKG monitor was attached, oxygen started, and a solution of rhythm-calming Lidocaine dripped into my vein.

By 11 P.M. the pain was severe and no longer controlled by morphine. Like everyone else, I found myself calling on God. And I didn't try to keep it quiet. Who cares when you're hurting?

By midnight my pain still had not improved. An elephant was standing on my chest. IV Morphine and Demerol were like water in their feeble attempt to comfort me.

"Cure me or kill me," I prayed out loud, tears of agony falling like rain from my cheeks. "Please, God, just stop the pain. Only you can spell relief!" And that perhaps was the most profound statement I've ever made.

I squinted up at the monitor and a block in the normal conduction of the heartbeat had appeared from nowhere, bursts of crazy beats also there. My forty years as a cardiologist told me this was a typical setting for sudden death. One moment here, the next moment gone. I tried to think of the resuscitated patients who insisted that the moment of death was painless; about how they

hated it when we brought them back into the world of pain—
except those who were having a hellish time in the after-life. No
glimpse of glory there. I was beginning to look for that heavenly
moment.

It was daylight when I came around, and thankfully by then,
the pain had trickled down to a dull ache. Through the haze I
could see we were on the second floor and there was a commode
chair next to the window, a beeping monitor overhead, oxygen up
my nose, and a prison of side-rails all about. A blood pressure
cuff was on my right arm, an I.V. in the left, and, like a hot poker,
a catheter had been jammed up the penis for good measure.
When I looked about, I was a prisoner. So this is how it felt to be
on the wrong end of a stethoscope!

I was still half in dreamland when the nurse came in. I asked,
"Did the runs of crazy heartbeat improve?"

Her eyes told me I did not need to know such things. "You
don't need a pacemaker, if that's what you mean, doctor," she
snapped. Roughly placing the tray on the bedside table, she
turned and slammed the door. Some bedside manner.

I would not say I was a "patient" patient. I was not. I found my
thoughts counted for nothing, my reasoning was disregarded, and
my identity amounted to a number on a bracelet. Family contact
was limited to five minutes on the hour. Telephones were forbidden. No books. No television. No nothing. Watch the walls and
wait. Finally, I dozed.

I came awake when the shift of nurses changed and urgently
pleaded for bowel movement privileges. Rather than having to
deal with a messy bed, they said yes. I took five steps to a bedside
commode that had a ferocious flush and that aspirated painfully
unless you raised your buttocks to prevent an air-tight seal with
the seat.

There was another engineering marvel: the toilet roll could not
be reached while sitting. And when I stood up to retrieve the
toilet paper, I saw how naked I really was down there below
the minishirt, things quite apparent to everyone who passed by
the open glass of the hallway.

I made a dash for the reclusive security of the bed, but the
catheter got in the way and made me pause at the sight of my
reflection. In the mirror I saw a chimpanzee dressed in socks and
tripping over the long tail of a urinary tube. It soon became obvi-

ous why some patients say they would rather die than go back to the hospital. It was also obvious why patients in office examining rooms say they don't look so good with their clothes off.

Although I was getting a taste of my own medicine, I nevertheless started some serious thinking. Maybe the humanists were right. Why invoke God every time you're sick? By using powers of the mind maybe I could have taken care of myself. A stronger positive mental attitude. Mind over matter. The popular humanists had suggested self-reliance, self-assurance, self-knowledge and self-esteem: that I should learn to tap into that inner potential of the "god energy within." If god is all and all is god, and I'm part of it all, then I should be able to *will* myself to get better. That's what this positive thinking is all about.

But none of this worked for me. I had already tried these powers to no avail. Self-help becomes a ludicrous joke when you get right down to it. I needed some power greater than me. I didn't need self-esteem; I needed God-esteem.

So I flipped open the Bible to Isaiah 66:2, where the Lord declared, "This is the one I esteem: he who is humble and contrite in spirit" (NIV). Then I looked in the concordance and nowhere could I find "positive thinking" or "self-esteem" listed in the Bible. If it didn't come from the Bible then it had to come from man, and so far, man hadn't helped me too much.

A GLIMPSE OF GLORY SEEN

In fact, two or three days later, at the zenith of all this attempted self-confidence, all hell broke loose, and the pains returned with a vengeance.

It was the elephant again. The sweating, the vomiting, the near black-outs. All that time of self-mustered mind-over-matter had been wasted. Indeed, I was *not* the captain of my soul. I had been spitting into the wind and it was coming back on me.

Suddenly there was a thud followed by a flurry of skips and palpitations and then a sickening quiet. Then nothing.

Then unexpectedly, suddenly, stars came raging past in a torrent, popping out of black velvet and sizzling past like bright meteors with long white tails. Nothing seemed to make sense. I realized it wasn't the stars which were moving, but that it was *me*, moving at an enormous speed, hurtling toward a far light of awesome beauty that was filled with tinkling chimes and fantastic metallic echoing. No voices, no tunnels, no beings, no time—and, strangely, no pain! A glorious ecstasy was all around. I asked myself, "Is this what it feels like to die?" And then came the solemn yet unsettling realization of it all: I was beholding a glimpse of glory.

Suddenly I was five years old and my father was crying bitterly. I had bumped into a bucket of scalding water he was carrying to fill the bathtub, badly burning my young body. I was wrapped in a blanket. The ambulance was late. I was not supposed to live.

With another flash, I was seven years old and we were at the beach. I couldn't swim. I lost my footing and couldn't find the bottom. Frantic air hunger clawed from panicked lungs. Then a strange peacefulness settled over me. Hands reached down to lift me out. Gasping, I looked up to see my father again.

I was being shaken and something hit me in the chest. A voice vaguely called, "Doctor Rawlings! Doctor Rawlings! Are you all right?" Then more shaking. "Come on, wake up! You're not drowning, you're hallucinating." The face was blurred, but I knew the voice. It was the head nurse.

She explained that during one of the long heart pauses I was thrashing about as if in a convulsion. A flatline on the monitor and its resultant alarm made her dash into the room to find erratic body movements and to discover that the EKG attachments had become loose at the wrists, perhaps relating to the flatline.

"How long was I out?"

"Less than two minutes," she replied, replacing the electrode pads. "I was about to call a code, but when I hit you on the chest you came around."

Looking back on it all, I must have entered some sort of a time warp, one foot in this world and one in another, perhaps reminiscent of those survivors of head-on auto crashes who recount a long life-review in only a split second just prior to impact. Such moments must be a place where time has no meaning.

A stalled heart can recover so fast that you wonder if it ever needed thumping in the first place. Perhaps that had occurred in my case. But the other way of dying, the "twitching" heart, must have maintenance CPR until the heart is jump-started with an electric shock to calm the quivering muscle into a unity of contraction. Many twitching heart deaths occur, and I remember one such ventricular fibrillation in particular that occurred at Erlanger Hospital in Chattanooga.

"I've shocked him three times already," complained the medical student. We were working on a patient with septic pneumonia who had just been coded over the hospital's intercom.

"So what?" I said. "Give him another bolus of Lidocaine and bicarb and shock him again." The medical student continued his awful bed-bouncing CPR technique and I was afraid he might break a couple of the patient's ribs in the process. Of course, this was preferable to having a dead patient!

In spite of this, a slow heartbeat eventually emerged and another patient had survived. Unfortunately, this patient mentioned an extremely negative experience during the CPR—one horrible enough to save for a later chapter, where we'll list it among other horrors.

There is a vital difference between the early and late stages of death. Clinical death occurs when both heartbeat and breathing have stopped but life can be restored by CPR or resuscitation. Clinical death represents an early and reversible stage of death—something man can do.

However, if life is not restored within a few minutes, then the sensitive brain cells die, followed by gradual death of the body cells, until rigor mortis finally sets in. Rigor mortis is the stiffness of biological death, that irreversible death that requires a resurrection, but not a resuscitation—something man cannot do.

HEART ATTACKS CAN GET YOU THERE

As with many severe heart attack victims, I had a glimpse of misery follow my glimpse of glory. During the treadmill exercise performed several days later, my blood pressure went soaring and the EKG sagged in the wrong places. This meant poor coronary blood flow in still another vessel, and to determine if additional heart attacks were pending, a coronary "angiogram" would be needed.

Under local anesthesia, I watched the TV screen while my partner Charlie inserted the hollow catheter into the groin artery and advanced the tube under fluoroscopic guidance back up the blood vessels to the heart. Contrast solution was then injected into the mouth of each coronary vessel supplying the heart, and x-ray video pictures were made.

Looking at the overhead screen from my recumbent position, I could see the damaged part of the heart that was not contracting. If the chest were surgically opened at that moment, I could picture in my mind that my heart would probably look like the heart of an autopsied victim I had seen a long time ago in one of our local hospitals. That autopsy was conducted by the foulest doctor I think I have ever known.

"What's the matter, boy—you gonna throw up?" the forever-burping pathologist said, poking his finger through the mushy black and blue substance of the heart attack. As he turned the heart around in his hand, the bruised area became readily visible, but the plugged coronary artery causing the attack was hidden by a thick layer of fat.

"Looks like somebody hit it with a hammer," he quipped as he dissected away layers of fat obscuring rock-hard arteries.

Finally, somewhat adjusted to his grossness, I asked, "How often do you find this much fat?"

Using the dull end of the scalpel, he scratched his head. "Haven't seen a heart attack yet that didn't have a lot of fat." Grabbing a handful of fat, he lifted the heart to eye level. "Never used to see so much. But nowadays, everybody's got it. A determined fat America is gorging itself into a society of fat people. People are as fat on the inside as they are on the outside."

I noticed as he said this that his own fat belly draped like a big apron over the autopsy table. Even his tiny eyes were almost obscured by his fat cheeks.

Then he seemed to come up with a grand idea. "Open yourself a clinic for fat people, boy! You'll laugh yourself all the way to the bank. Mark my words, treating fat people will be the big thing of the future."

While giving this advice, he was deftly and unemotionally dividing the victim's skull with a buzz saw. I queried, "What do you think causes people to have so much fat?"

"Dunlop's disease," he laughed, displaying bad teeth.

I should have known better that to ask, but I nibbled. "What's that?" I asked.

"Dunlop's disease? That's when your belly done lopped over

your thighs." I smiled grimly at my mistake. I had taken the bait hook, line, and sinker.

I should have told that obese, rude pathologist to look at his own abdomen, but the tube in my groin dragged me painfully back to the present. I knew that it would take maybe six to eight weeks before the soft area in my heart could heal into firm scar tissue—at least for minor activities. I was determined to be a patient patient and not an impatient patient as Raymond Boyce had been a week before.

Raymond had stayed home from work for three days with "indigestion." Feeling better, he returned to work on the fourth day. Loading some boxes with another employee, Raymond suddenly grasped his chest, turned blue, and dropped to the ground. A few gasps later, he was dead.

Raymond's autopsy revealed a large, soft bulge remaining from a heart attack that had occurred a few days earlier. He had returned prematurely to work, and the soft bulge had ruptured like a weak place in an inner tube, suddenly and unceremoniously dumping his life's blood into his chest cavity. It is not unusual for people to die a few days after what they think is "heartburn," giving them more than an adequate glimpse into the hereafter.

In my own case, the procedure showed the right coronary artery had completely closed and the other vessels were okay. There was no need for bypass surgery (implanting extra vessels), balloon angioplasty (squeezing them open), atherectomy (reaming them open), or laser treatment (vaporizing them open).

Of course, that was back in 1980, when most of these treatment options were not available. What was available, and still remains as first-line treatment, was clot-dissolving drugs to reverse early heart attacks before permanent clot closure occurs.

Vic Bond, my instrument flight instructor, was one who benefitted from these drugs. Apparently a man in good health, he nearly died quite suddenly. Initial IV streptokinase, the first available clot-dissolving drug, resolved both pain and sweating quite early, a procedure quite new to medicine.

Every half hour he received strep until blood pressure, pain, and EKG changes had recovered. Then IV heparin was added to prevent recurrence of clots until an angiogram procedure was done which showed multiple vessels involved, and bypass surgery was done. No glimpse into glory occurred in Vic's case.

You say this could never happen to you? You say you're not at risk because you jog, swim, play tennis, and work out in a health club? That you are immune because you eat only healthy foods and have good cholesterol levels? These are ideal things, but every day we bury heart attack victims with normal cholesterol levels who appear healthy. Several had their health club membership cards in their wallets.

Unfortunately, in 25 percent of heart attacks there is no warning at all. They just drop dead. This is the essential reason why every household should be acquainted with the medical gospel of CPR. Immediate CPR can keep half the sudden deaths alive until qualified help arrives. Simple training is available through the Heart Association or the Red Cross.

Who is most likely to develop coronary disease? Those people predisposed by high blood pressure, diabetes, high cholesterol, smoking habits, obesity, inactivity, and those with a clear family history of the disease.

If you are one of the predisposed, when will a possible heart attack likely happen? Strangely, the event is more likely to occur during sleep, when the blood flow is sluggish, the blood pressure low and the heart rate slow. It is then that clots form and attach on the roughened walls of hardened arteries. Predisposed people should be more afraid of going to sleep than going to work, since activity induces only 15 percent of coronary events. Eighty-five percent actually occur while doing nothing, like sleeping or watching TV.

Because of dietary tradition, the United States continues to be the second leading nation in the world in the frequency of hardened arteries and heart attacks. Americans like fat because a high-fat diet tastes good. The tradition of lard biscuits, so to speak, may be the problem. "I make lard biscuits because my mother made lard biscuits" is the usual answer. Poor countries, unable to afford fat diets, may die of starvation, but not heart attacks. Perhaps because they can't make lard biscuits?

OTHER CAUSES OF DEATH—WHOM DO YOU RESUSCITATE?

Although victims retrieved from death are the most reliable source for analyzing possible experiential trips to heaven or hell and back, increased CPR training among the populace has placed resuscitation in the general public marketplace where an all-out grasp at survival is frequently miraculous, but, on the other hand, rare occasions may result in thankless prolongations of terminal illnesses or a limited recovery which results in a permanent vegetative coma. Decisions for resuscitation relate to the cause of death, and for this reason the most common causes of death will be briefly reviewed.

Who would you resuscitate out on the street? The decision can be difficult. But when in doubt, resuscitate. For example, Mrs. Autrie Mullins, a twenty-eight-year-old mother of two, came into the emergency room of Hutcheson Memorial Hospital in Ft. Oglethorpe, Georgia, unconscious and cyanotic. Heart and breathing had stopped. Although her pupils were widely dilated, the young emergency room doctor continued a meticulous resuscitation.

"Widely dilated pupils," I said over his shoulder. "The classic sign of brain death. Do you know that?"

The doctor nodded and I shrugged. "Call me when you give up and I'll sign the death certificate for you." I closed the door and went down the hall to another patient.

Fifteen minutes later the phone rang. "She's sitting up and wide awake," he exclaimed excitedly. "You better come over."

Sure enough, Mrs. Mullins was sitting up and beginning to talk coherently. By the next day she was walking around on the ward, still with these huge, dilated pupils. They were from the herbicide she had used to spray her garden. The point is, widened pupils do not always represent brain death. No thanks to me, this woman is living today and raising her two children. She, incidentally, like half or more of other resuscitees, said she had no afterlife experience at all.

Whom, then, do you resuscitate? Every case must be quickly evaluated since the brain has only a four-to-eight minute survival time without blood flow.

Victims of accidents, the fourth most common cause of death, are always a must for CPR in witnessed choking or drowning, but you wouldn't want to see it used in cases of crushed skulls and mangled bodies.

How about strokes? Some stroke patients recover fully while others die or become severely incapacitated. In doubtful cases you might try, since strokes affect about 500,000 Americans each year, killing one-third of them, leaving another one-third severely disabled, and allowing the other one-third to recover nicely.

How about a bleeding stroke? Paul Hogan, alias Crocodile Dundee, suddenly burst a blood vessel in his brain while trying to bench press 290 pounds in a Sydney, Australia gym. Terrible pain, he said, the room going out of shape and the ceiling lifting up. But in Hogan's case he recovered without any resuscitation. He now says, "It makes me appreciate every day as it comes along."

Would you resuscitate an Alzheimer's patient? Not if the family has signed an advance directive requesting that no resuscitation be done. But suppose there is no family? No directive? Alzheimer's robs its victims of memory and reason, afflicting four million Americans and gradually leading to total disability and killing 100,000 per year.

How about the AIDS victim? Would you resuscitate them? The patient might want you to, but professional rescuers try to use ventilation masks to prevent oral contact with unknown victims. While herpes (fever blister disease) and TB have been transmitted by direct mouth-to-mouth breathing, no HIV transfer of infections has been reported. Nevertheless, the Center for Disease Control estimates 1.5 million Americans are currently HIV positive, 165,000 already manifesting the active form of disease, with nearly 65 percent already fatal. If resuscitated, you must remember, they will die again.

How would you recognize the manifestly contagious AIDS victim? Be suspicious if the victim has inexplicable weight loss as if he or she had cancer. The AIDS disease was correctly named "slim" or "skinny" in 1982 when it was first discovered in fishing villages along the shores of Uganda's Lake Victoria. Other characteristic manifestations would be black spots on the outside or the white spots on the inside—but who's going to look inside the mouth or delve into other orifices looking for "white spots" before doing CPR?

Similarly, would you resuscitate a cancer victim who has no hope? How would you know who is curable and who is not, unless you have documentation in hand? About seventy-six million Americans now living will eventually have cancer. This amounts to one in three people and will involve three of every four families. This year alone, the rate of death in the United States will be about 1,400 per day. But some can appear externally healthy when cancer is internally spread everywhere. Some people say such victims should be resuscitated to be better prepared for death. And then die again?

Briefly, the most common cancer is now lung cancer, occurring more in women than men because women now smoke more than men. Breast cancer will affect one out of every nine women today; while in men, cancer of the prostate will strike one of every eleven males, 80 percent after the age of fifty-five. Cancer of the large bowel maintains the same rate as it has in the past, while cancer of the pancreas is the "silent one," involving the digestive organ deep in the upper abdomen. While the pancreas has become the fifth leading cancer killer, there is no cure.

By performing this simple statistical review, perhaps you have an inkling of the most likely cause of your own death, and are more mindful of some of the dilemmas presented in CPR.

Finally, there are four simple questions usually found on the lips of dying patients. Sometimes they are unspoken. The first is, "What will be the cause of my death?" but this is usually evident to them by the time they enter the hospital.

The second is, "What does it feel like to die?" We will discuss this in the next chapter.

Next is the third question, "Is there life after death?"

And the final question: "Is it 'safe' to die?"

What is your answer to the dying patient? And to yourself?

2

RESUSCITATED

COLLECTIONS

Because the debate is hot and heavy, we will spend some time with the methods and history of collecting CPR cases, since much significance has been attached to post-resuscitation experiences. By denying the existence of negative events, a whole new religion has developed from near-death experiences. However, since the cases are plentiful and may include your own family, you may wish to collect your own series of cases and to make your own conclusions.

The cases I will present were collected by professional people making on-the-scene interviews while CPR was in progress: doctors, nurses, and paramedics involved with ambulances, emergency rooms, and intensive care wards. Many people who were with me in teaching life-support systems for the American Heart Association in hospitals and medical schools in many countries for many years have also contributed their experiences. The courses we taught involved CPR, ventilators, drugs for shock, central lifelines, restoring and maintaining heartbeat, restoring breathing, and reversing coma. It served as a good base for early interviews of victims who reported experiences at death's door, because it was the very time when negative and fearful experiences would be difficult to conceal.

After publishing some initial negative cases several years ago, I found myself running counter to the grain of other authors, pushed into the fray of controversy; thrown to the sharks, so to speak.

THE AUDACITY OF IT ALL

A relic of a 007 thriller, a Texas billionaire traditionally challenged his guests with a shark-infested swimming pool. "It takes guts to get ahead in this world," he said. "There are six man-eating sharks in this pool. If any of you are daring enough to risk your life against them, I will help you form a new business."

The billionaire gestured with his hand. "Whoever can swim across from here to there and come out alive on the other side can have any one of three choices: my beautiful daughter's hand in marriage, half of my business assets, or all of my oil fields."

Hearing a loud splash behind him, the billionaire turned to see a man flailing in a frenzy with his clothes on, churning the water for dear life. Somehow fulfilling the quest, the bedraggled man miraculously emerged unscathed on the other side.

"My dear fellow," the billionaire said to the victim, "you have accomplished something unattainable by anyone before. Now I will honor my commitment. Which reward shall you have—my daughter, I suppose?"

"No, sir, not your daughter."

"Half my assets, then?"

"No, sir, not your assets."

"Then you want all my oil fields?"

"No, sir, not those either."

"Then what do you want?"

"I want to know who had the nerve to push me in!"

Well, to this day I don't know who it was that pushed *me* in. Finding the first hell experiences, probably to the concern of authors reporting only euphoric glimpses of glory, was probably the very situation that pushed me into the pool. The initial shove undoubtedly occurred the day Charles McKaig fell dead in my office during an EKG treadmill exercise. That day everything turned upside down. It was the day I was thrown to the sharks.

Previously I was a cynic. To me, patients who reported an after-death experience were a little crazy. I was a heart specialist skeptical of spiritual things. We had been taught to treat the body, perhaps a little of the mind, but spiritual things? They belonged to the psychics and the shrinks.

The possibility that spiritual issues could emanate from CPR would have frightened even old doctors Kouwenhoven and Jude in their original closed-chest experimentations at Johns Hopkins Medical Center back in 1960—much less today, when over 100,000 lives are saved each year by modifications of their technique.

It now borders on the fantastic to realize that clinical death experiences have become the only experimental link between ancient prophesies and modern science.

WHAT IT FEELS LIKE TO DIE

When asked about his thoughts on death, Woody Allen replied, "I am not afraid of dying—I just don't want to be there when it happens." Perhaps this universal fear of death relates in a large part to fear of the unknown. But if the unknown could in some way be revealed—if we could find out what might exist beyond death's door and how it felt and how to get there—then much of the fear of death could be removed.

People might feel more secure if there was a U-Haul truck following in the funeral procession, carrying all their possessions with them to the afterlife, an idea dating back to ancient Egypt. The truth of the matter is that, barring a rapture, none of us will leave this world alive. Each will have their turn with death, which happens to be the most democratic event in history, whether we like it or not.

Through the ages man has predicted life after death but only in the last thirty years has resuscitation become so efficient that a whole new population has appeared to interrogate concerning death, its sensations, and its meaning. Most of these people represent the unexpected deaths, half of them responding to simple external heart compressions and mouth-to-mouth breathing, no instruments required. With these new techniques it is not surprising that renewed interest in the death process has swept the nation and our schools and colleges have now introduced more courses on death and dying than on sexuality.

What does it feel like to die? Everyone wants to know, but no one wants to ask (and even fewer want to try it). Yet the answer is

essential because it will affect each of us. Surprisingly, death survivors tell us that the moment of death is absolutely painless.
Painless! Nothing at all. No choking or smothering. Nothing like
that. "Feels like fainting," they say, or "like a missed heartbeat,"
or "a lost breath." "Less than anesthesia for surgery." These uniform answers came from several hundred patients summarized in
the first book, *Beyond Death's Door*.

Most people are deathly afraid of dying. They say, "Doctor,
I'm afraid of dying." But I have never heard one of them say,
"Doctor, I'm afraid of judgment." And judgment is the main concern of patients who have been there and returned to tell about
it.

Among those 20 to 40 (some say 60) percent of resuscitees who
claim a spiritual experience, the experience of heaven or hell
becomes so real that the victim is transfixed by every detail, recalling every sequence and every event. But contrary to the literature, as we shall emphasize again and again, these experiences
are not all good experiences. While a positive case might say, "I'll
never be afraid of death again, it was so beautiful there," the
negative case might say, "It's not dying I'm afraid of. It's returning to that awful place again!"

What about the 40 to 80 percent who report no experience?
Often they have no clear-cut explanation or else they don't want
to talk about it. Of course, the absence of any experience might
cause an assumption that death is oblivion, a void. But for some
reason, few of the patients seem to reach that conclusion.

Since nearly eleven million people have already had near-death
experiences, the cases are quite common. You may know of some
among your own friends. If so, why not collect your own cases?
Always make the interviews as confidential as possible; preferably
one-on-one where there is no fear of being overheard or ridi-
culed. It is a very sensitive subject.

Unfortunately, medical personnel in general are afraid of such
interviews, leaving them to ministers and psychologists who don't
see the patients until some time later, after the resuscitation has
been completed—and this is the very time when negative events
are hidden in the closet with the other skeletons. For some peculiar reason, medical people just don't want to be associated with
spiritual matters. Maybe it's pride. Maybe they're afraid of criti-

cism. Maybe it's too personal, making them vulnerable to their own spirituality or mortality.

Many people feel uncomfortable discussing spiritual experiences. One of the publishing agents reviewing this present manuscript refused to read further because she "couldn't cope with such morbid subjects—too depressing, too discomforting," she said. As you would guess, personal problems surfaced, and a few minutes later she said, "A friend of mine is dying in the hospital and her doctor insists that she is denying her condition. Well, isn't that her right? Isn't it less painful to deny than admit that you're dying? So why do you doctors insist on reminding people that they are dying when they don't want to know about it?" A good point, but such objections remind me of the old expression "Ignorance is bliss."

On the other hand, most dying patients already know that they are dying and most doctors actually try to avoid the dying patient as much as possible. The dying process represents a personal defeat to some doctors, while others continue to treat when there isn't any cure to be had. Some doctors doggedly keep their patients alive when they really know the situation is lost. It only prolongs the misery while raising horrendous hospital bills and raising the spectre of "passive" euthanasia.

WHY HELL CASES ARE NOT REPORTED

If the interview is delayed just a little bit—much less days, weeks, or months after the fact—only the positive experiences will be found. The negative experiences have long since been relegated to the painless portions of the memory, the victim apparently unable to coexist with this painful memory. Intolerable situations often lead to other solutions such as a personal religious conversion, a situation sometimes difficult to detect unless the patient volunteers the information. Thus, hell cases are not reported.

Hell cases also remain unreported because of personal ego and the embarrassment of it all. Patients don't want to discuss a matter that confirms ultimate failure in life, an overwhelming defeat, a slap in the face. Since the experience destroys self-esteem, pride conceals the error. Nothing more than human nature. The average doctor, for instance, will relate only his most impressive diagnoses and say nothing of past mistakes. Should we expect less from the patients?

The psychologists and psychiatrists (who write most of the books on the subject) never seem to encounter negative cases. Delayed interviews? The timing factor? Because they weren't there? Because they have never resuscitated any of their patients? Not in their line of business? All of the above?

Perhaps the greatest reason for the paucity of negative reports is the defective method of data collection. Methods are used that disregard the simple bell curve distribution for population studies and scientific information. There are invariably two extremes to any curve, and bias results when investigation is limited to only one end of the curve while the other end is disregarded or purposefully omitted.

To broaden the exposure data of the authors who write of euphoric NDEs and OBEs, I have offered some of the negative experiences we have collected for their personal touch and interview, but they have all refused. One author declined because negative data would interfere with positive results already collected. Another passed because the information would modify conclusions already published. A third, the legendary and broadly respected Dr. Elisabeth Kubler-Ross, would not say why she refused but declined the offer anyhow. Such lack of interest in broadened research is troubling.

Come to think of it, there might be still another reason why negative cases are not reported. Clinical death, reversible if heartbeat and breathing can be restored, is a unique category of experiences because they brush close to the door of biological death. Unfortunately, this unique category has been mixed and diluted into the greater category of general "near-death experiences," which includes life-threatening situations where consciousness and heartbeat were not necessarily lost and where no type of death occurred in any form. For instance, NDEs include situations where resuscitation was never required. The victims may have thought death was at their doorstep, or they may have contemplated death during an illness, or they may have had an accident or a long and precipitous fall. Sometimes they could be scared to death, expecting death from robberies or muggings. But in most cases vital functions did not stop and they did not go through death's door.

Don't say make-believe prayers. . . . they can dissect your soul like a surgeon's scalpel.

The NDEs without clinical death happen to be the least likely group to experience negative events. The resuscitated groups most likely to report negative events are those whose interviews were initiated during the CPR.

As mentioned, some additional negative material can be found hidden in good reports if one looks closely for a religious conversion precipitated by a hell-like event that required an urgent resolution.

Such was the case of Charlie McKaig. We will mention his case again because he had a positive experience obscuring the preceding negative one, and this initiated a whole chain of events.

Of course, some authors may not be happy about these cases, since negative experiences of any kind would prove embarrassing to the emerging "Omega" philosophy where everyone goes to heaven with no type of judgment involved. Proponents of this philosophy say that those who were returned to earth "because their time was not yet," are drawn inexorably toward a heaven on earth—a utopia directed by the unidentified light that furnished the glimpse of glory. The Omega concept is such an emerging, massive, encircling thing that it will be presented again in this book.

A CASE REVIEWED

The whole thing occurred late one day in 1977 when the other doctors had left Diagnostic Center to finish rounds elsewhere. Pam Charlesworth was finishing an EKG on a patient with chest pain.

"It's normal," she said.

I shook my head. "Hook him up again and this time exercise him enough to reproduce the pain. A smoldering heart attack could still be there."

The treadmill rumbled to life, moving Charlie McKaig, a forty-eight-year-old mail carrier from LaFayette, Georgia, at a progressively rapid rate. Pain reappeared along with sweating and breathlessness. An unusual humming noise from the monitor caused us to look up to see an unexpected run of ventricular tachycardia (rapid, dangerous heartbeat). This was followed by a very long pause in the beat and then followed by slow, widened beats and then by a flatline.

Surprisingly, Charlie continued to talk for a while, unaware that his heart had stopped. Four or five seconds later, he looked suddenly dumbfounded. It was as if he were about to ask a question. Then his eyes rolled up in his head and he fell, the treadmill sweeping the body away like so much trash.

This reminded me of similar problems occurring in the heart lab where the heartbeat stops for some reason, but amazingly, the patient continues to talk for a while. Hitting them on the chest or making them cough repeatedly usually starts them up again so the procedure can be completed as if nothing happened.

The CPR technique that we used on Charlie has since been modified by employing sequential chest/abdominal compressions at a rate of eighty per minute. The artificial breathing technique is the same. Details are available at your local American Heart Association or Red Cross, and the method is listed in the Appendix.

With Charlie's head sharply extended, chin toward the ceiling, one of the nurses breathed "the kiss of life." Another nurse started the IV for medicines. By then an underlying block in the heartbeat had appeared on the monitor. That means the heart was not conducting the beat properly and a temporary pacemaker would be needed for the heart to respond to the CPR.

Using a large-bore needle, I entered the big vein under the collar bone, then threaded the pacemaker wire in the right side of the heart and attached the wire to a pulse-generator box to initiate every beat, not missing a stroke.

But blood was spurting everywhere. Whenever I stopped pushing on his chest in order to adjust the pacemaker, the heart would stop, and Charlie's eyes would roll up, he again would sputter, turn blue, and begin to convulse.

With bare hands, just like you can, I would reach over and start him up again. But this time he was screaming the words, "Don't stop! I'm in hell! I'm in hell!"

Hallucinations, I thought. Most victims say, "Take your big hands off me, you're breaking my ribs." But he was saying the opposite: "For God's sake, don't stop! Don't you understand? Every time you let go I'm back in hell!"

When he asked me to pray for him, I felt downright insulted. In fact, I told him to shut up. I said I was a doctor, not a minister and not a psychiatrist. But the nurses gave me that expectant look. What would you do? That's when I composed a make-believe prayer.

I made him repeat the make-believe prayer word for word to keep him off my back. Meanwhile, I resuscitated with one hand and adjusted the pacemaker with the other. "Say it! Jesus Christ is the Son of God, go on and say it!" I said. "Keep me out of hell, and if I live, I'm on the hook. I'm yours. Go on, say it!"

And then a very strange thing happened that changed our lives. A religious conversion experience took place. I had never witnessed one before. He was no longer the wild-eyed, screaming, combative lunatic who had been fighting me for his life. He was relaxed and calm and cooperative. It frightened me. I was shaken by the events. Not only had that make-believe prayer blown out the soul of Charlie McKaig, but it backfired and got me too. It was a conviction I cannot express even to this day.

Since then, Charlie has outlived three permanent pacemakers, and it has been difficult to believe that this miserable prayer of mine had opened the road to my own salvation. A spiritual bonus for the simpleminded. The lesson? Don't say make-believe prayers. They can work. And they can dissect your soul like a surgeon's scalpel.

And that's what stimulated me to search for the mysteriously missing hell cases.

And that presented another problem. Why did the hell cases never question where they were or why they were sent there? And why did the heavenly cases, on the other hand, wonder if their experiences were bona fide? The quest for answers would prove to be my holy grail—to question those who were about to shake hands with death and those who had been beyond death's door.

MANY BIBLES ON THE SUBJECT

Charlie's hell experience forced me to dust off the old Bible that night, and to look at other books of faith as well. All these faiths seem based on the afterlife, but their ideas are different. One book of faith often refutes the other. So which doctrine is more authoritative? It was important that I know for myself. I felt my own life was too important to entrust to any one denomination or any one minister. Which book of faith represents the truth? To compare with the Judeo-Christian Bible I selected the *Tibetan and Egyptian Books of the Dead,* the *Vedas,* the *Upanishads,* the *Bhagavad-Gita,* the *Tripitaka,* the *Agamas,* the *Avesta,* the *Tao-te-King,* the *Kojiki,* the *Talmud,* and the *Koran.*

Surprisingly, most of them described both a heaven and a hell. But each claimed their own god or tradition as the only way to heaven. More generous, however, were some of the eastern faiths. They allowed that all roads lead to heaven.

While several of these books of faith claimed miracles, none compared in number and veracity with those contained in the Judeo-Christian Bible. In addition to miracles, there was still another area unique to the Judeo-Christian Bible: the area of prophecy. Precise accuracy for past prophecies suggested a similar expected accuracy for future prophecies. And I found another astounding thing: the slightest errancy in prophecy mandated the death penalty. The Judeo-Christian prophets had to be right.[1]

What about today's modern prophets—the fortune-tellers, the mediums, the clairvoyants, the astrologers—would they bet their lives on the outcome of their prophecies? None of today's psychics are 100 percent accurate, and this becomes a marvelous focal point to differentiate the psychic secularist, who *can* be wrong, from God's psychic, the prophet, who can *never* be wrong. To me, the insignia or proof for the one true God is the inerrant accuracy of Judeo-Christian biblical prophecy.

With this in mind, I made it a point to visit the graves of most of the world's religious founders during my teaching travels. And I was amazed. All of the graves were occupied except one. And that empty grave belonged to the only religious founder who claimed deity. It was Jesus Christ.

Because Christians represent a minority of the world's faiths, we shall look for the influence of other faiths upon near-death experiences in foreign countries and attempt to correlate these with the findings of other authors.

A TYPICAL SEQUENCE

Resuscitated reports for most faiths have a remarkable similarity in form, with many of them encountering the light at the end of the tunnel. But then the sequence diverges. Because the identity of the light in most instances is based on assumption, it is not surprising to find cases of deception. Deception is in the good and not in the bad. And this is interesting.

Both good and bad experiences are recorded in other faiths, and occasionally in those people with no faith at all. "Near-death" groups (the majority never "dead" in the first place) will be considered in a separate chapter because they are so varied (dreams, drugs, accidents, life threats, death-bed apparitions) that they seldom present complete analyzable sequences which otherwise typify the resuscitated clinical–death groups.

The bad experiences? They miss a step or two here and there and alter the sequence. They occur more swiftly, arriving rapidly, frequently leaving after a struggle. Since the negative sequence varies, let's first look at the sequence of a typical good clinical death experience:

1. During clinical death, the person leaves his body, usually experiences a heightened sense of awareness and euphoria, and is often surprised to see the likeness of himself remaining behind.
2. Looking down, the individual may recall details of events in the room, noting specific items of clothing and conversation, but finding himself unable to communicate with the living.
3. The spirit of this person soon discovers another world, sometimes entering directly, but frequently through a tunnel.
4. Encountering a "being of light," the person may undergo a pictorial life review. Thought-transfer may replace the need for both speech and travel.
5. In a reunion of sorts, the person may have a chance encounter with relatives or friends who have died before. (It should be noted the victim did not himself conjure or "call up" the dead, but went to the spirit world himself.)

6. The world they describe is exquisite beyond words and thus defies adequate description. The specific environment varies.
7. A barrier (a fence, a wall, a river) may next be encountered, an obstruction separating what might be called a "meeting ground" from possible "judgment ground."
8. Attempting to pass this barrier, the victim is returned to the body, often because it was "not yet their time," being resuscitated or electrically shocked into the world of discomfort and pain.

While the positive cases often wish they had not returned, the negative cases are invariably relieved. Value concepts and purposes change for both groups, especially the hell cases. Interestingly, some cases claim to be endowed with special psychic gifts or powers, and deciphering the good from the bad can be difficult.

HOW TO COLLECT CASES

Since eight to eleven million near-death victims have claimed near-death experiences, screening for interviews should be practical. A marked change in life-style should be evident, or you shouldn't waste your time with the interviews. Some of them could otherwise be nightmares, daydreams, or wishful thinking. But if the very life of the individual was changed, then make sure that the experience was not also influenced by drugs. Next, verify from the records if this was a clinical death or merely a near-death event. Clinical deaths cause permanent changes in those that have an experience.

Compare your cases with the composite model just listed. Note that most drug-induced experiences do not depart from this world. They may see bugs, snakes, or other things, crawling across the hospital room, but note that the events occur in this world—not another world.

Robert Louis Stevenson had his experiences in this world when he wrote *Dr. Jekyll and Mr. Hyde.* The inspiration was induced by the cocaine he used to alleviate the discomfort of tuberculosis. He was able to write firsthand about the struggle between good and bad, the stimulus of highs and lows allowing him to complete the entire book in just three days. Edgar Allen Poe and other composers, artists, and writers through the ages used the inspiration of drugs for their work, as do many of the mediums today. A hell on earth but not elsewhere.

Another distinction of clinical death from dream states concerns the item of recall. The resuscitated individual may recall precisely what occurred in the room while clinically dead. They may be able to reconstruct the scene, identify persons in the room, tell where they were standing, what they said, and also what they were wearing. It was as if they were fully awake when they were completely unconscious, no heartbeat or breath.

Lastly, analyze the experience by the sequence itself. The steps in the pattern of clinical death experiences are the same, as if they all had the same dream last night. No collusion or foreknowledge elicited.

DISCERNMENT OF FINDINGS

If the resuscitation experiences were not nightmares but a strange combination of nearly identical sequences, of post-conscious visual recall, of ethereal transportation to another world, and all of it resulting in changed lives, could these distinctive events possibly point to a life after death?

There is a contention here. Some say no, that other causes of imagery could include acidemia, hypercapnia, and hypoxia, all related to reduced blood flow to the brain which does occur when there is no heartbeat. It is true that certain stimulated areas of the brain can produce images, but there is no sequence, no consistency, and no predictability. Out-of-this-world experiences rarely, if ever, occur from the damaged brain, while in-this-world images are not uncommon. Induced images and hallucinations consistently pertain to this world, this environment.

What is the significance of the light at the end of the tunnel? Many psychic researchers believe the light represents a common compassionate force, a force of unconditional love existing for all who die regardless of faith, a force where nothing negative is ever found.

Most Christian theologians, in contrast, hold the opposite view —that the "compassionate light" could indeed be Satan or one of his angels masquerading as an angel of light or as a minister of righteousness (2 Cor. 11:14), deceiving many. A force trying to convince the unsaved that salvation is not needed. They say that if Satan could convince people that there is no judgment or accountability at death, then there would be no need to trust in Christ, and Christ would become superfluous. And Satan would win.

Hindering the universal adoption of the now popular "Omega point" (where events are invariably glorious) is the patient who has seen hell itself during his OBE or NDE. It is this testimony that bothers and upsets the commonly accepted interpretation that all is good. It is a devastating blow.

It is my contention after reviewing many cases that Satan could appear as Lucifer, the angel of light, to deny and reject the existence of evil, and thereby show that everything is good and okay out there.

But everything is not okay out there. Since the beginning of time the spiritual battle has continued between these two forces, and for nearly two thousand years the Scripture's warning and admonition have always been there:

> Enter by the narrow gate; for wide is the gate and broad is the way that leads to destruction, and there are many who go in by it. Because narrow is the gate and difficult is the way which leads to life, and there are few who find it.
>
> (Matt. 7:13–14)

In Christianity, Jesus Christ represents the only gate. On the other hand, Satan wants us to believe that no gate is necessary. In a nutshell, this is the very crux debated by all authors investigating near-death phenomena.

The bitter debate thus rages among authors over the existence of hell—or no hell—in clinical death reports. In my reports, therefore, I would like to identify with Luke. Luke is my hero, another physician, and he started his Gospel reports with this introduction:

> Many have undertaken to draw up an account of the things that have been fulfilled among us, just as they were handed down to us by those who from the first were eyewitnesses. . . . Therefore, since I myself have carefully investigated everything from the beginning, it seemed good also to me to

write an orderly account for you . . . so that you may know
the certainty of the things you have been taught.

(Luke 1:1–4 NIV)

Of course, Luke was talking about Christ and other important
things and not about CPRs and OBEs and NDEs, but nevertheless, with that understanding, I would like to offer you an opportunity to enter the arena of debate as I "write an orderly account
for you . . . so you may know the certainty of the things you
have been taught."

3

HEAVEN
AND THE
ANGEL OF LIGHT

"My temperature was almost 106 and I was having cardiac arrhythmias. I felt an incredible pain. The wall of my uterus was ripping apart. I was in septic shock, going into labor. As I lost consciousness I heard a voice shouting, 'I can't get her blood pressure!'

"And then within the tiniest fraction of an instant, I was out of my body and out of pain. I was up on the ceiling in a corner of the room, looking down, watching doctors and nurses rush around frantically as they worked to save my life. Then one of the doctors, really upset, yelled obscenities. And that somehow turned me over.

"Now I was in a sort of tunnel, a cloudlike enclosure. . . . I felt wind brushing against my ears, except I didn't have ears. I was there, but my body wasn't.

"I began to feel the most incredible, warm, golden, loving feeling, and the feeling was also a wonderful, warm, golden light. I was in this light, a wisdom, and that wisdom was the final word. The wisdom loved me and at the same time it knew everything about me. Everything I had ever done and felt was there for me to see. I wanted to proceed into the light and stay there forever, but I was shown that I had to go back and take care of my two children.

"In that same fragment of a second, I was back in my body,

back in all the pain. My son was being delivered, and I heard everybody screaming, 'She's back!' I was so upset, so angry to be ripped away from the most wonderful peace in all the universe. And then they told me my son had been born dead."[1]

This was the transforming experience of a Philadelphia nurse named Grace Bubulka, since moved to Los Angeles. Meeting loved ones and encountering a barrier were evidently some of the steps not mentioned in this case, but the God-inspired origin of the NDE seemed likely for her.

Kimberly Clark Sharp, age twenty-two, collapsed on the sidewalk outside a motor vehicle bureau in Kansas. "Suddenly there was an explosion under me and reaching out to the farthest limits of my view was this light. . . . It was so bright, the sun is not as bright, yet it didn't hurt my eyes. It filled up everything, and I was in the center of it. I was back with my creator. This light was all love. . . . I was being given information, in a communication between myself and the light, and I understood everything I was told . . . It was heaven, more than ecstasy. It was a reunion of the highest order."[2]

The quoted article failed to mention, however, that these events confirmed Kimberly's commitment to Christianity and convinced her to establish a much closer relationship with Jesus Christ. These were unquoted items that Kimberly privately mentioned to me when we were taping segments for "Beyond the Line," a secular TV serial filmed by Barton-Prinz Productions in Vancouver, B.C.

The encounter with a light seems to be the most common event noted in most near-death experiences. Visualization of events transpiring in the room is a somewhat less common experience, although the complete sequence of events often typifies clinical deaths where resuscitation is required rather than the sketchy sequences noted in near-death experiences where no loss of heart and lung functions occurred.

It was in mid-1988 that the medical emergency team arrived at the side of Sir Alfred Ayer, an Oxford professor afflicted with pneumonia, in the intensive care unit of London's University College Hospital. By that time, the slow heartbeat displayed on the monitor had dwindled into a flatline.

Working as a team, the doctors were able to restore Ayer's heartbeat four minutes later, the heart now pumping on its own.

During this four minutes of "death," as Ayer later described, he encountered an exceedingly bright light which, in some mysterious way, made him cognizant that this intense light was responsible for the very governance of the universe.

Professor Ayer, an avowed atheist, considered this a positive or heavenly experience, bordering on ecstatic wonder. Ayer now concedes he is no longer certain that death is the end of everything. But it is not clear from his description if he now accepts God, the Creator, the Governor of the Universe, as the sovereign of his life, or if he conceives that any known deity were involved, much less Jesus Christ.

As with some of the glorious reports that are beginning to appear, the reports are incomplete. Most of my experience concerning positive observations involved Christians who made positive identifications by seeing Christ on the cross, or identifying nail marks and such. But there are some recent good experiences claimed by atheists who might have seen still another angel of light—the one called Lucifer, the Deceiver, the one whose very name means light, the one assuring that everything is okay out there, the one advocating a free ride for everyone with no redemption, no penalties, no prerequisites. That intriguing problem will be one of the investigative purposes of this book as we both proceed to ferret out these things together, and compare these cases with the opposing cases, the ones who apparently went to hell and back.

Since a Gallup Poll indicates near-death experiences have touched between eight and eleven million Americans, the traditional religions are also disturbed that many NDEs experienced love, joy, and forgiveness from the light in the tunnel without belonging to any particular faith. To explain this, the traditionals say that satanic delusions are being offered for the express purpose of deterring the unsaved from finding true salvation.

Secular skeptics, on the other hand, conveniently dismiss the whole near-death experience as the product of hallucination from chemical change in the oxygen-deprived mind. Unfortunately, experiments with the oxygen-deprived mind do not reproduce these findings. In fact, the hallucination theory cannot account for a whole list of things found in bona fide experiences: the power of transcendency, experiences that occur in another world, positive visual reconstruction of events at the scene of the emergency, the remarkable reproducibility of sequences, and the resulting miraculous change or turnaround in people's life-styles.

Thus, retrieved death experiences present a challenge to the ecumenical question of what happens when you die. Everyone wants to know, especially since both near-death and resuscitated events occur in the marketplace everyday. The information is abundant and we should make use of it, because all through history man has predicted life after death, but only now do we have a new population for source information—those who claim to have been to heaven or hell and back.

In years gone by, lifesaving methods were pitifully poor, offering little source material for investigation of the death experience. Medieval methods of retrieval included such things as jostling the victim on a horse, hanging the victim upside down, whipping out the evil spirits, using bellows to blow air into the body, or rapidly raising and lowering the arms. But today, fifty percent of unexpected deaths will recover with today's CPR, and the resulting population is huge, a population that can't wait to report the good experiences and try to forget the bad ones.

Even in ancient times heavenly expectations for the after-life were evident in the artifacts left in Egypt's ancient tombs, left in the literature of Plato's *Republic* (written four centuries before Christ), and left in the art of Hieronymus Bosch's first depiction (around the year 1500) of the now-famous "tunnel of light" portrayed in his Flemish painting, *The Ascent into the Empyrean*. In the late 1800s Gustave Doré engraved a heavenly tunnel of light whose walls were composed of myriads of flying angels. It was entitled *Dante and Beatrice Experience the Beatific Vision*. Eventually came the age of resuscitation, permitting the capture of previously unrecordable experiences.

Now for some random good experiences for your own evaluation. Bleeding internally a few days after surgery, Barbara Harris in 1975 reported a variation in the usual sequence during her retrieval experience. At first she was looking down on her own body in the bed. "I felt calm and peaceful." Then she entered a total blackness where she felt the pleasant warmth of her grandmother, dead for fourteen years, as she embraced her. "I could feel what she was feeling," Harris said. Then a low droning noise began beckoning her and the next memory was waking up in the hospital bed.[3]

Robert Helm suffered cardiac arrest during knee surgery on November 7, 1979. "I was conscious of a tunnel with an intense light at the other end. I was going toward it at a really blinding speed. The walls of the tunnel were blurry at first, but then I noticed they were what appeared to be planets or stars." Going through the light, he found himself sitting on a rock in the middle of a beautiful lake, and next on a magnificent street. Subsequently, he saw Albert Einstein and others seated at a "wonderful computer" that had something to do with "destinies." On the street he said, "There was a band of angels singing. I was a total agnostic. I had no belief in angels or any kind of heavenly being." Since then, Helm says he is not afraid of dying. "It is without doubt, the most wonderful experience I've ever enjoyed." With a sweeping gesture he points to our present environment and says, *"This* is hell."[4]

During a firefight in Vietnam on May 29, 1969, Captain Tommy Clack had an explosive hit him in the foot. "I was immediately thrown into the air, and when I landed on the ground, I sat up and realized that my legs, my right arm, and my right shoulder were gone. . . . All of a sudden I was out of my body, looking at them working on me, and then they covered me with a poncho, indicative of death. We arrived at a MASH unit, and I was taken into an operating room. I watched them cut off my uniform, and at this point a massive bright light permeated the room. It was a wonderful, warm, good thing, like looking into the sun. Then . . . I was back out at the battlefield. Around me were people I had served with who had died. . . . They tried to get me to go with them, but I would not go. Then, in the blink of an eye, I was back in the operating room, watching the scenario."[5]

Carol Zaleski, professor of religion at Smith College in 1987 published a book called *Otherworld Journeys: Accounts of Near-death Experience in Medieval and Modern Times.* In the book she suggests that some hallucinations might be a vehicle for an encounter with something deeply true. Speaking of near-death experiences, she says, "I think it would be just like God to speak to us rather hard-of-hearing human beings in a form that we can hear."

Diane Komp, professor of pediatrics at Yale University, agrees. Having stood at the bedside of near-death children for twenty-five years, she writes a convinced Christian conclusion about what

she has learned in helping dying children and their families pre-
pare for death. In one case, Dr. Komp sat to comfort a family and
their seven-year-old girl who was dying from leukemia. Children
have a convicting openness without grown-up inhibition. The little girl managed the final energy to sit up and say, "The angels—
they're so beautiful! Mommy, can you see them? Do you hear
their singing? I've never heard such beautiful singing." Then the
girl died. Dr. Komp said, "The word that most closely describes
what I felt is 'gift.' It wasn't just that the child was given the gift of
peace in the moment of her death, but that this was a gift to her
parents."[6] Elsewhere in her talks, Dr. Komp does not hesitate to
mention Christian discoveries in her descriptions.

Dr. Melvin Morse, a pediatrician in the Seattle suburbs, has
found a greater tendency for near-death experiences in children
than in adults, their simple reports less influenced by cultural
effects. Early in his book *Closer to the Light,* young Katie did not
remember drowning in the YMCA pool, and, although resuscitated by Dr. Morse, she was not expected to live. She recalled
that out of the darkness a tunnel opened and "Elizabeth" came
out and accompanied Katie back through the tunnel where she
saw her late grandfather and met several other people including
two new friends who played with her, Andy and Mark. Finally,
Elizabeth, who seemed to be a guardian angel for Katie, took her
to meet the Heavenly Father and Jesus. When Jesus asked if she
wanted to see her mother again, she replied yes, and then she
awoke.

Dr. Morse, who has interviewed more than seventy such children, reports another case. When Jamie Untinen was five years
old she almost died from spinal meningitis. Later she drew a
picture of what she saw: three angels and Jesus sitting on a log.
He was "very nice" and told her it was not her turn to die.[7]

Typical of several cases, a male orderly in Canada suffered
cardiac arrest and floated first through darkness and then over a
brightly lit field of clover where there were beautiful smells and
music and a brother beckoning to him. Suddenly he felt pain
again and found himself back in the emergency room. He called
his lawyer and arranged not to be resuscitated the next time. The
expected fatal heart attack subsequently occurred, but his attending nurse "felt okay" about it because she understood that "he

was really ready to pass on and what was waiting for him was something wonderful." But his nurse didn't say what it was.[8]

Was this "something wonderful" just a field of clover or something else? Nothing further was related or explained other than the general impression that "everything is okay" out there.

It should be mentioned that some of these victims were quite surprised to find unquestioned approval in their particular case, skeptical of their acceptance into such a pleasant afterlife.

In other cases glorious feelings occurred when the figure they found was on a cross or when some other insignia of God's identification was perceived. These cases were ecstatic in their precise identity of the being of light and in the appropriateness of their location.

In the above cases, who is this being of light? Does the identity change to be convenient to the circumstance? And in each case is the light's identity assumed, counterfeit, or reliable? Lucifer, we are told, claims to be the light, the son of morning. But Christ also claims to be the light, the Son of God, who "gives light to every man coming into the world" (John 1:9). Which light is which? Christ said there would be counterfeits and that only a few would welcome him and receive him. "But as many as received Him, to them He gave the right to become children of God" (1:12). Does this intimate there should be more bad cases than good ones?

Whenever I encounter these problems, I seek help. I covet the opinions of theologians and lay people, and whoever is expert in the field. One of the lay opinions I obtain is from Dr. Jerry Jones, a family practitioner in the suburbs of Chattanooga. A brilliant agnostic, his god seems to reside in both people and money. For these reasons I seek his humanistic viewpoint to keep the theologians in balance.

One day I asked, "What do you think of this light they all seem to marvel about?"

He replied, "Perhaps the light represents some sort of supernatural intelligence." I poured more coffee from the thermos on my desk and he added, "Otherwise, why would the light consistently appear in most of these events?" Jerry was about forty-five at the time, medium build, prematurely graying, always wearing the doctor's white coat.

"Drugs don't do these things," he said. "Drugs don't cause

experiences in another world. But the thing I don't understand is why the light seems all-forgiving and why everyone is given another chance. And why are they all good experiences and no bad ones? Dreams are not that way. Nothing is that way. Not even life and death are that way. Is this light saying you're going to get something for nothing? That's like the sucker's promotion at the casino table, only he's shooting craps for your soul. There's a big lie somewhere in the woodpile."

"I think you're right," I nodded, "but I don't know why. The light appears to be too good to be true in many of the cases I've seen. If both Christ and Lucifer claim to be the 'light,' which is the counterfeit? Rarely, I've noticed that atheists see ecstatically good events also, perhaps concluding that god is 'all', that god includes nature, and that god includes themselves. If they are all god, then Jehovah, the Creator of the Universe, does not exist. I recall that one of them called the experience with the light 'a baptismal awakening to the brotherhood of mankind—and that it illustrated the ultimate good within us all.' Could this constitute the religion of the future we've heard so much about? The evolved right of divine man to enter heaven?" I said to Jerry, and it bothered me as I said it.

"There's a dichotomy here—a split," Jerry contended. "Many people are convinced they saw Christ—so this is one being of light. Who does that leave for the other?"

I shrugged. "That's the problem. There must be two. The Bible says Christ is the 'true light', but Lucifer makes the same claim because the word 'light' is in his name. Now, if Satan could change faces and dress as Lucifer, the angel of light, couldn't that account for some of the inappropriate positive reports?"

"I don't see why not," Jerry replied. "Like opening a door on Bourbon Street . . . for a quick peek into glory. Yes, it could work! A clever deception. Nobody would need this God of yours because they've already been stamped and approved. No salvation necessary. It would debunk the need of any faith or any commitment if the individual knows there is no accountability beyond death, that everybody is bound for heaven."

Finishing his coffee, Jerry stood at the window and we both looked out at the first few drops of rain. "It seems to me that some religion of universal salvation is coming," I said, "where accountability of all traditional faiths, including the faiths of

Karma, will be replaced by the new global faith where 'god is all.' A religion promoted by near-death experiencers who say you cannot lose. If not absorbed into heaven, they say you are sent back with another chance to make the world into another utopia for mankind."

These thoughts really disturbed us both. Nearby thunder rattled the windows and the rain poured down in buckets. Jerry put a hand on my shoulder. "How in the world would some dying patient discern which light is which? Which might be the angel of God and which might be Lucifer?"

I walked back to the desk for more coffee. "Maybe hell is surfacing to capture more and more of the uncommitted. Maybe it's like the preachers say: to know the spirit you have to test the spirit—to find out whether the light rejects Jesus' teachings or in any way denies that Jesus is the only Son of God. They say that Christ can never lie or deny Himself, but it seems that Satan loves to do either one."

The significance of things seemed heightened at the time by shaking thunder and streaks of lightning, wind scouring the panes with torrents of rain. And I paused to wonder what it was all about.

THE ANGEL OF LIGHT IDENTIFIED

It was the next day, the sun bright through the window, as I looked down at a third pint of blood draining rapidly into a pale, restless white male, age nineteen. No recordable blood pressure, a faint pulse in the neck, the chest bruised from resuscitation. The surgeon was scrubbing and I was listening to the heart. Two of the four stab wounds were gushing blood to one side. While preparing him for anesthesia, the patient said feebly:

> They were working on me in the ambulance, but it wasn't me. I was over to one side looking on. The one with the blood all over his coat put his fist in my belly trying to stop the bleeding. The other, a girl I think, was pumping on my chest.

> But I was out of there. I was going fast through blackness when this big light came rushing in on me.

> The light was real bright, and in some way it made me realize the good and bad I had done.

I saw my brother, two years younger than me, no traces of the crash. My mother was alive. She wore the same dress. She put her arm around me and we all walked through these beautiful green fields.

There was a rock wall. Mustn't have been three feet tall, but I couldn't climb over. On the other side I saw this person hanging from a cross and he spoke to me. But I could not reach him.

Then that awful pain in my belly came back. I was on the table and they were putting a mask over my face. God! The operation hadn't even started!

As in this case, many of my patients are Christians, and the glimpse of glory seems so real, God so near, that they want to recount the event to any cooperative listener. There is no ambiguity. They identify this brilliant "being" as Christ himself. No question of counterfeit. They describe the brilliance similar to the apostle Paul's description (in Acts chapters 9 and 26) of Christ's brilliance. (To me, confronting God would surely be a near-death experience in itself, but Paul had still another NDE at Lystra when he was stoned and left for dead. We will discuss that incident later.) But this was Paul's first NDE, if you consider it as such a thing:

> When one day about noon, sir, a light from heaven brighter than the sun shown down on me and my companions. We all fell down and I heard a voice speaking to me in Hebrew, "Saul, Saul, why are you persecuting me? You are only hurting yourself."
>
> "Who are you, sir?" I asked.
>
> And the Lord replied, "I am Jesus, the one you are persecuting. Now stand up! For I have appeared to you to anoint you as my servant and my witness. You are to tell the world about this experience and about the many other occasions when I shall appear to you."
>
> (Acts 9:3–6 TLB)

In Paul's experience, however, the light was so bright that he was blinded for three days. This appearance of light was only one of fifty-two instances where light is mentioned in the Bible, the "true light" identified as Christ in John 1:9.

This is probably the light said to have been glimpsed by many patients. But not all lights are good. Some evil lights are biblically mentioned as counterfeits, and there are many faiths that mention "beings of light." These faiths include those denominations directly worshiping Lucifer, and those offering the "Luciferic Initiation" into the New Age, a subject we will save for later.

In addition to testing the identity of the light, whether or not it in any way denies that Jesus is the only Son of God, remember to look for the evidence of profoundly changed lives, as in the following example. A retired and well-to-do accountant was a Christian-turned-cold following the death of his mother several years previously when her leg was amputated. In spite of his most fervent prayers, she died, and he concluded, "God is as deaf as a stone idol. He has no use for me, nor I for him." Subsequent to that time, the patient himself got into trouble:

> In the hospital elevator, I actually felt my heart stop and then I stopped breathing. I remembered saying, "So this is it."
>
> The next thing I was looking down from the ceiling in the intensive care unit. There was this young doctor in a white coat and two nurses bent over me. The doctor was yelling "get this" and "get that!"
>
> Next thing, I was going through this dark passage. I didn't hit any of the walls and at the other end I walked out into an open field. On the far side was this endless white wall which had three steps leading up to a doorway. I entered. Up on the landing sat the dazzling figure of an old man in glowing white robes. He seemed to be looking down into a big book and studying.
>
> As I approached I felt an overwhelming reverence and I asked, "Are you Jesus?"
>
> He said, "No, you will find Jesus and your loved ones beyond that door." Then he looked again in his book and nodded. "You may go on through."
>
> On the other side of the door I was amazed to find a brilliantly lit city, reflecting what looked like the rays of the sun, only diffused and suspended with particles of radiance. The roads were all made of gold. Some sort of shining metal covered the domes and steeples in beautiful array and the

walls were strangely smooth, not quite like marble, but made of something I had not seen before. Even the air smelled good, and faint music was there.

Then I saw two figures walking toward me and I knew immediately who they were. My mother and father who had died years ago. My mother was an amputee at the time of her death, but now she had two legs and was walking!

"You and father are beautiful," I said. And my father said to me, "You are also beautiful. Just look at yourself and see how you glow."

Then I noticed that one building was much larger than all of the others. It looked like a football stadium with the open end radiating a blinding light. I tried to look at the light but it was too brilliant. Many people were gathered in front of this building in an attitude of prayer.

I pointed and asked my parents, "What is that?"

"In there is God," they said. I will never forget that scene.

As we approached the next place, the place where Jesus was supposed to be, I felt as if I were hit and everything became dark. A jolting power went through my body and it hit me again in the chest, arching my body upward. I opened my eyes and I grabbed at the heart machine's paddles before they could shock me again.

This was another positive identification of Jesus (or of his angels) as the being of light. The positive identification of this light is of tremendous importance to these people, reinforcing the very core and conviction of their faith. Notice that this particular patient was deep into the sequence and had advanced beyond the sorting ground, beyond the barrier, beyond death's door.

———

In the late 1970s Assistant Secretary of the Navy James E. Johnson was in his car waiting on a traffic light in Washington, D.C. He was talking to attorney Jack Snyder when his words were cut off by screams of crushing metal as the car was rear-ended at high speed, hurling him into the steering column, wedging him into the dash. Everything went black. A moment later he found himself floating toward a light which was as dazzling as a brilliant sunrise as he gazed down on the scene of the accident without the slightest desire to return to the lifeless body tangled in the wreckage below.

I flew headlong through a dark tunnel at accelerating speed toward the shimmering light I sensed was Christ. . . .

Inside this light was a celestial city, like a castle in the sky. The translucent golden streets glowed with the brilliance that illuminated the whole city. . . . I knew I was in heaven.

Soon I saw Ken, my son who had been called to heaven years before. He was dressed in dazzling white. . . .

Then I recognized my father-in-law, with his special way of smiling and that little squint in his eyes I had known so well. "You'll be all right," he said. "Go on back. Go on back. Go on back."

My own mother and father joined the chant. My mother pointed to the light and asked, "Did you see Him?" I answered "Yes," with deep reverence. Caught up in the pervasive love and total peace of that place, I could not imagine leaving. Yet I knew I must. My time had not come.

The accident scene came into focus again. Suddenly, I felt very heavy, as if someone had laid an iron weight on top of me. As I began floating downward toward my body, a growing sensation of pain filled my consciousness.

The shimmering light of heavenly love slowly dissolved into a harsh, flashing red light. I was back in my body.[9]

After he was extricated, moved to the hospital and x-rayed, Secretary Johnson felt exuberant, as if divinely healed. The ambulance attendants and the doctors only laughed when he announced he would walk home that same day, fully recovered. But he did just that.

Such personal experiences concerning a specific Christian afterlife have been recently obscured by a plethora of non-Christian positive experiences coming from surprised agnostics who were "touched" by this magnanimous, understanding, all-loving, "compassionate being," who found no fault, no undeserving circumstance. They thought this being of light had to be good, since they were obviously permitted a "glimpse of glory," a glimpse that seemed to assure that heaven would be their destiny.

The bona fide Christian event, on the other hand, so radically influences their lives that they must tell others, often writing books about their experiences, as did Richard Eby in *Caught up into Paradise* and Betty Maltz in *Glimpse of Eternity*.

So it appears that unique clinical deaths, not the generalized catch-all wastebasket of near-death experiences, contain the strong thread of cohesiveness, identifying a consecutive progression of events that yield analytical comparisons. In fact one of the clinical deaths in biblical times may have involved the apostle Paul. Instead of permanent biological death—"It is appointed for men to die once, but after this the judgment" (Heb. 9:27)—Paul may have experienced a clinical death in the city of Lystra where he was stoned and left for dead by a murderous mob of people who resented both his ministry and his miracles (2 Tim. 3:11).

By timing, this may have occurred when Paul was "drawn up into paradise" where he "heard things so astounding" before he was returned to his physical body. This was recorded in his second letter to the Corinthians, as described in the third person:

> I know a man in Christ who fourteen years ago—whether in the body I do not know, or whether out of the body I do not know, God knows—such a one was caught up to the third heaven. And I know such a man—whether in the body or out of the body I do not know, God knows—how he was caught up into Paradise and heard inexpressible words, which it is not lawful for a man to utter. Of such a one I will boast; yet of myself I will not boast, except in my infirmities. (2 Cor. 12:2–5 NIV)

THE BEING OF LIGHT UNIDENTIFIED

The majority of the literature is burdened with all sorts of "beings of light," but many of them are unidentified, the viewer overwhelmed by the brilliance or possibly diverted by the beautiful environment. Any assumptive identification was often nebulous, the figure assumed to be a prominent representative of their faith. Yet the light usually remained unidentified. Unless the being of light was identified by reliable word or sign, there was no way for the victim to know exactly who he had encountered or where they came from. It could have been Lucifer himself masquerading as an angel of light unless the spirit was tested through the acknowledgment of his name and his relationship to Jesus Christ or some other deity. Some Christians can only say they knew it was Christ because of the confirming witness of the Holy Spirit within them.

Let me give you an example of the "no-accountability" problem we're addressing. In 1980 I was sitting next to an attractive, well-groomed woman of fifty-two. We were on a national TV talk show by David Susskind out of Miami. The female guest was announcing to the world the marvelous news that "heaven's gates are open wide to everyone who dies. No one is left out. Everyone should know."

During her resuscitation from an automobile accident she received a "vibrantly transmitted" message from a "beautiful being of light." The vibrations forcefully demanded "unconditional love" for a world that had no sin. That was why she was sent back: To announce the global message of love, the new planetary consciousness for a new religion which would proclaim the divinity of mankind.

It was not until the commercial break that I got to know her. In the act of lighting up a cigar, she informed me that she was a friend of Madalyn Murray O'Hair, President of the American Atheistic Society, an articulate lawyer who was to get the best of me during a subsequent TV debate in Detroit. I was beginning to understand the source of the vibrations which proclaimed heaven as a free ride for everyone.

It was perhaps ten years ago I first recalled the words this woman was using—buzz words like *global* and words like *planetary, paradigm, new world order, age of enlightenment,* and *transpersonal psychology.* These are new names for old concepts that have been redesigned and modernized for the new age in which we live.

LUCIFER THE ANGEL OF LIGHT

Many religions associate their leaders with light, and, as mentioned, in the Christian faith both Jesus and Lucifer claim to be light. To repeat, it is crucial in near-death studies to determine the source of this being of light—whether the source is a reliable representative of God, or a luring mirage of evil that imitates God as a forgiving Force. A force which could change Dr. Jekyll into Mr. Hyde, a change Johanna Michaelson and others observed in their spirit guides.

Light of all sorts is presented in NDE/OBE reports, more often in those without clinical death. This unidentified, beautiful figure could conceivably represent the imitator, the one whose name in most monotheistic faiths means "light bearer." It comes from the Latin *lucis-ferre,* or Lucifer. Lucifer is so beautiful that he is also known as "the morning star." Could this be the same "Angel of Light" seen by those of little faith and the uncommitted?

I asked myself why the deceptive angel is beautiful. Would it be poor salesmanship if Satan appeared as Satan? Instead of repulsive demonic beings, could Lucifer and his angels cunningly appear as "servants of righteousness" and deceive many people? The Bible says yes. The potential for the "Angel of Light" to be Lucifer instead of God is emphasized again from another translation of 2 Corinthians 11:14–15:

> And no wonder! For Satan himself transforms himself into an angel of light. Therefore it is no great thing if his ministers also transform themselves into ministers of righteousness, whose end will be according to their works.

While hell is just plain hell and offers no possibility of deception, the Christian must be wary of the wonderful reports so eagerly claimed in the majority of near-death experiences. The experience may give false assurance, the survivors having no opportunity to make theological inquiries. The impostor, of course, would be the one who denies Jesus is the Christ, the Son of God, but the figure of light may be non-committal on the subject or cleverly avoid any self-identification at all (1 John 2:22). Yet the ministers say those who know Christ now will also know him then.

In what other ways could you detect the fraudulent? "Unconditional love" is something uniformly dispensed by this light, says researcher Elisabeth Kubler-Ross. "God *is* love," we are also told by Christian teaching. But God is sinless. He unconditionally loves the sinner but punishes the sin. What is sin? The ministers say that rebellion against God is sin. To me, a layman, it seems that sin would also include thumbing your nose at God, "God-damning" this or that, or maybe just turning your back on God as if he never existed.

In this context, would a God-sent angel of light see no sin in each passerby? Would the true angel of God consider unrequested absolution as everyone's humanistic right? Isn't repentance a vital part in receiving Christ's atonement? Would the non-Christian get a pat on the back or would he receive specific admonitions? Of course, we don't know the destiny of those who did not return to receive another chance at life.

But other faiths also see the light at the end of the tunnel. They assume it is one of many messengers or gods of their own faith. For instance, the Hindu often assumes the light to be the "Yamdoot" or death spirit. But it seems remarkable to me that the figure of light never identifies itself as Brahma, Vishnu, Shiva, Krishna, Buddha, Allah, Matreya, or any one of the other deities. The Jew may identify the figure as one of Jehovah's angels or prophets. The Christian may be sure the light is Christ himself. Some have seen Christ on the cross and feel a surge of spiritual confirmation that encourages their purpose in life.

But misrepresentations by the light do indeed occur. I have interviewed several cases which confirm this. One is in the following report.

It occurred one day while I was covering at Plasma Alliance for Dr. Durwood Kirk, a retired urologist undergoing surgery at the time. Plasma Alliance extracts blood from paid donors to obtain immune globulins for the manufacture of vaccines. While screening applicants for carriers of hepatitis or AIDS, I noticed one donor with recent wounds that could introduce a blood infection into others. So I started the questioning routine.

This was a self-assured, husky white male of twenty-one years. He told me the residual bullet wounds in his chest required both resuscitation from coma and blood transfusions. Three small-caliber bullets had entered the left chest, one of them nicking the heart wall at the time.

During CPR in the ambulance, he told me he had an out-of-the-body experience. He was surprised by the heavenly light surrounding him. He felt welcomed by the light. The light was "understanding." No ridicule or rejection. The sordid parts of his life were not examined and no mention was made of the couple he had killed three years before during a robbery in a parking lot. Only "peace and love" were communicated. This was his story:

> The trouble all started when we were dancing. She had been working the bar earlier in the evening, so I thought she

was available. We walked out on the floor and started dancing very close, our bodies touching.

I've danced with all types of women, but this was the
strangest-feeling woman I've ever danced with. I found out
that my partner was actually a man, dressed in a woman's
clothing, complete with padded bra, wig, and a mouthful of
lipstick!

I personally hate homosexuals, and now I was dancing
with this gay who was a cross-dresser to boot! I gave her (or
him) a shove and beat her up. She ran from me over to the
bar. I ran after her, but she pulled out a gun hidden under
the bar and shot me three times in the chest.

Keeping the patient on the subject, I asked, "After you had
been shot, what about the tunnel you saw and this all-forgiving
light? How did you feel about that?"
He thought for a while, then threw up his hands in despair.

Well, it felt good to be in this beautiful place, you know,
but I kept wondering why the light never asked me about my
beating the heck out of the cross-dresser. And the light never
mentioned the two killings from the past.

I was glad he didn't ask me about those things, but if he
was from God, why didn't he? I thought about bringing it up,
but said to myself, "Why knock a good thing?" and kept my
mouth shut. I knew I should be in hell instead of this nice
place, but I kept quiet.

Looking around and lowering his voice, he said, "Doc, does
God ever make mistakes?"
This report helped crystallize my thinking. It was evident that
Satan very often masquerades as God, and that one simply must
analyze the reports to discern if the "being of light" is from God
or not. For example, is the being all knowing and truthful, as God
is, or seemingly forgetful (such as the murders and misdeeds in
this case)?

And in all the other NDE reports that are positive and glowing,
does God overlook the miscreant's past? Does the light automati-
cally grant absolution? Or could that particular God-like being be
forgetful because it is not from God?

Recently other survivors have openly questioned the being of

light and this unrequested forgiveness. I would think that unconditional love sometimes has "conditions." For instance, I can remember conditions as a child. My father would withhold
chastisement if I said I was sorry and asked his forgiveness. Unconditional love? Yes, my father had that, also. He loved me so
much, in fact, that it would make him cry when he spanked me.
But he was not "all-forgiving" unless I "fessed up." How much
more, I wonder, would our heavenly father be forgiving, still loving us unconditionally, if we fessed up? I found the answer in
1 John 1:9. "If we confess our sins, He is faithful and just to
forgive us our sins and to cleanse us from all unrighteousness."
Healing may be in the asking, but sometimes the light never
seems to question the need for forgiveness.

Can the light be all-forgiving and just at the same time? Even
the current form of Hollywood Hinduism does not offer the forgiveness that is spontaneously dispensed by the light. Karma
never forgives. Karma mandates mercilessly that one must burn
off in today's life the misdeeds of previous lives. Karma, the reason of reincarnation, does indeed imply accountability after all,
and this is disturbing news to reincarnationists who insist there is
never any accountability. Karma, in actuality, proves to be a cruel
means of refining one life after another, until you finally get it
right.

From what source, then, do the New Age religions explain this
light that dispenses unconditional forgiveness? By definition, it
could not be from karma and reincarnation. Perhaps it comes
from the "religion of resuscitation," the one now based on the
uniformly beautiful near-death reports. It is called the Omega of
unconditional love, the magnanimous passport to heaven for one
and all. The permanent glimpse of glory.

Of course, the heavenly cases are always ecstatic about the
marvelous results. But it does seem strange that none of the hell
cases have ever cried foul to the being of light in charge of their
destiny, nor have they complained of the unfairness of their predicament. The common conclusion of such survivors is that hell is
just plain hell, as we shall see in the next chapter.

4

HELL
IS JUST
PLAIN HELL

THE PERSUASION OF HELL

The patient said his life was a living hell. In his sixties, this large gray-haired farmer would fall to the floor unconscious, hitting his head, resulting in lacerations requiring sutures. Each time, his heart seemed to start up again or shift into very fast rhythms. CPR assistance was often required until an electrical jump-start could be accomplished in the hospital. He called this uncertain existence "a living hell," awakening to considerable pain and good-sized hospital bills. His circumstances were approaching futility until we finally inserted a pacemaker.

By the time Medicare got around to reviewing the records a year later, they decided the correcting pacemaker had been unnecessary because it did not fulfill the criteria listed in Medicare's code books. It did not matter that the "sudden death" episodes, which had occurred on eight occasions in ten months, were no longer a problem. They ruled the pacemaker expenses must be repaid by me, the patient, and the hospital.

The appeals court judge at the beginning ruled that "the fact that the patient appears to be doing well at the moment does not prove that he needed the pacemaker." Shuffling more papers, he shook his head. "Nowhere in the books is 'multifocal ventricular tachycardia'—or whatever you said it was—listed as an indication for using a pacemaker."

Unfortunately, I stood up and said something. "I know it isn't listed, your honor, because your Medicare books need updating." That obviously didn't settle too well, so I hastily added, "But, more convenient to the cause, the patient has consented to demonstrate the need of his pacemaker for his survival."

The judge went through a few more papers before he nodded his approval. Quickly placing the patient on the floor, I hooked him to the monitor and arranged the necessary magnets and paddles. I knew the patient's heart was unable to beat on its own, but the judge had to be convinced.

Moving more papers around, the judge interrupted. "Do you intend to turn off the pacemaker?"

I shrugged, gesturing with my hands. "When I turn it off he will stop existing for a while, but that will allow your honor to determine the need for himself." Then I started deprogramming the pacemaker.

For an eternity there was an uncanny silence and then the judge suddenly slapped the table and stood abruptly. "That won't at all be necessary, doctor." Another long pause. "After further deliberation, the court rules this pacemaker is both necessary and justified. Case dismissed!"

Like Solomon and the baby, the judge's timely decision avoided the patient's potential transient encounter with heaven or hell.

It was an interesting case, illustrating faith in the unseen. Although the judge was not able to see the pacemaker, he was nevertheless willing to accept someone else's word that it existed and that it served a vital function. Like the pacemaker, there are an abundance of other unseen things we are told exist and have vital functions. Sometimes things are best left alone, however, and not manipulated or challenged, but accepted on faith. This is important because faith in the unseen is the hope of all religions.

Surprisingly a Gallup poll[1] listed a full 78 percent of the public believing in heaven and a whopping 60 percent believing in hell. Among those claiming no religious belief, 46 percent still believed in heaven and 34 percent in hell. On the subject of prayer, even among those who do not believe God has ever existed, 10 percent will still pray daily to some spirit or another. In comparison, 70 percent of religious believers pray daily.[2]

It would seem that most people have some belief in hell; otherwise hell wouldn't be used as one of the most popular words in our lexicon. It is often a word relied upon when the vocabulary is limited, but it is also cultivated by intellectuals, who consider hell to be a myth. Disparagingly, the people who believe in hell the least need to remind themselves of it the most, which strongly suggests an outward rejection of inward uncertainty.

Of all the religious books in the world, each purporting to be an exclusive authority in spiritual matters, none speaks in more detail about hell than the Judeo-Christian Bible, addressing hell more frequently than it does heaven, admonishing "wide" is the way to destruction and "narrow" is the way to life; that "many" shall find the former but "few" will find the latter.

If this is true, if negative experiences have been predicted to be much more plentiful than positive ones, then why isn't this reflected in all the near-death reports? Why don't dominantly negative reports occupy the mainstay of post-resuscitation literature? The truth remains that the negative reports are there (i.e., on the lips of the survivors), but the observer has to be on the scene to capture them before they are swept away into painless areas of the memory.

It is interesting to note that similar negative data are available in the deathbed scenes, but, again, someone has to be there at the right time to record them. Dr. Ian Stevenson and Dr. Justine Owens, researchers at the University of Virginia, are now encouraging a study expressly designed for early interviews of resuscitated patients and other near-death experiences. On-the-scene interviews should uncover the present disparity in the bell curve.

HISTORY OF HELL

Hell itself has always been the believer's worst nightmare, always wondering if it is safe to die, continually reaching for reassurance.

"I preach a literal hell," says Rev. Morris Chapman, past president of the Southern Baptist Convention. "The Bible calls it a 'lake of fire,' and I don't think that definition can be improved upon."

In contrast, many churches sponsor little talk these days about a literal, punitive hell as a real possibility after death. "My congregation would be stunned to hear a sermon on hell," says the Rev. Mary Kraus of the Dumbarton United Methodist Church in Washington, D.C., whose parishioners view God as "compassionate and loving, not someone who's going to push them into eternal damnation."

When I asked my former minister, Dr. Matthew McGowan, and the present minister, Dr. Ed Byrd, of Central Presbyterian Church in Chattanooga, why they did not preach more about hell, the answer was, "because the congregation wouldn't like it."

Today, in the minds of modern scholars, a literal hell just doesn't exist anymore. "Once we discovered we could create hell on earth," says John Dominic Crossan of DePaul University in Chicago, "it became silly to talk about it in a literal sense."[3]

By most accounts, hell has all but disappeared from the pulpit rhetoric of mainline Protestantism, and hasn't done much better among evangelicals. Hell has gradually disappeared, so to speak, and no one seemed to notice where it went. Until now.

Now, the baby boomers seem to be returning to American traditional religion seeking answers to basic questions of faith and morality in a world filled with pervasive violence and hatred. A Gallup Poll taken in 1990 amazingly shows that more Americans believe in hell today than they did in the generally more pious years of the 1950s.[4]

Ours is the first generation ever that has been afforded an opportunity to approach some answers. We now hear from a population that has been through preliminary death to claim and report the ancient biblical beliefs of a life beyond the grave. This phenomenon is one of the rare connecting links between scripture and science.

Besides Judaism, hell can be found in some degree in almost every religion of the world with the probable singular exception of the North American Indians, where purgatory is replaced by the happy hunting ground.

In Islam, for example, which shares common roots with Christianity and Judaism, hell is reported to be a huge "lake of fire," traversing beneath a narrow bridge over which all souls must pass if they are to enter paradise. Those who fall from the bridge, the ones found unworthy by Allah, enter one of seven layers of hell, a burning "bed of misery." Even the Arabic word for hell, *Jahanna,* has the same derivation as the Hebrew hell, *Gehenna,* literally the place of incineration. This is the place to which the Ayatollah Khomeini condemned Salman Rushdie for writing *The Satanic Verses.*

For those following the New Age Hinduism as a hope of escaping the concept and punishment of hell, there await some relatively unknown surprises. Instead of one hell, the Hindus have a total of twenty-one hells in all, affording an opportunity for the bad *karma* (the evil which one commits during a lifetime) to be burned away.

There is, on the other hand, no judgment day in Hinduism. You pay as you go. In the long run, however, the very wicked are placed in the "lower hells" where they may be boiled in jars, scorched by sands, or devoured by birds.

While the philosophy of the New Age ignores the possibility of hell, it also ignores the hellish possibility of humans returning as animals (rather than humans) in the next life. The scriptures of the ancient Hindu *Puranas* emphatically outline that one's karma may transfer a very bad human into a very lowly animal, commensurate with their crimes while human. Thieves of grain, for instance, could return as rats, or misusers of food as roaches.

Buddhism represents the followers of a man named Siddhartha Gautama, who broke from Hinduism in 600 B.C. to travel to Asia, similar to the way Mohammed broke from Judaism in 600 A.D. to form Islam. Buddhism speaks of a multitude of hells as temporary stops in one's journey toward Nirvana, an apparent blissful state of nonexistence, the person becoming a nonentity in a rather blitheful sea of nothingness. Tibetan Buddhists will also speak of "eight cold hells" for the wicked. Thus, hell is not unknown to other reincarnationist religions, although the New Agers are probably not aware of the thought.

Jainism and Taoism, variants of Buddhism and Hinduism which travelled toward the Pacific Rim, religions which also predate Christianity by centuries, also believe in hell. While Jainism believes in millions of hells, Taoism, primarily the Chinese religion, talks more of Buddhist paradises with only a few hells reserved for special punishments.

Concerning the Christian view of hell, in the third century Origen thought it was "remedial," while others thought hell a "place of annihilation," and still others "a place of eternal fire and tor-ment." Even Dante's imaginary description of hell recorded in *The Divine Comedy* of the fourteenth century depicts flaming levels of hell, which happen to parallel the descriptions given in the Muslim Koran seven centuries earlier.

Further Christian confusion occurred when both Martin Luther and John Calvin viewed hell's punishments as "eternal" but "figurative," defined mainly as an ostracism from God. Later, in the Second Vatican Council in the '60s, Catholicism ecumenized the potential for "all souls" to make it to heaven, although purgatory might be a "temporary requirement" for some.

Some cultic views have also found their way into the church. The three main ones have one thing in common—they deny the teaching on an eternal hell. Universalism assumes that all men have immortal souls and all will be saved. Annihilationism assumes the immortality of the soul, but teaches that God, at judgment, will annihilate all who are not saved, their immortality taken from them. Conditional immortality assumes the soul of man is not immortal and therefore those not saved are simply never resurrected to eternal life and they cease to exist.

Thus, the Christian doctrine of hell entered the present century in somewhat fragmented fashion, although recent events have changed the motif. These events include the resurgent experiences with violence, suffering and hate (perhaps an earthly taste of hell); the convincing reports of hell encounters after clinical death; and a return to fundamentalism where hell today remains a vital central doctrine—a doctrine inextricably linked to the concept of salvation through the death and resurrection of Jesus Christ. This doctrine holds that hell is neither allegory nor metaphor, but a place. A place which, if successfully renounced by the New World Order, would hopefully make unnecessary the need for personal salvation. That repudiation is, of course, the new gospel proposed by most NDE researchers and the appealing secret desire of most: that there is no hell.

Eternity could be a "hell-of-a-long-time" to pay for outright denial of hell, or for procrastination in determining one's beliefs, and another reason why these negative resuscitated cases become so fascinatingly crucial. To the people who have been to hell and back, those who claim to have experienced it and who returned to testify, the fact of hell is as certain as the moon and the stars and the visible heavens.

The Christian Bible, interestingly, does not always portray hell's fire as a fiery place in every passage. While the fate of the impenitent is certainly portrayed as "the hell of fire" (Matt. 5:22 RSV), and "the unquenchable fire" (Mark 9:43 RSV), it is also related in other ways to "the outer darkness" (Matt. 8:12 RSV), the place where the "worm does not die" (Mark 9:48), a state called "destruction" (Phil. 3:19), a separation "from the presence of the Lord" (2 Thes. 1:9), and "cast out" from the Kingdom of God.

No matter the description, it's a hell-of-a-place to be. Whether a place of torment or a separation from God, resuscitated patients are determined never to experience that place again. From some sort of horrendous fear, often too difficult to express in words, a plethora of conversions or sublimations (concealed in areas of unreachable memory) appear as possible escape mechanisms.

Only a few of the hell experiences relate to descriptions of the final judgment found in the book of Revelation. They more closely correlate instead to Jesus' description of the beggar and the rich man when they both died and their spirits left the body to begin a spiritual existence. In the heavenly world the beggar was comforted by Abraham himself; in the hellish world the rich man was begging for water for the tip of his tongue "for I am tormented in this flame" (Luke 16:24). From Jesus' description, it seemed to be a fiery place of desolation without hope.

Jesus was always adamant about the place, talking more about hell than heaven, distinctly familiar with the place where he said most people would go. Although only 40 percent of ministers preach hell, and while researcher Carl Johnson maintains that 70 percent of all clergy deny the very doctrine of hell,[5] it seems that Jesus thought hell was a very important subject to remember.

TO HELL AND BACK

Pacemakers are a common source of clinical deaths. A twenty-three-year-old male experienced repeated fainting whenever heart block (conduction failure for beating) suddenly recurred. The periods of unconsciousness were becoming more frequent, suggesting a poor outcome.

The block was inherited. Both his father and brother had pace-makers for the same birth defect, both still living. Fortunately, we were all set up for the pacemaker implant when the natural heart beat stopped permanently and a near-death experience occurred. The patient is talking to me:

> You were watching the television monitor to guide the pacemaker wire inside my heart. That's when it stopped. I was blacking out and then you hit me on the chest, saying 'excuse me.' Then your fist came down like a hammer. I saw that scared look in your eyes. Someone was yelling. Something crashed over to my left and everybody went crazy. You started shoving on me with both hands and then I was out of it.
>
> I was floating, pitch black, moving fast. The wind whistled by and I rushed toward this beautiful, blazing light. As I moved past, the walls of the tunnel nearest the light caught fire. Beyond the blazing tunnel a huge lake of fire was burning like an oil spill. A hill on the far side was covered with slabs of rock. Elongated shadows showed that people were moving aimlessly about, like animals in a zoo enclosure.
>
> An old stone building was on the right, mostly rubble, with different levels and openings crammed with people trying to move about.
>
> Down the hall I saw an old friend who had died. The last I recall, they were dragging the river for him; he had been involved with gambling. I yelled to him, "Hi there, Jim!" He just looked at me. Didn't even smile. They were taking him around the corner when he started screaming. I ran, but there was no way out. I kept saying "Jesus is God." Over and over I would say, "Jesus is God."
>
> Someway, somehow, I got back as you were putting in the stitches. I loved every one of those stitches. Only God could have gotten me out of a mess like that. I'll never forget it.

When I saw this patient later in the office he wasn't the shy young man I had known. He told the nurses about the positive experience of the miraculous recovery, but never mentioned details of hell nor the reason why he was there.

Like so many negative experiences, this patient had no recall of scenes or activities that occurred in the room. He saw the being of light at the end of the tunnel, but the light soon turned into blazing fire, igniting the tunnel walls as he went by. He called it the "fire of hell." Several other people saw the heavenly light turn into a foreboding ring of fire.

Somewhat similar observations were made by Nancy Bush, President of IANDS (International Association for Near-Death Studies), as she encountered several different negative near-death experiences (now about fifty) that her predecessor, Kenneth Ring, had apparently failed to see or failed to report.[6]

Drs. Moody and Ring, both now actively engaged in the para-normal—Moody into mirrors and crystal balls and Ring into UFOs—reviewed several thousand NDEs in the Evergreen Study and reported that less than 1 percent (actually only 0.3 percent) had hellish experiences and would have us think that life after death is, after all the evidence is reviewed, entirely a heavenly affair.[7]

Going to hell and back becomes life's most frightening adventure.

Fortunately, a few observers are beginning to disagree. One of the disagreements was by researcher Dr. Charles Garfield who noted, "Not everyone dies a blissful, accepting death. . . . *Almost as many of the dying patients interviewed reported negative visions (demons and so forth), as reported blissful experiences,* while some reported both (emphasis mine)."[8] Note his ratio of roughly 50/50 for negative/positive. I am not the only researcher claiming large amounts of existing negative material!

Perhaps we should look closer into clinical deaths for hidden evidences for hell. Some of the so-called "good" cases report personal skirmishes with demons and evil forces on their way to the light, as if part of a constant struggle between good and evil for the spirit or soul of man, even while on the way to this glimpse of glory.

In Demetria Kalodimos's excellent study, "A Glimpse of Glory," a documentary between September and October, 1992, on WSMV in Nashville, Tennessee, she interviewed one resuscitated woman who found herself in a frightening void, "totally alone,"

before she eventually saw the light. In the same film, a Mr. Tandy
Hawks was confronted by a menacing voice that called him "ugly
names," becoming "more violent" as he approached the light.
Young Hawks eventually reached the light and this glimpse of
glory caused his conversion to Christianity, losing friends as he
became compelled to share the good news.

Lee Merritt was a young man featured in the film who became
aware of "demons within the walls" of the dark tunnel. "The
darkness was so real you could touch it and it would burn," he
said.

The negative sequences, except for the ravaging scenery, seem
more abbreviated and rapid than the heavenly ones. Frequently
they would see people or friends who had died, but there was no
apparent "barrier" (a wall, a river, or some physical boundary)
which was found in many pleasant experiences that separated the
meeting ground from possible judgment areas.

Gleaning the literature for similar negative experiences in ancient times was mostly a futile endeavor because there was no
effective resuscitation available to recover clinical deaths. However, hell was always there in deathbed visions, those foreboding
events prior to death, and also the hell from drugs and dreams
dating back to Freud's experiments and beyond.

When people used to die at home in yesteryears, family observations of deathbed experiences were common. Today, however,
death scenarios are hidden in nursing homes and hospitals where
the family is constrained from constant attendance. Most hospital
personnel in attendance seem disinterested and dispassionate, ig-
noring spiritual events, sometimes afraid of them because of
things they don't understand.

When I asked why no hell-like events had been reported in
these institutions, the reasons given were that no one was there at
the time, or the patient was influenced by the toxicity of an oxygen-deprived mind. The oxygen-starved mind, however, happens
to be one of the least likely circumstances to produce extraterrestrial experiences or decisions.

Both the deathbed experiences of yesterday and the resuscitated experiences of today were not all infallibly good in spite of
the volume of positive near-death reports you read about. Many
of them, those not talked about, were frighteningly bad.

For instance, some gruesome experiences in the past were described on the deathbeds of Voltaire, King Charles IX of France, Queen Elizabeth in 1603, Ethan Allen, Thomas Payne, David Hume, and Edward Gibbon.[9] Even at that time the negative experiences, as they are today, were hidden from public view and not reported. Proud families of the past naturally mentioned only the favorable events. It is no different today. Positive events are given liturgy by the family of the deceased while dismal events remain closeted with the other family laundry.

Resuscitation was first introduced in the 1970s. Prior to that time, negative experiences were found only in protracted illnesses or comas. In 1948, for example, George Godkin of Alberta, Canada related a despairing near-death affair in the midst of a prolonged critical illness:

> I was guided to the place in the spirit world called Hell. This is a place of punishment for all those who reject Jesus Christ. I not only saw Hell, but felt the torment that all who go there will experience.
>
> The darkness of Hell is so intense that it seems to have a pressure per square inch. It is an extremely black, dismal, desolate, heavy, pressurized type of darkness. It gives the individual a crushing, despondent feeling of loneliness.
>
> The heat is a dry, dehydrating type. Your eyeballs are so dry they feel like red hot coals in their sockets. Your tongue and lips are parched and cracked with the intense heat. The breath from your nostrils as well as the air you breathe feels like a blast from a furnace. The exterior of your body feels as though it were encased within a white hot stove. The interior of your body has a sensation of scorching hot air being forced through it.
>
> The agony and loneliness of Hell cannot be expressed clearly enough for proper understanding to the human soul; it has to be experienced.[10]

While the descriptive language is flavored by the times, the negative experiences are much the same today. There is no relationship to occupation, education, or circumstance. Affluence has never altered the outcome.

While some of the "good" experiences believe the purpose of the light was to encourage them to mend their ways and "do better" when they were sent back, some cases are beginning to wonder if they really belonged there, accountability not even mentioned. But the hell-like cases always know they came to the correct place. No mistakes. No questions. An example is the Sunday school teacher, a Baptist, who had three separate death experiences from three separate cardiac arrests, the first two from heart attacks. The last arrest was the complication of an unexpected cancer of the rectum, and we didn't try retrieval methods that time. The first of these clinical deaths displayed snakes and fires and things so horrible that it resulted in a religious awakening. He said he knew he was not the Christian he should have been. Some sort of a conversion resulted and the second clinical death produced a wonderful, heavenly experience, the one that he wanted in the first place. At the third and final death, both he and I were sure what the results would be. He was the one who was able to reassure me.

In separate clinical deaths occurring in the same individual, which itself is a rare thing, it's always bad-to-good conversion. I've never seen a transition from good-to-bad. The significance? It appears there's nothing like a little bit of hell to dramatically change life's purpose and attitude.

The same was true for the mother of a despondent fourteen-year-old girl. She swallowed the same sedative capsules her deranged daughter had used to dispose of herself two weeks previously. The mother decided to follow in the footsteps of her distraught daughter. Yet, instead of finding her daughter, who had been mentally ill, she found hell staring her in the face. After being resuscitated, she formed a support group for family survivors of teenaged suicide victims, discovering that 85 percent of those people who failed suicide were quite glad to be alive. She discovered they just needed somebody to listen, somebody to understand, somebody to love them.

Hell experiences are not uncommon among the glamour and money moguls of Hollywood, probably because the hell experiences are publicized (if they were ever revealed), making good copy in the grocery store checkout lines. Such sensationalism is always the substance of newscopy, particularly when some TV evangelist can be photographed in the red light district.

Except for tabloid literature, negative cases supposedly never occur. But the cinema world does have its negative side. Curt Jurgens, a German actor and idol, had a negative experience when his heart frequently stopped during much of the four hours it took Dr. Michael DeBakey in Houston to replace part of an aorta (the main blood vessel):

Soon I had a feeling that life was ebbing from me. I felt powerful sensations of dread. I had been looking up into the big glass cupola over the operating room. This cupola now began to change. Suddenly it turned a glowing red. I saw twisted faces grimacing as they stared down at me.

I tried to struggle upright and defend myself against these ghosts, who were moving closer to me. Then it seemed as if the glass cupola had turned into a transparent dome that was slowly sinking down over me. A fiery rain was now falling, but though the drops were enormous, none of them touched me. They spattered down around me, and out of them grew menacing tongues of flames licking up about me.

I could no longer shut out the frightful truth: beyond the faces dominating this fiery world were faces of the damned. I had a feeling of despair . . . the sensation of horror was so great it choked me.

Obviously I was in Hell itself, and the glowing tongues of fire could be reaching me any minute. In this situation, the black silhouette of a human figure suddenly materialized and began to draw near. It was a woman in a black veil, a slender woman with a lipless mouth and in her eyes an expression that sent icy shudders down my back.

She stretched out her arms toward me and, pulled by an irresistible force, I followed her. An icy breath touched me and I came into a world filled with faint sounds of lamentation, though there was not a person in sight. Then and there I asked the figure to tell me who she was. A voice answered: "I am death."

I summoned all my strength and thought: "I'll not follow her any more, for I want to live."[11]

Interestingly, in this account and others, there was an absence of the "beings of light." In the glowing positive accounts dominating current literature, this Black Angel, the Angel of Death, is seldom mentioned. Dr. Phillip Swihart of Montrose, Colorado, a clinical psychologist, had been attacked, beaten, and kicked nearly to death, and ended up in the hospital. In the operating room, awaiting exploratory abdominal surgery, he felt some strange presence before the darkness came:

> This experience was, to say the least, unbelievable. Every detail, right up to the present time. It all took place in what seemed just a fraction of a second, and yet it was all very vivid.

> All the time I was watching my life go by, I felt the presence of some sort of power, but I didn't see it. Next, I was drawn into total darkness. Then I stopped. It felt like a big hollow room. It seemed to be a very large space and totally dark. I could see nothing, but felt the presence of this power.

> I asked the power who I and who he, or it, was. Communication was not by talking but through a flow of energy. He answered that he was the Angel of Death. I believed him. The Angel went on to say that my life was not as it should be, that he could take me on but that I would be given a second chance, and that I was to go back.

> The next thing I remember I was in the recovery room, back in my body. I was so taken in by this experience that I did not notice what kind of body I had, nor how much time had elapsed, it was so real—I believed it.[12]

Encounters with a "death angel" are more frequently reported in negative than positive experiences and in cases of terminal illness than elsewhere.

In and out of prolonged coma, one female patient of mine described a "hooded, faceless messenger" of death which circled over her bed, grim darkness appearing about the room "as if death and life were waging a battle." Death won before any known sequence evolved that we could report.

Among all the negative experiences, the scenes and environment of hell seem to vary. Regardless of the environment, however, hell is just plain hell. It is not of one stereotyped sort, but it doesn't matter—going to hell and back becomes life's most frightening adventure. Some will see demons and hideous things, but to my knowledge none have seen the devil. Some will see the turbulence of hell, lakes of hell, or layers of hell; others will see the fires of hell as Rev. Kenneth Hagin described in his account, going through a "pit-like" entrance.[13]

Still others describe lakes of fire, fire on the mountains, or fire

in the deserts—or no fire at all. They can find themselves in a
pitch-black space where they are required to perform punitive
tasks, as in the case of a patient who was resuscitated in the
excitement of the Knoxville football stadium and later transferred
to our clinic at Diagnostic Center:

> I was moving through a vacuum as if life never ended, so
> black you could almost touch it. Black, frightening, and deso-
> late. I was all alone somewhere in outer space.
>
> I was in front of some type of conveyor belt which carried
> huge pieces of puzzle in weird colors that had to be fitted
> together rapidly under severe penalty from an unseen force.
> It was horrible. Impossible. I was shrieking and crying. I was
> deathly afraid of this force. I knew it was Hell, but there was
> no fire or heat or anything that I had expected.
>
> I was alone, isolated from all sound, until I heard a mum-
> bling, and I could vaguely see a kneeling form. It was my
> wife. She was praying at my bedside. I never wanted to be a
> Christian, but I surely am now. Hell is too real.

In both the United States and in India, afterlife apparitions are
commonly reported, but the experiences show many differences.
The Americans, predominately Christian, tend to see only one
supernatural being and later may encounter family and friends
who have died before. The people of India, predominately
Hindu, do not usually see family or people, but do see some of
their many gods or religious figures.[14]

The influence of positive and negative reports are remarkably
different. Heavenly reports, depending upon the identity of the
light as good or potentially evil, either serve as a convicting rebirth for the Christian, or a rebuff of the moral world to encourage hedonism—eat, drink, and be merry, that all will be well.
Negative events, in contrast, command a redirection of moral
values and objectives in life. Hell is so profound that it provokes
convictions, and conversions, and a compelling new life-style.

Of all those who have been to hell and back, I wonder why is
there no report of anyone seeing Satan, or Lucifer, or Pan, or
gods of hell? It bothered me so much that I took this disturbing
problem to David Mainse, founder of 100 Huntley Street, Toronto's global evangelistic television network now transferred to
Crossroads in Burlington. He used Revelation 20:10 as a refer-

ence to indicate that the devil has not yet been cast into the "lake of fire." He said this is the reason why the devil has never been seen in hell. Other theologians, such as Ben Haden and Ed Byrd, tend to agree that Satan is still alive and well, but not yet in hell.

From my own viewpoint as a doctor, I imagine that if I had a hell experience I would expect to see something previously pre-programmed in my mind, something from Halloween. Something from a dream. I imagine I would see a figure in a red suit with horns, cloven feet, and a pitchfork. Something projected from youth, books, movies or plays. You know, the traditional devil. But no one has reported this.

Although the devil was never visualized, one of the possible "helpers" or "herders" was described by two physicians, themselves resuscitated, something that only three of the initial three hundred cases had seen: the figure of a human body with a goat's head, a he-goat, worshipped in the classical times of Mendes in Egypt. It was one of the evil beings of the day, representing the power of wealth and fertility. And it was called the Baphomet.

Since hell has been recognized from classical times, whatever happened to hell in modern times? How did it gradually get diluted down over the years? Why did we try to get rid of it?

HAS
HELL

DISAPPEARED?

Hell seems to have been diluted into oblivion, the fires of the damned drowned in today's thought. Yet the residual concepts of hell have withstood centuries of criticism and still appear in the scriptures of most religions in the world except for some rebelling cultic offsprings.

The term "cult" apparently describes those groups who claim allegiance to the Bible and yet deny its basic teachings. These groups are different from the "occult" groups which deal more with mediumism and spiritism, although they frequently overlap, half of them obtaining direct revelations from the spirit world. They have splintered from mainstream Christianity in part because of a denial of an eternal hell. And so it seems that everywhere hell becomes one of the dividers of sects, denominations, and individuals. Even divisive politics doesn't touch the divisiveness of hell.

Whatever happened to hell? The following are some of the cults listed by John Ankerberg and John Weldon in *Facts on Life after Death*. Listed also is each group's divisive opinion about both heaven and hell along with its founder's quotations.[1]

1. *Christian Science,* founded by spiritist Mary Baker Eddy, teaches that "there is no death." They believe that "heaven

and hell are states of thought, not places. People experience
their own heaven or hell right here on earth."

2. *Edgar Cayce,* a spiritist and New Age prophet, said that
"the destiny of the soul, as of all creation, is to become One
with the Creator" and that no soul is ever lost.

3. New Age cult leader Sun Myung Moon of *The Unification
Church* believes that "God will not desert any person eter-
nally. By some means . . . they will be restored."

4. *Mormonism,* founded by occultist Joseph Smith, argues,
"The false doctrine that the punishment to be visited upon
erring souls is endless . . . is but a dogma of unauthorized
and erring sectaries, at once unscriptural, unreasonable, and
revolting."

5. *Jehovah's Witnesses,* founded by Charles Taze Russell maintains that the wicked are forever annihilated because "the
teaching about a fiery hell can rightly be designated as a
'teaching of demons.'"

6. *The Church of the New Jerusalem* (Swedenborgianism),
founded by spiritist Emanuel Swedenborg, emphasizes that
God "does not condemn anyone to hell."

7. *Eckankar,* a New Age religion founded by Paul Twitchell
and Darwin Gross, insists that "there is no death". . . and
that there is no eternal hell.

8. *Lucis Trust* and The Arcane School/Full Moon Meditation
Groups, established by New Age spiritist Alice Bailey, argue
that "the fear of death is based upon . . . old erroneous
teaching as to heaven and hell."

9. *The Love Family* (The Children of God), founded by spiritist David Berg, views hell as a temporal purgatory: "The lake
of fire is where the wicked go to get purged from their sins
. . . to let them eventually come . . . out."

10. *Rosicrucianism,* an occult philosophy, declares that "the
'eternal damnation' of those who are not 'saved' does not
mean destruction nor endless torture," and that "the Christian religion did not originally contain any dogmas about
Hell."

11. *Unitarian Universalism* confesses the following: "It seems
safe to say that no Unitarian Universalist believes in a resurrection of the body, a literal heaven or hell, or any kind of
eternal punishment."

12. *The Theosophical Society,* founded by medium Helena P. Blavatsky, declares, "we positively refuse to accept the . . . belief in eternal reward or eternal punishment." Hence, "Death . . . is not . . . a cause for fear."

13. The spirits everywhere proclaim their allegiance to cultic teachings, declare Ankerberg and Weldon. "Ramtha," the spirit speaking through medium J. S. Knight, claims "God has never judged you or anyone" and "No, there is no hell and there is no devil." "Lilly" and other spirits channeled through medium Ruth Montgomery argue that "there is no such thing as death" and that "God punishes no man."

There are also variations within orthodox churches concerning the belief in hell. Some believe in purgatory, a waiting place where sinners are penalized until all sins are purged away, after which they are translated to heaven. The major support for this doctrine, according to theologians Habermas and Moreland, comes from 2 Maccabees 12:39–45, a disputed book written after the completion of the Old Testament and prior to the New Testament, and considered by most Protestants to be an apocryphal book that is not part of the true canon of Holy Scripture.

"The Bible says nothing about purgatory or the need to be purged after death," Ankerburg and Weldon say. "Rather, the Bible claims that Christ himself did all that was necessary to earn our joyous entrance into God's presence at death. Paul states in Philippians 3:9 that his right standing with God was not something he earned or secured through acts of penance or reparation" [and in Phil. 1:21 and 2 Cor. 5:8], "that at death, we who are believers in Christ immediately go to be in Christ's presence."[2]

There seem to be a number of contributing factors involved in the continuing demise of hell in our society. For instance, hell has become the great enigma of modern humanistic psychology, which promotes the tenet that man achieves fulfillment by fully satisfying his wants, not by denying them. In other words, if it feels good, do it. They say we can trust only what our five senses can perceive, and it is rights and liberties that are emphasized instead of duty and obligation. They deny the existence of hell, of course. They say it just doesn't fit.

To further defang the stigma of hell, many intelligent researchers support a belief in a "force"—not the god of traditional faiths

—but more like the force portrayed in Star Wars. Many of the culturally elite also play Dungeons and Dragons and equivalent games with spiritual entities. These players seldom question the games' source or purpose, convinced that it represents the good or "positive" side of the force. The bad or "dark" side of the force is rarely considered, nor is the possibility that the bright side of the force might be Lucifer as the face on one side of the coin, with Satan on the other side. Two faces of the same force.

Is hell ever found in the medical literature? Researchers Osis and Haraldsson described a Hindu policeman in his forties who was afflicted with pulmonary tuberculosis. He yelled from his hospital bed, "The Yamdoot [messenger of death] is coming to take me away. Take me down from the bed so that the Yamdoot does not find me." Pointing out the window he said, "There he is." And at that moment, as if someone had fired a gun, "a volume of crows covering a tree outside the room suddenly flew away." The nurse said she "was appalled" and ran outside but could see no cause for the commotion. She reasoned that "even the crows themselves were aware of something terrible." A few minutes after this negative experience, the patient went into a deep coma and died. Several other cases illustrate that negative experiences can involve any culture, and suggest that unseen spiritual events can influence the environment.[3]

In a subsequent study of deathbed visions both in America and India, Osis also found "increasing numbers" of negative cases (actually 18 percent) who had "visions of horror." Osis went on to say, "They had fearful visions and didn't want to go [to punishment areas]. It was as if soldiers came to take prisoners—a real fear reaction."[4]

In a previous book, one of these same authors conceded that some patients seemed to be experiencing "hell," and he described it this way:

> The patient had a horrified expression, turned his head in all directions and said, "Hell, Hell, all I see is Hell." Another had the terrifying feeling of being burned alive. These are only two cases in our collection that strike a distressing emotional note—a small minority indeed when compared with the number reporting peace and beauty.[5]

It really doesn't matter whether it is clinical death, near-death, contemplated death, deathbed visions, dreams, or drugs. Indeed, there are negative experiences found in all of these. But, for some reason, no one wants to mention them. Is the hell-fire of Billy Sunday considered offensive today?

Preliminary to TV talk shows, including premier ones like "The Today Show," I was cautioned not to discuss the subject of hell, and not to mention the name of Jesus Christ or any religious thing which could be considered offensive to the audience. Perhaps they wanted the viewer to determine the "offensiveness" later in life—the hard way.

One prominent researcher emphasizes the "ease" and rapidity with which the beautiful side of evil can change, like a Dr. Jekyll to a Mr. Hyde, into a demonic being:

> I could clearly see the door of the room in which I slept, and I experienced the horrifying certainty that through that door would come an unnameable, dreadful creature. Enveloped in terror, yet still in my dream, I saw the door slowly open and beheld an apparition of my mother standing in the doorway. In my mind I can still see her as I saw her then, perfectly my mother in every detail of feature, and wearing the same brown dress I had seen her wearing when I left home a few days previously.
>
> The shocking thing was that I knew it was not my mother. I was completely aware that she was not present for she was at our home, about fifteen miles away. In my dream, she walked over to the bed where I lay asleep, bent over me, and woke me with a kiss. I awoke instantly to the unpleasant presence of a demon, with the disguise of my mother's form and likeness now entirely discarded.[6]

Similar deceptions were encountered in out-of-the-body experiences by Carl Jung, Johanna Michaelsen, and people like self-experimenter Robert Monroe, who is a close friend of Dr. Elisabeth Kubler-Ross. Monroe seems to have had something that plagues other authors dabbling in the metaphysical—encounters with demons—something usually publically denied.

> I started out carefully—and felt something on my back! I remembered the little fellow from before, and certainly

didn't want to try to go somewhere with him hanging on my back. . . . Then, as I was trying to hold off the first, a second climbed on my back! Holding the first off with one hand, I reached back and yanked the second off me, and floated over into the center of the office, holding one in each hand, screaming for help. I got a good look at each, and as I looked, each turned into a good facsimile of one of my two daughters (the psychiatrist will have a good time with this one)! I seemed to know immediately that this was a deliberate camouflage on their part to create emotional confusion in me and call on my love for my daughters to prevent me from doing anything to them.[7]

Dr. Raymond Moody, a foremost expert in near-death studies, now gives courses in contacting the dead from a converted Aesculapian Temple (the temple of a mythical god from Greco-Roman times) near Anniston, Alabama, that we shall discuss later.

Dr. Kenneth Ring of Connecticut University is now journeying into the spirituality of UFO encounters.

Dr. Elisabeth Kubler-Ross, a respected leader in the field of thanatology (the study of death), her material considered required reading in many hospitals, still communicates with the dead. The trio of Salem, Anka, and Willie, her own personal spirit guides, assist Dr. Kubler-Ross in important medical decisions and in her personal life. These spirits, she maintains, are the real highlight of her life:

Last night I was visited by Salem, my spirit guide, and two of his companions, Anka and Willie. They were with us until three o'clock in the morning. We talked, laughed, and sang together. They spoke and touched me with the most incredible love and tenderness imaginable. *This was the highlight of my life.*[8] (Emphasis mine).

Dr. Raymond Moody, a collaborator and personal friend of Dr. Kubler-Ross, claims he could not find a single description of a religious heaven or hell in cases he reported in his first book, *Life After Life:*

Through all of my research, however, I have not heard a single reference to a heaven or a hell anything like the customary picture to which we are exposed in this society. Indeed, many persons have stressed how unlike their experiences were to what they had been led to expect in the course of their religious training.[9]

By the time of his second book, when the sample size had increased, Dr. Moody apparently found the critical material lacking in the first book. Not only did he find heavenly experiences, he also found some surprisingly negative ones as well:

Several people have reported to me that at some point they glimpsed other beings who seemed to be "trapped" in an apparently most unfortunate state of existence. Those who described seeing these confused beings are in agreement on several points.

[Dr. Moody continues by describing a woman who saw people who] seemed to shuffle, as someone would on a chain gang [and had] . . . this absolute, crushed, hopeless demeanor.[10]

This patient further related to Dr. Moody that "there were only shades and tones of gray," in this other world, and that everything she saw was "quite depressing."

Of course, the word "hell" was never mentioned, but the existence of this evil realm seems to be tinged by his present research. In his temple replica for mystical experiences, Dr. Moody advises caution to students as they attempt to conjure spiritual encounters through "scrying," an experiment using crystals and mirrors, warning them about unforeseen complications.

Even when demonic influences were already evident, investigators would maintain that negative near-death experiences never occurred or were negligible or insignificant. Kenneth Ring, psychology professor at the University of Connecticut, constantly claims that "nobody reported to me experiencing images of hell." Dr. Michael Sabom, before moving to Emory University, had also stated he encountered no hell reports, causing him to be "convinced that these [near-death] experiences are very real to the persons and are uniformly pleasant."[11]

These 'all good, no bad' statements from Dr. Ring and from Dr. Sabom, both members of the International Association for Near-Death Studies (IANDS) based at Hartford, Connecticut (which has collected more cases than any other organization), seem to be in direct conflict with other members of the organization.

According to Nancy Evans Bush, president of the IANDS group at Yale University Medical Center, negative near-death experiences are indeed present, and she has collected about fifty cases as of press time (1993), still a small percent of her studies, but they are beginning to surface. In fact, she categorizes the negative into three groups: The first group contains people who thought they were "losing control" in their NDE experiences; some suddenly saw the light in the tunnel "as a reflection of the fires at the gates of hell instead of seeing it as a radiant light." The second group felt they were caught in the frightening void of a "great cosmic nothingness," frequently resulting in a long-term despair. The third group saw a vision of hell where people were being "tortured or tormented." She also presented these observations when several of us appeared on a NBC-TV documentary entitled "A Glimpse of Glory," which was mentioned earlier. Ms. Bush's negative findings were also reported by Nora Underwood in an article "Between Life and Death" found in *Maclean's* Magazine, April 20, 1992.

Hell has become an amusing, fun place to be.

"Of course," concluded Nancy Bush during the TV interview, "a negative experience does not necessarily mean you are a bad person. It only means you have work to do to improve." The conclusion of a judgment, condemnation, damnation, or any sort of an evaluation or rejection appears to have been rejected.

But hell experiences are nothing new. They have always been there. However, retained consciousness for negative events can be quite transient and should be immediately recorded before becoming erased from all knowledgeable recall. This particular psychological principle (usually called *repression* or *selective forgetting*) has been recognized for some time, although overlooked by the very psychologists and psychiatrists who prefer to promote the good life and the benevolent dispensation of a heavenly reward for humankind.

The renowned psychologist F. W. H. Myers, for example, had

repeatedly emphasized that experiences in the coma state rapidly fade from memory if not immediately recorded. A scientist without philosophical bias, he put it in this way:

> It is possible that we might learn much upon questioning dying persons on their awakening from some comatose condition, as to their memory of any dream or visions during this state. If there has in fact been any such experience, *it should be at once recorded,* as it will probably fade rapidly from the patient's supraliminal memory, even if he does not die directly afterwards.[12] (Emphasis mine)

Still another reason for emphasizing and recognizing the existence of negative experiences is that they are not any more uncommon or rare today than they were in the past. Of the several emergency rooms still being monitored for the present study, two more hell cases have been reported as I write this manuscript. The reports are samples from one hospital in one city—this time, Memorial Hospital in Chattanooga—collected by Mary Ann Hickman and assistant head nurse Dotty Gilbert. They report that Ira Anderson (not his real name), a sixty-two-year-old male suffering an acute heart attack, had to be restrained because, using his words, there were "demons coming after me." Fighting the staff, writhing and kicking off the creatures, feet running in place as if to escape, nurses and doctors pinning him to the stretcher, he eventually blacked out. After the cardiac arrest rhythm had been corrected by electric shock, the demons seemed to follow him as he went to the intensive care area where, regaining his consciousness, they pounced on him once again. Review of the records showed no medications to account for the demonization.

In the same week and in the same emergency room, Ruby Tinney and charge nurse Nancy Humphries reported a thirty-eight-year-old heart attack victim, who, with blood-curdling screams, kept yelling he was in hell and demanding that a pastor be called.

Just prior to that, to illustrate the frequent intermixture of good and bad events, Nancy's mother, sixty-year-old Rebecca Love, developed anaphylactic shock in the same emergency room resulting in a positive experience.[13]

The increase in hell-like experiences is probably related to in-

creased nurse awareness, rather than to increased incidence. Hell
has always been around, interwoven into most cultures, and is not
the product of the current preoccupation of videos, books, and
magazines which depict violence and evil as if they were the first
to discover hell in its present earthly form.

By immunizing the public to the trauma of violence and evil,
the media does, however, encourage permissive concepts and a
bland indifference concerning evil. In this way hell becomes an
everyday event no longer to be feared, reducing the traditional
malevolent connections with Satan. Much like the MTV awards
suggest, hell has become an amusing, fun place to be, where amorality is the accepted norm.

Gradual changes in moral standards and traditions have discarded unpleasant reports in favor of gratifying ones, thus loosely
changing attitudes and ethics. And now it has come to some
resuscitated atheists with wonderful reports: "There is no condemnation, no worry," says one; "Only unconditional love," says
another; "I'm okay and you're okay and everybody goes to
heaven," say some others.

Worse than that, near-deathers are now visiting hospital bed-
sides with the reassuring message, "Look, no need to be concerned. No religious beliefs are needed. I've been there, and the
light shows love for everyone." Then, as death closes in, they may
say, "Let me stay until you see the light. The time is short, and
there is nothing to fear." Spiritually, then, they die naked, the
final path warped at a crucial time.

Few if any of these Omega near-deathers are aware of the
biblical passage that "Satan himself transforms himself into an
Angel of Light [and] his ministers transform themselves into ministers of righteousness" (2 Cor. 11:14–15). Or perhaps they
couldn't care less. But the light they see, as Nancy Bush has
pointed out, may yet turn into fire.

The interpretation of the light, therefore, is based solely upon
the victim's intuition where no guidelines or rule books are in
place. Without a Bible, a spiritual standard, a guidance system, a
road map, the victim can become disoriented and lose direction.

Consider the story of a world-famous physician who flew himself to several medical conferences. His name was Andreas
Gruntzig, the young founder of angioplasty, the coronary remolding technique to avoid by-pass surgery. One night while Andreas

was blindly penetrating a heavy rainstorm on his return to Emory University, the plane's main guidance system failed unexpectedly.

The old ball-and-needle was the only remaining backup guidance system to keep the wings level. Limited to this system, Andreas could not tell whether he was going up, down, right, or left. With wings apparently level, seeing nothing, blindly trusting in his own instincts, Dr. Gruntzig confidently flew the plane directly into the ground. No guidance, no destination, no life. Secure within himself, ordinary man literally doesn't know which end is up.

If the Bible is our guidance system, then hell is unequivocal, because the place is specifically named fifty different times. Remember that Christ talked more about hell than he did about heaven.

The patients who have been there are also unequivocal and quite certain of the place. These people do not consider hell to be a deception sent from Satan. They understand that such deceit would be counterproductive for the cause of evil. Hell's exposure of hell would obviously be self-defeating and self-destructive.

Jesus explained it this way: "Every kingdom divided against itself is brought to desolation, and every city or house divided against itself will not stand. If Satan casts out Satan, he is divided against himself. How then will his kingdom stand?" (Matt. 12:25–26). This message was important enough to be repeated in the book of Mark (3:23, 26) and in the book of Luke (11:18).

This is the reason we should never reject or disregard negative experiences, or conveniently avoid the subject, merely because they do not support our personal beliefs. Nor should any authors fail to report such cases because they are incompatible with their previous publications or future TV talk show programs.

If there is a hell, if the Bible is true, if these patients had a glimpse of hell instead of glory, then we must each decide for ourselves, *Is it safe to die?* Intriguing the mind and baffling the soul, it is perhaps one of life's most important questions. The answer lies no more than a few heartbeats away.

6

NEAR-DEATH
EXPERIENCES

Perhaps one of the most contested subjects debated, next to politics and religion, is near-death experiences. Since there are two schools of thought, which should we follow? The ministers, on the one hand, claim NDEs are either the chemical hallucinations of a blood-deprived mind or Satanic delusions to convince the unsaved that salvation is not required. Secularists, on the other hand, believe that NDEs are all real and that they are all good. They feel that the consistent reports of good NDEs in the next life represent a benevolent message that insures a guarantee of heaven. This uniform acceptance by the angel of light has inspired a new philosophy called "Omega," which has been referred to previously, and which will be a recurrent subject in this book.

Omega serves to indicate two things: There are no prerequisites for entrance into this heavenly place, and those who are not accepted but are returned to earthly life are constrained to move the world toward peace and brotherly love, which is called the "Omega Point."

Of course, the introduction of negative cases would tend to unsettle the Omega concept, the concept of a uniform glory seen by all faiths and nonfaiths alike.

Obviously, both schools admit that death is not oblivion, that NDEs are valid and true, compounded by a combination of visual

reconstruction of events, astoundingly similar sequences, transformation into another world, and remarkable changed lives that
result—a combination that cannot be duplicated by hallucinations, drugs, or fevers.

To investigate other possible causes, Schoonmaker measured
blood oxygen levels at the time of his patients' cardiac arrests.
Those who had near-death experiences had sufficient oxygen
present for normal brain functioning.[1] In Morse's studies, there
was no more oxygen deprivation measured in those children with
near-death experiences than without these experiences.[2] Concerning the euphoria produced when trauma–induced polypep-
tide proteins are released into the bloodstream and attach to the
brain's endorphin receptors to relieve pain, none of these were
capable of producing sequences, nor do they produce beliefs or
decisions. Electrical stimulation of various parts of the brain
could not reproduce the sequences either.

Apparent psychic phenomena are also inexplicable—how blind
individuals with NDEs report visual reconstructions of clothing
colors, types of jewelry, and other visual details occurring in the
room; how victims visualize events and people located in other
rooms and how they see loved ones in another world, with no
prior knowledge of their deaths.[3]

Other psychic phenomena can appear as residuals of deeper
NDEs. Some claim clairvoyance, forecasting accidents and illnesses; others claim an aura capable of causing electrical interfer-
ences with automobiles, computers, or the burning out of light
bulbs; telepathy is mentioned by others; and some claim an ability
to heal. Different gifts, I suppose, but of unproven source.

Although close occultic connections are characteristically
found by many near-death researchers (as we shall point out),
this does not mean, as proposed by some members of the clergy,
that all near-death experiences are occultic and unbiblical. Theologians Habermas and Moreland, after carefully examining NDEs
from a biblical viewpoint, believe that near-death phenomena
may also have occurred in scripture, referring to Stephen's predeath vision (Acts 7:55), and Paul's trip to heaven (2 Cor. 12:1–
5), the latter perhaps occurring at the time Paul was stoned and
left for dead in Lystra. "Also," these authors continue, "going to
be with Christ is precisely what the Bible says will happen to the
Christian after death. So if believers experience this after a very

close call with death, why should we object on biblical grounds?
. . . At the same time, it doesn't follow that all near-death
experiences are satanic counterfeits. Some even appear to follow
biblical expectations. Dying is a natural event and does not auto-
matically involve aspects of the occult, as some other activities
do." Therefore, Habermas and Moreland conclude, "each NDE
needs to be viewed according to its own merits."[4]

From the religious and philosophical viewpoint, NDEs remain
the only known research study that attempts to document relatively inaccessible beliefs on the subject of death and dying. This
is an important subject since Gallup and other polls indicate that
70 percent of Americans believe in life after death, and have
since 1944 when the surveys began. Seventy to 80 percent continue to believe in heaven and 50 to 60 percent in hell.[5]

To review, near-death experiences consist of a conglomeration
of circumstances. The term "near-death," first coined by psychiatrist Raymond Moody, includes such diverse things as acute
fright, attempted suicides, near murder, severe accidents, electrocutions, drug trips, anesthetics, near drownings, hangings, poison-
ings, combat experiences, and falls from great heights. Some of
this NDE group will have out-of-the-body experiences and some
will not, sometimes depending upon intensity or depth of the
experience. OBEs, a much larger group of experiences, will be
discussed in the next chapter.

Also mixed into this hodgepodge of NDEs are the terminally ill
patients with their deathbed visions, both good and bad. The
deathbed really represents a separate category of people who
await sure death, irreversible death, biological death, their deaths
without any recognizable sequence, the spiritual scenes of one
usually distinct from those of others. And they are not all good
either. Some are horrible.

Unfortunately, this near-death menagerie becomes a cloak to
hide, dilute, and absorb the unique clinical deaths where both
heartbeat and breathing have stopped, the ones most likely to
have both an analyzable sequence and changed lives. For this
reason we shall separate clinical death from near-death experiences.

Let's first consider the near-deaths of accidents, then look at
deathbed visions in the rest of the chapter, separating the good
from the bad, and finally examine suicide attempts.

ACCIDENTS

"Coming right at me is this black car passing an eighteen-wheeler. Two lanes and nowhere to go. I'm a goner, so I hold my breath. In a split second a dumb video flashes back in my brain. I am in the fifth grade and throwing an eraser at the teacher, and next I am twelve years old and running away from home. In college, I am getting married.

"Then I wake up in a ditch with a broken arm, the car on top of me, and the other car gone. How can this be? Seeing my whole life in a split second?"

I nodded understandingly. "A time warp like those other near-deaths we presented in the slide lecture. Perhaps you had one foot in eternity."

I handed him something to read by Albert Heim. It was about a mountaineer who fell during a climb in the Alps. As he was falling, he not only saw his fate but wondered about the loved ones left behind. Countless pictures of his past life appeared. All this took place during the five to ten seconds he was falling before he hit the ground.[6]

There are more than a score of other cases in Albert Heim's series paralleling the head-on vehicular collisions of today: mountain climbers who fell from precipitous heights but lived to tell about it. With breath-taking sensation they recall the last thoughts before impact and what it all felt like. Several of them recalled complete life reviews, while others remember only the echoing screams while going down. Still others remember the unreality of the whole thing by a denial: "This really isn't happening to me." This is similar to the denial that occurs when the doctor informs the patient of an incurable cancer: "It just can't be me!" Sometimes they die persisting in this denial.

Acute confrontations seem to produce more out-of-the-body experiences than the slow deaths of terminal illness where more spiritual entities tend to intermittently appear.

The following OBE occurred during a precipitous fall from a ridge, a safety rope saving the victim at the last second:

Then suddenly this feeling [of falling] was superseded by a feeling of complete indifference and detachment as to what was happening or likely to happen to that body. I seemed to stand aside from my body. I was not falling for the reason that I was not in a dimension where it was possible to fall. I, that is, my consciousness, was apart from my body and not in the least concerned with what was befalling it.[7]

In those cases where death is slow or delayed, as in cancer, strokes, heart, lung or kidney failure, there's plenty of time for complete life reviews and all sorts of contemplations, but if life is short and death approaches swiftly, there may be only enough time to see the flashbacks common to situations described by victims of rapes, accidents, wars, robberies, drownings, drugs, electrocutions, and such. All these near-deathers, of course, have the potential for out-of-the-body experiences.

OBSERVATIONS AT THE DEATHBED

Involved in reviewing emergency situations and sudden deaths for three and a half decades, I knew I needed additional experience with terminal diseases and more of the deathbed scenes. To accomplish this, I spent the last two years in nursing homes studying terminally ill patients.

At seventy-two, Maria Ratinsky was a drawn, tight-skinned woman living on a roll-away bed in an overheated room. She had scleroderma (hardened skin) and not long to live. That morning on rounds I found both Mr. and Mrs. Ratinsky in the same small bed.

"I know it's against the rules," she explained sheepishly, "but it is so cold and Marvin keeps away the chills." She knew she was dying, now skin-and-bones, her hard skin ice cold to the touch, the disease now on the inside of her. She had probably a week or two left, unable to swallow because of the internal involvement.

There was love there, I saw that, and something behind the worn eyes that I didn't quite understand. I realized I knew a lot about death but not much about love. I turned, not knowing what to say, and moved out of the room. Maybe I was learning after all. It was these slow deaths—strokes and cancers—which gave something to say in their eyes and in their touch. Thanatology, the study of the dying, had love and deeper meanings than I had thought.

Instead of consistent flashbacks, some of the dying patients will

experience "flash-forwards," taking a peek into the future, something psychics keep looking for in their crystal balls.

While the apparitions of the dying patient have no analyzable
sequence of shared repetitive events, they are something marvelous to behold. In the early stages, usually before the nursing
home, are questions like "why me?" "Could the diagnosis have
been a mistake?" "What have I done to deserve this?" After the
rejection and reaction stages of dying come the stages of recognition, regression and, finally, resignation. Some of the stages are
omitted. During recognition the questions become more covert
and sometimes not outwardly expressed: "What does it feel like
to die?" And inevitably they wonder, "Is there a life after death?"
Some ponder their relationship to God and wonder, "Is everything 'good' out there?" Death is approaching, and they are dying
to find out what death is all about.

> **"When death is chasing you in the emergency room, there is no atheist."**

Regression occurs when remorse, depression, with-
drawal, and worthlessness dominate. Self-esteem doesn't work and suicidal tendencies may next appear. Resignation occurs when waiting is at an end. This is the last stage, the time when they could use some really good news.

As with acute near-death events, chronic death is also near and
frightening. But in a different way. While there is a saying that
there are no atheists in foxholes or in the emergency room, seldom are there true atheists on the deathbed. They may want
release from pain or misery, but they are also looking for something more. And the underlying password is the same for all:
"God help me!"

Even Madalyn O'Hair, one of the world's leading atheists, may
someday add her name to that list who say "God help me!" or so
I told her one day during a televised free-for-all we had in Detroit. She responded rather forcefully: "You are a farce, Rawlings,
because there is no God." The attack was bitter and she seemed
to enjoy it. "And there is no life after death, either! The patients
you found were obviously deluded!" She was sitting very low in
her chair, spraddle-legged like a man with quite a bit showing,

although nothing was visible to the cameras in front of us. "You're completely wrong, Rawlings," she continued. "Because on your deathbed you will find oblivion and nothing else."

Well, for some reason I was inspired to heights of oratory. "In the emergency room you will be no different from anybody else," I said, leaning forward. "When your turn comes you'll call on God like all the rest of us. When death is chasing you in the emergency room, there is no atheist."

However, the oratory didn't last very long. In her late fifties at the time, gray-haired and overweight, Madalyn O'Hair reared back and let loose the sharp sword of belligerence, a masterful vocabulary and blunt proselytizing for atheism placing her above the rest, both as a lawyer and the founder of the American Atheistic Society.

Fortunately, the unseen audience soon jammed the phone lines. The first call was my salvation. "Lady, you're just plain sick," the caller said. Starting at that moment Madalyn switched her attack to the camera instead of me.

Well, I suppose you win a few and lose a few. But the invariance hypothesis is still there. Whether in the emergency room or on the deathbed, they call on God. Whether they wish to or not, the average person invokes God, especially so in the hellish experiences.

Of course, the family will try to conceal any embarrassing, hellish experiences observed on the deathbed. This masking of deathbed reports causes most authors to assume that deathbed experiences, as with all other NDEs, are all good experiences with no relationship to religion, philosophy, race, or circumstance. Statistical bias results when the whole picture is not analyzed, especially when good experiences replace the converted bad ones. But researchers seem recalcitrant and show no interest in the negative possibilities.

Negative deathbed visions, as with negative clinical deaths, almost never question the reason why they are confronted by their present circumstances. Because of this unquestioned acknowledgment, negative experiences prove more reliable than the positive ones, since deception seems possible only in the positive ones.

Why are most of the reports beautiful? If Satan should appear as Satan, it would horrify the victim. It would turn him from his ways and dispel the aura of unconditional love and acceptance.

On the other hand, if Satan should appear as Lucifer to be the angel of light, the victim might feel secure and comfortable in the seduction of this angelic fate. However, deception is less apt to occur on the deathbed since the offer of "another chance," a recovery to normal life, is somewhat ludicrous in these circumstances.

Concerning other countries and other faiths, deathbed experiences can also be positive or negative, but relate to the culture and religion of the individual involved. As we said, negative deathbed visions in India may involve a messenger like the Yamdoot or the messengers from the gods of destruction, Shiva, Kali, or Pan.

While dying Christians may see angels, Jesus, or the Virgin Mary, the predominantly Hindu culture of India would hope to see Krishna, Vishnu, Yama, or one of the friendly gods. According to Osis and Haraldsson's study involving a large number of cases gathered in America and India, visions did not seem related to medication, age, sex, or education; and religion only "slightly" facilitated such experiences.[8]

These same authors, while gathering data for the Parapsychology Foundation, evaluated many other deathbed reports. One little girl, age four or five, was anxious and fearful as she arrived at the Ervin Hospital in Delhi. She had been telling her parents for three days that some god was calling her and that she was going to die soon. She seemed to be seeing and hearing something but did not describe it. Although she appeared well, she kept repeating, "God is calling and I am going to die." Strangely, she died the following day. The diagnosis made was a "gradual circulatory collapse which had no apparent cause."

There were two explanations the authors proposed for the girl's death: she either received a death call by ESP or died "as a result of self-suggestion."[9] This explanation is not unexpected if the authors are participating in occultic mysticisms.

Interestingly, none of the deathbed visions I have encountered suggest that reincarnation would occur—that they would return to earth as a newborn or would inhabit another person already born. This concept of "possession" was surprisingly offered by reincarnationist expert Ian Stevenson to explain inhabitation of those already born.

POSITIVE DEATHBED VISIONS

As we mentioned, all NDEs consist of both good or bad experiences, although most authors report only the pleasant ones. As with dreams, some of these NDEs can be nightmares of negativity. Since the family does not talk about negative deathbed experiences, let's start with the good reports.

> When nineteen, while engaged in teaching school, she [Helen] took a severe cold which developed into tuberculosis and terminated her earthly life at the age of twenty.
>
> During Helen's illness . . . young friends who called upon her would afterward say, "One would not think Helen was going to die. She speaks as if she were going on a most delightful journey!"
>
> . . . The next day Helen said, "Ma, you thought I was asleep yesterday while you were sitting by me. I wasn't, and two angels came into the room. The walls did not hinder their coming. . . . [Then the mother placed a hand on her daughter's forehead and said] Helen, I think you are very near home. Have you any fear?"
>
> "Not a bit," Helen replied. "Call the family, so that I may say good-bye to them."
>
> As they gathered about her she bade each one a loving farewell, telling them she was going to Heaven, because of the blood of the Lamb and enjoining them to meet her there.
>
> . . . They asked if she would like to have them sing, and she replied, "Sing until I die—sing my soul away!"
>
> . . . Then, as the dying girl's eyes closed in death . . . she saw something glorious beyond conception.[10]

Deathbed visions seem to vary with the degree of consciousness at the time. Those with strong convictions are more likely to have positive visions while those of little faith struggle to discover anything good.

John Knox, as an example of the expectations of many Christian founders, died in 1572 with the fervent words: "Live in Christ; live in Christ, and the flesh need not fear death. . . . Now it is come!"

This quote is but one of a large number listed in *Pebbles from the Brink,* by M. C. Pritchard, published in 1913 and loaned to me

by David Mainse. *Pebbles from the Brink* received its name for Sir
Isaac Newton's profound reflection made in 1727 shortly before
his death:

> I do not know what I may appear to the world, but to
> myself I seem to have been only like a boy playing on the
> seashore, and diverting himself by now and then finding a
> smooth pebble or a prettier shell than ordinary, while the
> great ocean of truth lies all undiscovered beyond me.[11]

A discovery in this "ocean of truth" was found a little later by
Samuel Johnston: "Believe a dying man. Nothing but salvation in
Christ can comfort you when you come to die."[12]

Even pre-Christian Aristotle, the great thinker, was groping for
the missing link as he died: "In pollution I entered the world,
anxiously I have lived in it, miserably do I depart from it. O Thou
cause of causes, have mercy upon me."[13]

Other great men have had similar thoughts while departing this
world. William Pitt admitted, "I have, like other men, neglected
prayer too much to have any ground of hope that it can be effica-
cious on a deathbed; I throw myself on the mercy of God through
the merits of Christ."[14]

It may surprise students of evolution to learn that in the closing
days of his life, Charles Darwin reportedly embraced his previous
biblical faith. According to Lady Hope of Northfield, England, a
friend frequenting his bedside, some of the following occurred:

> It was one of those glorious autumn afternoons that we
> sometimes enjoy in England when I was asked to go in and
> sit with Charles Darwin. . . .
> He was sitting up in bed, propped up by pillows, gazing
> out on a far-stretching scene of woods and corn fields, which
> glowed in the light of a marvelous sunset.
> "What are you reading now?" I asked.
> "Hebrews," he answered. "The Royal Book I call it."
> Then, as he placed his fingers on certain passages, he com-
> mented:
> "I made some allusion to the strong opinions expressed by
> many on the history of the Creation and then their treatment
> of the earlier chapters of the book of Genesis."
> He seemed distressed, his fingers twitched nervously and a

look of agony come over his face as he said, "I was a young man with uninformed ideas. I threw out queries, suggestions, wondering all the time about everything. To my astonishment the ideas [of evolution] took like wild-fire. People made a religion of them."

Then he paused. . . . "I have a summer house in the garden which holds about thirty people. It is over there (pointing through the open window). I want you very much to speak here. I know you read the Bible in the villages. Tomorrow afternoon I should like the servants on the place, some tenants, and a few neighbors to gather there. Will you speak to them?"

"What shall I speak about?" I [Lady Hope] asked.

"Christ Jesus . . . and His Salvation. Is not that the best theme?"[15]

These were said to be Darwin's last thoughts, apparently discarding his theory of evolution saying, "I was a young man with uninformed ideas."[16]

Deathbed visions and reports seem less common today, possibly because our forefathers were more indoctrinated in theological values or because we don't see as many dying patients at home because they are neatly tucked away in hospitals and nursing homes. Perhaps our emotions and communications have also withered. A sign of weakness in the new age. For instance, we no longer hold hands, and we seldom express our inner feelings. Emotions have grown cold.

In the new age in which we live, traditional moral values have been replaced with violence and indifference. No one seems to administer the tender care that was part of the deathbed scene in the old days. Today, Granny is dumped into the nursing home. And some of the families would actually rather see Granny in the grave. The family is too busy to look after her, and when Medicare runs out, some families have dumped Granny on the hospital stairs without leaving identification. They reason that the hospital might be obligated to take care of her if no identification can be made.

This is one of the reasons that deathbed scenes are seldom described today. The family is just not there. Many overworked

The most significant moment of life is death.

nurses and attendants, already too busy with other patients, could care less about spiritual matters. Except for caring for pain, bowel movements, and routine complaints, deathbed patients are usually ignored. Thus, spiritual matters are evaded by the frightened family and discounted by disinterested hospital personnel.

"We are not allowed to mention anything about faith or beliefs," said one nurse. This now seems to be the mandated rule for most hospitals, nursing homes, and hospices. When the patient asks about terminal concerns, either nothing is said or the subject is brushed away, and or the patient is referred to a minister.

However, many of these patients are programmed against ministers, not permitting the minister or the Bible into the room. On the other hand, patients often listen to the lay people—people like you or me. Patients are seeking an opinion of what it's all about. But if the spiritual gospel is not presented, the social gospel frequently is. Some of these visitors represent the new breed of near-deathers, reporting glorious "peeks of heaven"—which they eagerly communicate to the dying patient to allay his fears—that all will be well at death regardless of one's beliefs.

"Just hold my hand, and I'll help you to get through the tunnel to the light," one visitor said. The problem is that the patient, often spiritually destitute, may face eternity unaware of other options. Unaware because you and I have not presented these options or because the family has assumed that the patient's commitments have been made, when they are not secure at all.

"I just can't stand to see mother like this," the daughter of Mrs. Albrecht confided in the hallway. "The cancer makes her look and smell so terrible that none of the family can stand to be with her."

I said, "But she's dying and she knows very well when you're there and when you're not. It is very important that you be with her."

"But she keeps seeing crazy things."

"Then ask her to describe some of them. Talk to her. But don't ever leave her alone."

Uncannily, a beautiful death experience occurred to Mrs. Albrecht while the family was absent.

> "Is that you, Mark?" [her son].
>
> "Yes, it's me." [I held her hand].
>
> "Can you see the chariot and the angels? Do you see them?"
>
> "Yes, I see them," I said.
>
> "It's glorious. Be a good boy, Mark. Let the others know that I have gone."

Then she reached out and took a final breath or two. It was a great moment, but the family missed the whole thing.

The moment of death, a painless thing, can often be a glorious observation for someone there. Vigils can be arranged by shifts, because the most significant moment of life is death, most certainly for the patient and should be for the family. Some predeath events are quite inspirational, as in the following case of Ida Williams.

Late on rounds one morning I barged into the room to find the minister hovering over the bed, quietly reading from the Bible. Mrs. Williams, whose eyes were tightly closed, asked the minister to stop reading and turn down the bright lights.

"But the lights are not on," the minister said.

"Then the sun is too bright. Turn down the blinds."

Then she finally opened her eyes and pointed: "I see Him! He's here! See His hands! See the heavenly hosts! They're all here—Majesty unutterable! The most glorious morning of my life," she said, welcoming them. Slowly she eased back, the heartbeat fading, and the breathing stopped. Everything stopped, but the smile persisted. Coding was not even considered.

I moved to the window and looked out. It had been dark and raining all morning, long tears streaking down the panes.

NEGATIVE DEATHBED EXPERIENCES

While most literature readily admits that positive near-death experiences are plentiful, it claims that negative experiences are rare or do not exist—neither in near-death experiences nor in apparitions on the deathbed. One author estimates that negative experiences "may represent perhaps 1 percent of all reported cases, perhaps less." He goes on to say, "In my own experience, having talked to or heard the accounts of many hundreds of NDErs, I have never personally encountered a full-blown, pre-dominantly negative NDE."[17]

Now I can verify that negative experiences characterize many NDEs, some categories more than others, but deathbed visions are certainly included in this group, and if negative deathbed experiences are obvious, then why are none of them reported in other NDEs?

The same is true for clinical death survivors, which are now especially plentiful. I have offered several negative NDE patients for these authors to personally interview (including Drs. Kubler-Ross, Ring, and Moody), but they have declined, the cases apparently presenting a glitch for data they have already published. All-positive data surreptitiously introduces the new "religion of the NDEs," the religion worshipping heaven as a benevolent gift to everyone, a God-given right.

If negative deathbed interviews can be established as fact, then negativism in other categories of NDEs should also be considered possible, again suggesting that they are not all positive as had been claimed. Negative cases would be a stumbling block to New Age faiths.

Professor Ring opens the door for transposing deathbed data into other NDEs by stating that if we draw on "well-known . . . deathbed visions, which are certainly related to and partially overlap NDEs, we have a solid basis for extrapolating [the events] to NDEs proper."[18]

If the logic is true, if negative cases can be proven to exist in any of the NDE categories, then this would negate the claims of those researchers who insist that all dying patients are destined for heavenly places regardless of faith or belief. Further, if these negative cases can be proven to exist, and if some of those who saw the "glimpse of glory" have been deceived, then it suggests it may not be safe to die unless salvation has been secured before-hand.

According to beliefs of the leaders in the field, including the Shirley MacLainers, there is no god outside of nature itself. If God is within us, then we also are God. But by this logic there would be four billion gods running around on earth, each doing their own little thing. With no one in charge, each would have to make his own rules. After all, what feels good to you has to be right because you are a god. All along, Satan has said this very thing: eat the fruit and "you will be as gods," and "you shall not surely die," the messages channeled through the serpent to Eve, and therefore to ourselves as her progeny (Genesis 3).

But the deathbed is simply marvelous in resolving the problem. That's the time the patient realizes that he is not god, otherwise he wouldn't be in this predicament in the first place—he wouldn't be dying. It did not take Sir Francis Newport very long to see the light and resolve the problem.

> That there is a God, I know, because I continually feel the effects of His wrath; that there is a hell I am equally certain . . . being continually upbraided by it with . . . all my sins brought to my remembrance. . . . Why I am become a skeleton in three or four days? See now, then. I have despised my Maker, and denied my Redeemer. I have joined myself to the atheist and profane, and continued this course under many convictions . . . when my security was the greatest, and the checks of my conscience were the least.

In inexpressible horror, he cried out, "Oh, the insufferable pangs of Hell!" and died at once.[19]

A. B. Shaw, collecting his cases back at the turn of the century, tells of the son of a wealthy Texas farmer who was dying of a severe three-day illness of unknown type:

> All through the night previous to his death, he suffered untold physical and mental torture. He offered the physicians all his earthly possessions if they would save his life. He was stubborn till the very last; and would not acknowledge his fear of death until a few moments before he died; then, suddenly he began to look, then to stare, horribly surprised and frightened, into the vacancy before him; then exclaimed, as if he beheld the king of terrors in all of his merciless wrath, "My God!" . . . His wife screamed and . . . the dying man continued to stare in dreadful astonishment, his mouth wide open, and his eyes protruding . . . until he died.[20]

Another of several negative experiences recorded by Shaw included that of Mrs. J. B. in 1886:

> I called to see her during her last sickness and found her in a most distressing state of mind. She recognized me when I came in, and was loath to let me leave long enough to bring my wife, who was only three-quarters of a mile away; saying, "Devils are in my room, ready to drag my soul down to hell." . . . She would say, "See them laugh!" This would throw her into a paroxysm of fear and dread, causing her to start from her bed; but when I tried to get her to look to Jesus for help she said, "It is no use; it is too late!"[21]

Great men in the past have had deathbed recountals, but only two more will be mentioned. Napoleon Bonaparte in 1821 confessed to the Count de Montholon:

> I die before my time, and my body will be given back to the earth to become food for worms. Such is the fate of him who has been called the great Napoleon! What an abyss between my deep misery and the eternal kingdom of Christ.[22]

And then the self-reliant Voltaire, whose "pen was mightier than the sword," whose intellect and honors could never be excelled, was now excelled by a stroke that was slowly causing his death. When his friends visited, they described this unexpected situation:

> He cursed them to their faces; and, as his distress was increased by their presence, he repeatedly and loudly exclaimed: "Begone! It is you that have brought me to my present condition. Leave me, I say; begone! What a wretched glory is this which you have produced to me!" Hoping to allay his anguish by a written recantation, he had it prepared, signed it, and saw it witnessed. But it was all unavailing. For two months he was tortured with such an agony as led him at times to gnash his teeth in impotent rage against God and man. . . . Then, turning his face, he would cry out, "I must die—abandoned of God and of men!" . . . Even his nurse repeatedly said, "For all the wealth of Europe I would never see another infidel die."[23]

While covering in a local nursing home, I notice that these identical problems that recurred down through history are unchanged today. An illustration is the case of Mr. Bartholomy in the nursing home:

"What is it you see?" I said. Mr. Bartholomy was trembling and grimacing at something behind me. When I turned, I could see nothing there.

"They're coming again!" he repeated.

"Who's coming?" I insisted.

Mr. Bartholomy was then sitting bolt upright for the first time in a week, but kept looking toward the window. "They're prowling around over there just waiting for me to die. Make them go away!"

Putting a hand on his shoulder, I eased him down and I read his chart. I could see that no drugs had been administered, there was no fever, and no lab problem except anemia. Another eight pounds weight loss. But mentally, was he complaining of flash visions? Possible spread of cancer to the brain? From toxic paranoia? Endorphins? Anoxia?

By the process of elimination, it seemed more of a delusion or hallucination. But why should I pay attention to the delusions of a dying patient—anything can happen in those cases. Although it should not bother me, it did. I had to pay attention.

The chart indicated he was well educated, a Protestant, several grandchildren, but no family in town. He needed psychological or spiritual help of some sort, but I gave him a sedative shot instead. The apparitions ceased, but a little later that night he died. I realized he had been all alone and soulfully denied. I had failed to be a real physician.

I have thought a lot about that ever since. And it still bothers me.

SUICIDES

As with clinical death and deathbed experiences, many researchers also believe that suicide attempts do not present any adverse or negative experiences. They maintain that negative suicide experiences do not exist. No hell-type encounters or visions are mentioned, not even to those requiring resuscitation. I said to myself, *Were any of the reporting authors present during the CPRs of these patients? Had any of the authors themselves performed the resuscitation?*

Kenneth Ring, professor of psychology at the University of Connecticut and author of a book foreworded by Dr. Elisabeth Kubler-Ross, is an example. Professor Ring claims there is no essential difference among NDEs of illnesses, accidents, or suicide attempts. That they are all uniformly pleasant, presenting much the same results. Prof. Ring states:

> In my own experience, having talked to or heard the accounts of many hundreds of NDErs, *I have never personally encountered a full-blown predominately negative NDE . . .* however one dies, the NDE, if it occurs, is much the same . . . the invariance hypothesis . . . research on suicide-related NDEs by Stephen Franklin and myself and by Bruce Greyson has also confirmed my earlier tentative findings that NDEs following suicide attempts, however induced, conform to the classic prototype.[24] (Emphasis mine)

In spite of these glittering results, obtained from delayed interviews by personnel who were not there at the time of the events, there is, nevertheless, an occasional negative experience that slips through their coveted data. That, after all, is one of the central reasons I have written this book.

Dr. Raymond Moody, a close friend of Dr. Kubler-Ross and appearing together in medical symposia as fellow psychiatrists, describes a couple of interesting suicide interviews in *Reflections of Life After Life*. One interviewed suicide patient was an exception to the traditional "all-positive" rule. This particular patient was trapped by mental reruns of the same uncomfortable scenes which had occurred in the original suicide attempt, these recalls continuing "even while I was dead." Another of Moody's patients, some time after the initial suicide attempt, gave rather vague reasons to Dr. Moody why he would not repeat the attempt:

> No, I would not do that again. I will die naturally next time because one thing I realized at that time is that our life here is just such a small period of time and there is so much which

needs to be done while you're here. And, when you die it's eternity.[25]

Between the lines there might be suggested some disturbing experiences as the reason the suicide attempt was not repeated. Dr. Moody interestingly states "Absolutely no one that I have interviewed has sought a repeat performance of their experience."[26] Why not? It seems logical that anyone depressed enough to try suicide in the first place would try it again if the previous suicide attempt revealed a really beautiful experience for their release. Therefore one must assume they did not see the glimpse of glory that was allegedly seen by all other reported NDEs.

This situation could present a real problem. If a person contemplating suicide reads about all the wonderful, uplifting NDEs experienced by other people, they might assume that suicide could not only resolve their own depression but be uplifting, thus encouraging them to repeat the performance until successful. To me, this is utter subterfuge. I have never seen any good experience result from attempted suicide. Eighty-five percent were glad to be back.

Mrs. P. M. H. Atwater, a businesswoman who wrote *Coming Back to Life,* a book foreworded by Prof. Kenneth Ring, presented more liberal evaluations than did her cohorts. She recorded seven negative NDEs found through her own interviews and mentioned six others she had heard about.

Although the following client of Mrs. Atwater was not a suicide attempt but a victim of heart attack, the incident is listed here since it closely parallels the typical negative suicide descriptions that I have encountered. All attempted self-euthanasias have been uniformly negative, not positive. This presents, I think, Ring's "invariance hypothesis" in reverse order. It backfires.

She was chalk-white with fear when I arrived. While clinically dead, she had experienced an incident which went like this: she floated out of her body and into a dark tunnel, headed through the tunnel toward a bright light ahead; once the light was reached, she came to view a landscape of barren, rolling hills filled to overflowing with nude, zombie-like people standing elbow to elbow doing nothing but staring straight at her. She was so horrified at what she saw she started screaming. This snapped her back into her body where she continued screaming until sedated. As she relayed her story, she went on to declare death a nightmare, then cursed every church throughout all history for misleading people, with rubbish about any kind of heaven. She was inconsolable.[27]

After that, Mrs. Atwater mentioned an amazing deduction: "They admitted meeting what they feared most in dying, which confirmed and strengthened their already strong belief that their 'sins' would be punished."

In contradiction to Dr. Moody's observations, Mrs. Atwater comments that not only can suicide attempts be repetitive (as we know), but can actually be enticed (as we may not know) by the malignant deception of a previously positive NDE they experienced or by someone else's positive NDE that they read about (we will mention a case). To illustrate, Mrs. Atwater relates the following case:

> One woman who contacted me spoke of being hospital-ized twice for attempting suicide—many years after her near-death episode. She had formerly [in the NDE episode] experienced a scenario that was indeed soul-stirring and up-lifting; but with the passing of years and a life filled with tragedy and pain, the positive upliftment she had previously received seemed to fade. Memories of how wonderful it was on "The Other Side" prompted her to try killing herself so she could return. She failed both attempts and caused her-self even more grief. When last I heard from her, she seemed reasonably back on her feet and more sensible, stating that she now realized there was no escape and she had better get busy and solve her problems herself.[28]

Solve her problems herself? No escape? She was one of the termination contemplators, living either in the dread of death or wishing that death would actually occur. The challenge for pre-ventive medicine is to recognize and counsel the death wish be-fore it materializes.

This particular author, Mrs. Atwater, rebels from her compatri-ots when she says, "Not all suicide scenarios are positive, how-ever. *Some are negative.* . . . Just because an individual has had a near-death experience does not prevent him or her from considering and perhaps attempting suicide at a later date. I am aware most researchers claim the opposite to be true, but I cannot substantiate their claim."[29] (Emphasis mine)

Some of the more recent authors are encountering an increasing number of negative experiences in all categories of NDEs. Sometimes Mrs. Atwater finds a mixture of experiences, one of which was her own:

> I can personally relate to both of these cases for my third death experience was what I came to call an "emotional suicide." I willed myself dead and my body was too exhausted to argue. Whether or not I physically died is debatable here, but as far as I am concerned, I did die. This happened two months after an incredibly loving and wonderful near-death [non-suicide] scenario in which I was overcome with forgiveness and joy.[30]

However, Professor Ring and his previous colleagues of the IANDS group continue to confound the "invariance" that only one extreme of the bell curve exists—the good extreme. In collusion with Moody, Kubler-Ross and others, Ring seems to persist in the great white hope that only good experiences of unconditional love, without negative fears, will be found by each of us in the hereafter, thus spawning the philosophy that heaven's gates are open wide for everyone who dies. Professor Ring summarizes his findings this way:

> The great unanimity of these reports means that there is a consensus among near-death experiences concerning what it is like to die . . . that the experience of death is exceedingly pleasant. Indeed, the word "pleasant" is far too mild; "ecstatic" would be chosen by many survivors of this experience. *No words are truly adequate to describe the sense of ultimate perfection that appears to characterize the entry into death.*[31] (Emphasis mine)

The experience that death is "exceedingly pleasant," indeed "ecstatic," might induce the depressed and forlorn to attempt to get there ahead of time. And that's exactly what happened to the couple reported by the *L. A. Times*. These two lovers had read the uniformly glowing reports of the next life. The two were seeking the "glimpse of glory" suggested by the findings of Moody, Kubler-Ross, Ring, and the forerunners of New Age thought. Deeply in love, the couple decided to discover the good life beyond for themselves:

> The man and woman kissed each other time after time, then turned their backs to the bay and, holding hands, tumbled backward off the Golden Gate Bridge to their deaths. The man had left a suicide note in his car that indicated he had been "called" to enter the "other world." The note ended: "I love you all, wish I could stay, but I must hurry. The suspense is killing me."[32]

The appealing concept of reincarnation to find a better life has also tempted people to end the mediocrity of their present life. For example, on February 8, 1963, when Ronald Reagan was governor of California, John A. Brown was convicted in the city of Riverside for allegedly murdering a fourteen-year-old boy, to which he had voluntarily confessed. Governor Reagan pardoned him after Brown changed his plea to innocent and after tape recordings were found in the Riverside County Clerk's office which "proved Brown's original confession was falsified because he wanted to die in the gas chamber and be reincarnated [into a better life]."[33]

The core message to remember is that suicide attempts in lucid and responsible people have invariably been bad experiences in those cases I have encountered. I suppose it is possible that distraught minds of the mentally ill and irresponsible may not have a negative experience. I don't know this because I haven't had such cases.

The following experience of an Eastern Airline pilot was colored by the drugs and the alcohol he had consumed in his suicide attempt. But his case illustrates that almost anything (whether drugs or suicide) can produce negative experiences.

> Before they washed my stomach to bring me back, I saw ugly people squeezing through the window. They grabbed me and took me to this immense valley. There was fire there. I was watching people scurrying back and forth there, waving their arms and yelling. That's when I started vomiting. I realized where I was. They were washing out my stomach.

Most religious traditions give strong admonitions against suicide. The Judeo-Christian Bible emphatically states that the fullness of our time is in God's hands (Psalm 31:15), that murder is forbidden (Sixth Commandment), including murder of oneself (Exodus 20:13; 1 Corinthians 6:18–20). More specifically, our lives are not our own; they belong to God (Genesis 9:5–6; 1 Corinthians 6:19). And yet some suicidal Christians say, "It is my life, isn't it? It's mine to do with as I choose, including suicide if I wish."

Of course, those countries condoning suicide, or self-induced euthanasia, will usually extend the liberty to abortions and, sooner or later, to voluntary euthanasia, which usually doesn't remain voluntary very long, as we will discuss later on.

In the next chapter we will examine some out-of-the-body enactments which might fulfill this inquisitive desire to discover death without dying. Since death is such an unforgiving thing, out-of-the-body experiments could afford a rather exciting and challenging way to follow in the footsteps of death without a permanent exit visa. It could permit a means of analyzing the inevitable without entering death's door.

At least, that is the reason given by some experimenters who seek knowledge through out-of-the-body experiences.

7

OUT-OF-THE-BODY
EXPERIENCES

"Everyone will fantasize an out-of-the-body experience some-time in their life," Dr. Jerry Jones said as we approached the entrance to a doctor's office in La Fayette, Georgia. "I think OBEs are sort of an experimental rehearsal for death. Seeing what near-death feels like, you know, separating spirit and body and looking to make sure everything is safe out there. That way there are no surprises."

"What about those real OBEs that occur without fantasizing?" I asked. "Have you seen any?"

"Oh, sure." He nodded in the direction of the doctor's office. "Even the doctor here had an OBE just last week." He seemed reluctant to go on for a while. "The OBE happened when the doctor had been beaten pretty badly. Right here where we're standing. A truck driver was waiting here to teach him a lesson. He said the doctor had been fooling around with his wife while she was a patient in the office."

I stood back. "You mean the doctor had an OBE from getting beat up?"

Jerry nodded. "He was half-conscious for a while. The girls had to carry him home in their car. He told them something crazy about being out in space way up near the moon or something, and that he didn't know how to get back. I guess he could probably have jumped over the moon when the truck driver phoned him later to apologize."

"Apologize for beating him up?"

"No, he apologized for beating up the wrong doctor—it was his partner he was after."

Besides trauma, there are many other ways to experience OBEs, drugs being the fastest. Certain psychedelic drugs like angel dust (PCP), speed (LSD), and cocaine are readily available and are really quite reliable hallucinogens. They'll get you out of the body pretty quickly, and may offer "a cheap peek into heaven."

DRUG-INDUCED OBEs

Tal Brooke, now an accomplished Christian author and expert in the New Age and a classmate of Dr. Raymond Moody at the University of Virginia, chose LSD to experimentally obtain the thrill of the OBE he had heard so much about. This is what happened:

> There I saw millions of lights as if I were viewing the city of Los Angeles turned upside down. My mind exploded with knowledge; I was a poet, a writer; I knew every line of Shakespeare; I suddenly realized my capabilities were limitless. I wasn't *part* of the universe: I *was* the universe![1]

Drugs are the easy way. Although it may take longer, meditation is another way to obtain an OBE. Pursuing the meditation route, Shirley MacLaine soon melted into "one" with her surroundings. She became "part" of the sauna bath, "part" of the rocks, the water, the bubbles, things she vividly recounts in her book *Out on a Limb*.

We list drug cases here to illustrate that an OBE can be obtained without an NDE, in spite of the fact that most authors list out-of-the-body experiences as part of near-death experiences. In other words, near-death is not at all necessary to obtain an OBE, the experience of separating body and spirit.

Part of the person's experimentations with drugs and meditation is to obtain the "high" which usually accompanies an OBE. But there is a penalty for what they call a "cheap peek into heaven" with drugs. When the dreaded "low" occurs, the next high may require a larger dose. Then overdose miscalculations can occur. There are also individuals who have idiosyncratic reactions to even small doses, explaining the unexpected deaths for some of the first-time users.

Now, let's take a closer look at the drugs commonly used to attempt OBEs, a situation which, for all their purported recreational benefits, actually are deadly deceits.

LSD was the first drug to be used on a large scale. The introduction of this drug helped create the culture explosion of the 1960s, familiarizing thousands of people with the so-called marvelous wonders of the spiritual world, a world unknown and hidden to the conventional straight society of that day. Personal participation was the new key to enter the "cosmic consciousness," the same mystical game the yogis had experienced through centuries of meditation, often drug enhanced.

While the yogis and holy men found mind-altering drugs the best route for rapid transit, they used the older drugs mescaline and hashish, drugs that proved to be too slow for the fast-lane traffic of the modern psychic.

Professor Timothy Leary of Harvard, a more modern and intellectual psychic, introduced the next generation of hallucinogens called LSD-25. After administering hundreds of doses of LSD-25 to his college graduate students, Professor Leary took to the road. He became an academic celebrity along with some other distinguished Harvard professors, like psychologists Dr. Richard Alpert and Dr. Alan Watts who composed "The Joyous Cosmology" to discuss their own mystical encounters while "tripping on the fantastic."

Leary and Alpert then transliterated *The Tibetan Book of the Dead,* the ancient Buddhist text on the rituals of death, into a manual outlining the liturgy for taking LSD and entitled it *The Psychedelic Experience.* The book also taught reincarnation, karma, and self-divinity, along with the benefits of drugs.

It didn't take long before huge amounts of the new LSD became available, enough to spike gallons of Kool-Aid for the thousands of spectators participating in the 1968 "Summer of Love" rock concert in the Golden Gate Park. "Nirvana" in pill form thus became a reality overnight, music synergizing the rock into the underscoring message "down with the establishment."

With LSD encouragement, the hippie communes explored additional alternatives for abandoning civilization and going back to nature, with freedom of the spirit becoming an obsession. The new culture of anti-establishment and anti-materialism emphasized drugs, sex, long hair, and the need of a bath.

While on road tours waving a Ph.D. in psychology, Professor Leary promoted a new gospel that looked beyond death. He proclaimed,

> LSD opens the mind and releases an enormous amount of awareness energy. Here is a key to the mystery which has been passed down for over 2500 years; the consciousness expansion experience, premortem death and rebirth. It is possible to get beyond ego consciousness, to tune in to the neurological processes which flash by at the speed of light, and become aware of the treasury of ancient racial knowledge welded into the nucleus of every cell in the body. Psychedelics [drugs] can open this door.[2]

A few months after Leary's talk, Tal Brooke, then a graduate of the University of Virginia and Princeton and a frequent speaker at Oxford and Cambridge, decided to challenge this experiment. This time he took ten times the normal dosage of pure LSD-25. A fraction past midnight, he swallowed 3000 micrograms of the pure material, and within an hour he was "sitting on top of an atom bomb."

> My thoughts and perceptions began to fuse. Stars joined like drops of mercury across the night sky forming multi-colored webs—breathing and arching across the heavens, across galaxies and onto the very ground where I perched. . . .
>
> As a force drove my mind at a speed greater than thought, I could feel something far older than I suddenly start navigating my course. I passed ten thousand crossroads per second, and took the proper turn on each one of them. . . .
>
> My speed increased even more, as I became a diamond wedge cutting the finest possible arcs, from one juncture to another. . . .
>
> Then something happened. I lost all grasp of language and thought. I saw a doorway into a new universe. It was a pin-

point of light. To fight the acceleration required to approach it was to fight the mass of the entire universe. . . .

At the barrier of the pinpoint of light—I entered the eternal present. All thirteen billion brain cells within me seem to turn inside out, as though jumping to a higher gestalt and forming into a higher structure that was previously latent. Each cell recites one of my former names. . . . Once I enter the pinpoint of light, all ties with the world vanish. I enter the Unborn. . . . I had entered into the ocean of being . . . the clear light or the Ocean of Brahman. . . . I had been allowed to experience the highest mystical state, what the Hindus call *Nirvikalpa Samadhi.*[3]

So impressive were these phenomena that Brooke explored the occult for two decades. After spending two years in India as the personal disciple of the miracle-working Sai Baba, the superguru, Brooke became a consummate New Ager before the term had even been invented:

My beliefs were a composite of the best I could find from the East blended together with the most radical breakthroughs in the West—the new physics, new forms of psychology, psychic research, channeled information from such psychics as Edgar Cayce, theosophy, and creative ideas coming from the psychedelic subculture. The drama of life was to ride the wave and "trust the Force" as I saw my third eye open.[4]

The ultimate conflict, Tal said, was an overwhelming confrontation with the simple claims of Jesus Christ.

But for others, those seeking "truth" through altered states of consciousness, there seemed to be no escape once entrapped. It seems that ever since Eve altered her state of consciousness by eating forbidden fruit, people have continued to seek the fountain of satisfaction through mind-altered states, swilling the transient pleasures of sex and drugs to reach these states, only to thirst again. Lasting peace still eludes the human grasp. Instead of peace, they may be surprised to find a spirit entity capturing their souls or a drug addiction destroying their minds.

Some people on LSD never live to reach the drug depravity reached by others. Convinced they are superhuman, some users will jump out the window as if a bird, only to find they cannot fly. Louis Costello, sixteen years of age, was so confident in his LSD delusion that he took a plunge of nearly one thousand feet using an umbrella as a parachute. He barely survived a broken pelvis and fractured legs.

Now to classify some of the standard groups of mind-altering drugs that are capable of inducing the so-called glorious adventure of OBEs without NDEs, and mention their street names. The major groups include the narcotics, the depressants, the stimulants, the psychedelic hallucinogens, and the marijuana group.

1. The *narcotics*, used for pain, include opium, from the poppy plant; morphine, a derivative of opium; heroin (Horse, Smack); Demerol (cubes); Dilaudid (dillies); some forms of codeine (Percodan, perks); and Methadone, itself addicting and no longer advised as treatment support for narcotic addiction.

2. The *depressants*, used for nervous tension, include phenobarbital; Quaaludes; the valium group (mother's little helper); and alcohol, the most common offender.

3. The major *stimulants*, used for "energy and a high", include cocaine, from the coca leaf (coke, flake, snow, rock, or crack); and amphetamines (speed, meth, crank, or ice).

4. The typical *hallucinogens* (used for "escapes" and "trips"), include LSD (acid, microdot), mescaline (peyote, buttons, cactus flower), and PCP (angel dust, hog).

5. The last is the *cannabis* group, named after its most active chemical and used for "fun" and "relaxation," including marijuana (pot, hemp, grass, reefer, Thai Sticks); and hashish, compressed resins from the marijuana plant (hash or hash oil, the name "assassins" deriving from the word hashish).

It is usually possible to recognize a child or adult on a drug trip, and to sometimes specify the dominant drug involved. Obvious evidence would be needle tracks in the arms or legs from mainlining the veins. Drug paraphernalia may appear sooner or later, carelessly left around at the time of the "glory" or the "high." Absenteeism from work will appear, and personality changes of lying, cheating, or stealing will often emerge.

Each drug group will produce characteristic signs or findings. Narcotics produce drowsiness, euphoria, constricted pupils, and slow respirations. The depressants result in drunken behavior, slurred speech, and may lead to semistupor. The stimulants produce heightened alertness, insomnia, excitation, fast pulse, dilated pupils, and loss of appetite. The hallucinogens cause an array of unpredictable "trips" such as illusions, delusions, or hallucinations and may often initiate acute anxiety. The cannabis group relaxes inhibitions, produces a sense of well being and exhilaration, and often results in disoriented behavior.

THE HISTORY OF DRUGS

Since NDEs are often characterized as OBEs, and since OBEs can be imitated through drugs, predeath phenomena and their potential dangers can be evaluated for relative safety through experimentation.

When I came to Chattanooga, my first heart patient was staying in a private clinic on McCallie Avenue next to the famous Thomas House. As I entered the clinic, I saw a woman in labor, about to deliver a baby. No medical personnel were present, and the physician in charge was sitting on a sofa, sweating and shaking—in no condition to do anything. He was too nervous and weak to stand up and was shouting at people who weren't there. I yelled in his ear that his patient was about to deliver. He merely shook his head, and threw a syringe behind the sofa. His face was pulled to one side and saliva drooled down his chin. His pulse was fast and his pupils dilated. As I took his blood pressure he suddenly convulsed, knocking a lamp off the end table, and fell to the floor. The pregnant woman screamed in the next room.

After sedating both doctor and patient, I delivered the baby without difficulty, smacked it, and cut the cord. Behind the sofa I found several vials labeled "amphetamine." Dexadrine in pill form no longer satisfied his needs and he had been mainlining speed with a needle, leaving multiple tracks in the left arm.

His brother, another physician, finally arrived and mentioned the history of acute depressive states, self-treated with mind-altering drugs. Various uppers included a mixture of speed and vodka to get him through the day, then several downers would get him through the night. As drug dependency increased, he became more secretive, denying that any problem existed. A couple of months after I saw him, he dwindled to skin and bones, and died.

Since then drug refinements have exploded on the market. Speed, the poor man's cocaine, is now distilled into "ice," a product destined to become perhaps the most dreaded of present drugs. MDA, one of the current ice crystals, is called by drug abusers "ecstasy" or the "love drug." The glimpse of glory sought by most drug users lasts much longer with ice and requires fewer fixes to achieve the desired effect. In fact, the high with ice is said to last most of the day—up to fourteen hours compared to cocaine's meager thirty minutes. Ice, in other words, lasts twenty-eight times longer than crack, although both belong to the same stimulant group of drugs.

Because the fear of contracting AIDS through the use of dirty needles has reduced the mainline approach by vein, smoking or inhaling drugs is now the trend.

Either crack as the ultimate cocaine or ice as the ultimate speed can be readily smoked as a means to attain the purported predeath cosmic wonders and the dazzling OBEs.

The medical profession was first introduced to cocaine in 1884 by Sigmund Freud, the physician who was to become the revered father of modern psychology and psychiatry. His famous manuscript describing cocaine was simply entitled *On Coca*. Freud first used cocaine himself for depression. Then he attempted its use to treat a close friend addicted to morphine. Instead of curing morphine addiction, it resulted in addictions to two drugs instead of one.

Dr. Freud was also the first to use cocaine to facilitate OBEs produced by hypnosis, which was also his invention. In fact, hypnosis remains the basis of today's theories of the unconscious and subconscious, all based upon mesmerism or drug experiences, or both. Cocaine soon became a panacea when Freud enthusiastically recommended it for the treatment of asthma, sexual problems, drug addiction, and many other things. He considered cocaine his own drug and his own discovery. As a result, he became most depressed and disturbed when a competitor, Dr. Carl Koller, stole his secret and introduced cocaine's first clinical use in the form of simple anesthetic drops for eye surgery, still in use today.

Have you ever wondered what a cocaine "jag" feels like? Like all other psychic phenomena, this glimpse of glory can be insidious and portend both good and bad effects. Robert Louis Stevenson found this to be true in 1885, when, while using cocaine to alleviate the misery of his own tuberculosis, he experienced enormous mood swings that enabled him to write the renowned *Dr. Jekyll and Mr. Hyde* in just three days! The book itself is evidence that out-of-the-body transformations can be either gloriously beautiful or horrible, although the potential for the horrid and evil is ignored by modern-day writers on the subject.

Similarly, Edgar Allen Poe and several other authors, musicians, and poets, owe much of their mood swings into evil and macabre events to personal use of drugs. Thus the heaven and hell of drugs resemble the results of all other mind-altering states, whether OBEs or NDEs. This further refutes the "all good" philosophy of authors who collect data on these subjects.

Although cocaine was first tested by entertainers in the 1920s, it was not widely popularized until the movie "Easy Rider" appeared in 1969, showing it to be the "real thing" for subsequent motorcycle gangs. Following the popularity of LSD in the 1960s, cocaine became the "champagne of drugs" for the 1970s and the 1980s, possibly to be replaced by ice for the turn of the century.

Cocaine is an incredibly unpredictable drug in both dose and effect. Without warning, it can anesthetize or paralyze the respiratory system or the heart's conducting system. By constricting the coronary system, cocaine can produce sudden heart attacks or fatal rhythms regardless of the user's age. Cocaine took the life of Len Bias at age twenty-two while he was a basketball star at the University of Maryland. It also took the life of Rico Marshall, a high school running back who idolized Bias, at the age of eighteen. In May of 1989 Esteban DeJesus, the lightweight boxing champion who once beat Roberto Duran, died of AIDS, which he contracted by sharing needles while shooting up a concoction of heroin and cocaine. The list of the young victims goes on and on, and the numbers are increasing.

Unidentified mixtures of drugs, or "fruit bowls," have become a party grab bag, guests eager to discover what the next bowl will have to offer. When the bowl is first passed around, each person tosses in a favorite pill or capsule (plus optional unknowns of pretty color) and the next time around they must pick out one and subsequently describe their feelings of altered consciousness to the rest of the group. Then the procedure is repeated. Using drugs instead of bullets, they play an accumulated Russian roulette.

Still other types of parties expand the method to include seances, pentagrams, mystic rituals, and chanting. Drugs are often used to help call up spirits through incantations and magic mantra. With or without drugs, group meditations can do the same thing—conjuring up unknown spirits, bringing forth the dead, seeking secret information for personal power, or sometimes the euphoria of astral travel—things forbidden in the Bible.

When "it" takes control, when the spirit being begins to arrive unbidden, with or without drugs, thoughtful provisions have been made for a hotline for those cornered by evil spirits or enslaved to recurrent mental motion pictures. The parapsychology organizations which have been fostering OBEs and spiritual contacts are now providing for the unexpected side effects through standby advisory counselors. They have finally acknowledged that the spirit of the fox has entered the henhouse of the mind.

Alcohol is the last drug to mention as a cause of OBEs. Our greatest chemical preservative, alcohol is still our worst drug offender. Before the days of refrigeration and pasteurization, wine of biblical days served as the preservative of water. Noah, the first vintner, was probably also the first abuser, when, on at least one occasion, he consumed too much of his own wine. But it was centuries later before someone got the bright idea to add cheese and cholesterol products to wine parties. Do you think the additional consumption of cholesterol could have at all been involved in reducing Noah's longevity of 950 years to man's present figure of three score and ten? The French Paradox study showed that the mantle of the grape (red skins more than white) prolongs life and contains suppressant materials which lower the "bad" cholesterols and raise the "good" ones, thus delaying the onset of hardened arteries, the disease that has since been killing more Americans than all other diseases put together. Hardened arteries and heart attacks were conditions apparently unknown in Noah's day.

OTHER DANGEROUS OBE METHODS

Of course, drug tripping is only one of several OBE methods for spiritual contact. Others include seances, past-life recall, sorcery, witchcraft, shamanism, necromancy, fortune-telling, horoscopes, Ouija boards, Tarot cards, and things other than the Jesus Factor. The Jesus Factor, of course, involves the biblical constraints which strictly forbid all the above practices (Deut. 4:19, 13:1, 18:10–14, 18:20; Lev. 20:6, 27; 1 Sam. 28; Isa. 47:13; Jer. 10:2, 29:15; Dan. 10:13; Matt. 24:24; Eph. 6:12). They are forbidden not because the spirits are imaginary but because they are very real, representing many false gods. Attempted visual materialization of these spirits implies mental idolatry, violating the commandment "There shall be no other gods before me."

Almost everyone, when you really give pause to think about it, has had some sort of an out-of-the-body experience. Dreams, as we discussed, are a common example of induced imagery by self-hypnosis. Some are good and some are bad, but we have all had bad dreams. We know for ourselves that they do exist. Yet most authors prefer to think that nightmares or negative OBEs do not exist, which is such a strange paradox. It simply means they haven't looked far enough.

Michael Sabom, a cardiologist at Emory, also says he has encountered no significant negative experiences, after looking at 30 of his 116 interviews (26 percent) sometime within the first month, six of them sometime within the first day.[5] Of the positive reports, none of them were reportedly obtained on the floor or during the resuscitation, often the only time when negative cases can be detected. Why all the positive reports? Perhaps the tunnel of light turns into fire, or the angel of light changes faces, or there is a direct entry into the macabre—forcing conversions that lead to positive events, the only part the patient chooses to remember (as in the case of Charlie McKaig).

As mentioned in chapter 4, some of the positive OBEs from clinical deaths have negative encounters on the way to the eventual light of glory, as if the struggle between good and evil continue to the last moment. One woman encountered a frightening void. Mr. Tandy Hawks was menaced by a voice of violence. Lee Merritt found demons residing in the walls of the darkness.

One patient I interviewed yesterday by phone didn't want his name mentioned because he hadn't yet revealed the negative part to his family, the part where the nurses had to hold him down during the resuscitative efforts. He probably never will, since he says "the matter has already been settled, and things have changed where I don't need to worry about the future."

Self-hypnosis or deep meditation into daydreams can whisk a person away into distant lands or sometimes reprogram bodily functions. The Hindu gurus particularly favor hypnagogic meditation to program biofeedback to control such physiological systems as pulse rate and blood pressure. Biofeedback and self-hypnosis are now popularly used in pain control clinics across America. Meditation visualizations can also be used to call down spirit forces from the so-called astral planes. These contact mechanisms represent ancient shamanistic rituals of the witch doctor which have been revitalized, updated, and clothed in scientific terminology for current times so they won't be recognized as modern-day witch doctor practices.

Dr. Raymond Moody now specializes in selected fields of shamanism, giving instructional seminars for thought travel through mirrors and crystals in an occultic process called *scrying*, possibly a metaphor implying "scrutiny," although I am not sure of the exact meaning.

The name of Dr. George Ritchie also surfaces when speaking of thought travel, the person to whom Raymond Moody dedicated his book *Life after Life*. Ritchie's ethereal trips usually flitter from heaven to hell and back again, more or less at will, something Jesus himself said was impossible. According to Luke 16:26, Abraham said there was a "great chasm" separating the immediate worlds of heaven and hell which people encounter at death and no one is allowed to cross from one to the other.

In July 1991, Dr. Moody's seminar entitled "Frontiers of Consciousness" was held at the Omega Institute for Holistic Studies in Rhinebeck, New York. Subsequent scrying seminars were held at his retirement home near Anniston, Alabama, an old gristmill built in 1839. Dr. Moody says the home was modeled after the Temple of Aesculapius, the surrounding acres full of springs and a few snakes, as were the original temples. In these temples the people of the Greco-Roman period would gather to be healed by the pagan gods of nature, chief of which was Aesculapius, the mythical god of medicine whose father was said to be Apollo.

Dr. Moody conducts seminars in the Temple for psychic heal-ing, necromancy, past-lives invocation, fortune-telling, clairvoy-ance, ESP, and others. Demonstrations are given by Raymond's associate, Mr. Dan Brinkley, a man allegedly struck by lightning several times, resuscitated, and hence made clairvoyant. As a re-sult, Brinkley is convinced of the doctrine of self-divinity.

The core teaching in Moody's Aesculapian Temple turns out to be an ancient shamanism called "dream incubation experiments." These experiments involve scrying where hypnogogic states of altered consciousness are practiced. "Shamanism must come back," Raymond proclaims. "It is the essential ingredient."

Modern shamans represent ancient witch doctors dressed neatly in business suits, who use modern incantations to disen-gage the gears of one's mental faculties in order to subdue con-scious awareness and yield control of one's self to the spirit world —things God called an "abomination" (Deut. 18:11–14). The Bi-ble says we are forbidden to communicate with any spirits outside of the triune God: Jehovah, Jesus, and the Holy Spirit.

Witch doctors have changed their methods as history changes, but not their goals. The shamans of the American Indian, for instance, chewed peyote from the cactus flower to facilitate the visualization of the sacred desert coyotes. Some Catholics try to visualize the Virgin Mary and some Christians try to visualize Jesus—which seems virtuous but is not biblical. To mold and pro-duce an idol, when you give reason to it, the object must first be conceived and visualized in the mind before it can be constructed as an idol, and this could conceivably be part of idolatry. We are to know and think of Christ, but not to visualize him. "Casting down imaginations, and every high thing that exalteth itself against the knowledge of God, and bringing into captivity every thought to the obedience [not visualization] of Christ" (2 Cor. 10:5 KJV). Many of my theological advisers think that conceiving a graven image is the first step in the making of mental idols.

Ancient witchcraft or modern shamanism offer little differ-ences. Saul did the same thing in the Old Testament. Using the assistance of the witch of Endor, Saul summoned the prophet Samuel from the dead. After Samuel actually appeared, Saul at-tempted to obtain information concerning the outcome of a cru-cial battle. King Saul already knew that God had forbidden such practices (just as he does today), but Saul was desperate. As a result of his disobedience, Saul was first defeated in the mighty battle, then was beheaded without mercy. God does not like necromancy where the dead are brought down from another world. In contrast, the NDErs accidentally encounter the dead in another world. There is no meditative or intentional "calling up" of the deceased.

In Deuteronomy 18:10–12 (NIV), God forbids anyone who practices "divination or sorcery, interprets omens, engages in witchcraft, or casts spells, or who is a medium or spiritist or who consults the dead. Anyone who does these things is detestable to the LORD."

OBEs INTO PAST LIVES

Ian Stevenson, currently professor of psychology at the University of Virginia, is a staunch advocate of reincarnation. Stevenson seems convinced that spiritual "possession" of an individual by a previously deceased person may occasionally occur long after one's inception or birth to explain some of the peculiar déjà vu or "already seen" phenomena. This is especially confusing when the possession occurs while the donor is still living and has his own soul.[6]

Notice that this runs counter to the reincarnation concept. It makes you wonder who this possessing spirit really is—whether it is a deceased person or, in fact, a possessing demon.

Out-of-the-body experiences, on the other hand, are often used to prove reincarnation. For instance, one might conjure the scenery of a medieval pageantry as proof that one was actually there in a previous life (the déjà vu phenomenon). Since OBEs can reach into the past, some people are convinced they were Bonaparte, King Henry the VIII, Alexander the Great, or even one of the pharaohs of Egypt. This can be an embarrassing situation, however, when several people claim they were George Washington, when only one George Washington existed in history—considering there is only one soul for any one body.

There seems to be an unexplained discrepancy. Why doesn't anyone claim to have been a beggar or a cripple or a garbage collector? There were many more of these than there were George Washingtons. Instead of the plentiful poor, everybody claims to have been someone plentifully rich or important. And if they were important in the past, why aren't they even more important now, since the law of karma is constantly improving them?

If the original law of reincarnation has not been counterfeited but remains the true reincarnation of India, why don't more people recognize original transmigration and find they were animals in their previous lives? Why don't they remember being a rock or a tree or a worm as the result of their terrible misdeeds in previous lives?

The ideas seems ludicrous when you look at the people of India, the birthplace of karma and the cradle of reincarnation. Why haven't they become more affluent as karma improves them? Instead, the majority in India remain downtrodden, living in squalor, many still begging for food in the large cities. Why do the filthy poor still outnumber the filthy rich? If karma were true, then the well-being of the populace is antithetic to the principle.

India, a land predominately Hindu, also contains the Jaines who sweep the sidewalks in front of them so they won't step on their future Uncle Chandra, the bug who may be on his way up the ladder of evolution. The Parsees wear gauze masks to prevent inhaling an insect which might be a near relative awaiting a more benevolent future in the transmigration of things.

The more pleasant, westernized version of reincarnation (no bugs or rocks) has migrated from east to west, becoming the religion of the entertainment world in the United States. Everyone is seeking "the truth." Celebrities continue their sojourns back and forth to India as students of the system to learn how "to get it right." Gurus are sought as master teachers for meditation to obtain the ultimate glimpse of glory and self-realization into pure consciousness, and to seek the ocean of Brahma, that much sought-after sublimity of the astral planes.

Perhaps this is why Shirley MacLaine's books are so popular. Celebrities, seeking greatness for their higher selves, don't seem to see the evil or harshness of karma which keeps the heel of the caste system treading upon the poor. In Calcutta, for instance, the wealthy do not help the lower castes who live in the gutters because the downtrodden have obviously done atrocious things in previous lives, and must suffer their karma. If assisted in any way, the karma of the miserable people will only become worse in the next life since payment was withheld. Rationalizing their ability to help, they might say, "That is their karma, and this is my karma."

That was the same conclusion reached by Channappa Kundra, an intelligent chemical engineer visiting our local TVA system from Delhi. He was hospitalized and in his third day of an unexpected heart attack when I first saw him on rounds.

"Did you do something bad to deserve this?" I said rather tritely. "And won't you be delaying your karma if I treat you?"

"The heart problem is not my real karma." He then sadly shook his head. "I am also succumbing to cancer of the pancreas. As you can see, the body is wasting. The heart would be a better death. My karma seems so unduly cruel when I have tried to live so contritely."

He smoothed the wrinkles from his sorrel-colored gown as he pondered the predicament. "Our system is different than yours. What we call *at-one-ment* you call 'atonement.' Karma struggles to make us one, but it is also unforgiving. So tell me more about this mercy system of your God."

I sat beside him, explaining the system where all debts are paid "for all time" through Christ's one single offering—and does not involve the indebtedness of repeated lives and merciless karma.

I found the verse I was looking for the next day. "For by a single offering [not repeated life-after-life offerings] he has perfected for all time those who are sanctified" (Heb. 10:14 RSV).

"You mean the repentant Christian believer can be accepted without penalty payments for his past?"

"That's it in a nutshell," I said. "And another bonus: the Christian type of nirvana involves no identity crisis."

I lost track of Channappa when he recovered enough to return to India. By the time I searched for him a year later near the city of Agra, he had already died from the cancer.

ASTRAL TRAVELS

In the United States both reincarnationists and scientists continue out-of-the-body experiments—a peek into the spirit realm to supposedly determine its content, its nature, and its safety. In a unique experiment, Elisabeth Kubler-Ross used Robert Monroe's experimental time machine known as the M-5000 program, and it seemed to work. Tal Brooke had initially helped to construct the machine in Monroe's home residence outside of Charlottesville, Virginia and gives this description:

> Cables and sound equipment trailed through the house from central command, an isolated geodesic chamber of pyramidal glass rippled with colored lights, while pulse generators whirred and hummed to the syncopated beat of a synthesizer/organ.[7]

Mesmerized by the unusual rhythm of the sound tapes, Tal recalled that Monroe went "whooshing" out of his body at midnight from Charlottesville to travel at astral speeds to Stanford University. During other experiments Monroe would "whoosh" to the University of California at Berkeley or at Davis where a Dr. Charles Tart and an array of notable parapsychologists would be assembled at 9:00 P.M. their time. Monroe would ethereally arrive and look around the room, noting people, conversations, and even furniture arrangements. Then he would "whoosh" back into his body in Charlottesville and give Tart and his associates a long-distance phone call in California, exactly describing to them what he had just seen.

Tal said, "He [Monroe] was right on target repeatedly, astounding these scientists with the fact that there are other forces operating behind the machinery of the physical universe."

From such experiments there would seem to be a reality to the spirit world, no longer a question of mythology or make-believe. There is an actual power in these two opposing, separate, and antagonistic forces in the astral sphere.

For eons of time, these two forces have been at war. One force presents two faces: either the bright face or the dark face, either good or bad, but usually disclaiming they are one and the same. Orthodoxy, on the other side, maintains that God and two-faced Satan are completely different forces in the business of contesting for souls.

Further out than dream states, the vastness of astral travel would require special techniques. While the word "astral" pertains to stars, the phrase "astral travel" implies the ultimate celestial transportation of an out-of-the-body experience. This implies "whooshing" (as did Monroe) through an imaginary substance that exists beyond human perception, moving at the speed of thought—the speed of light very slow in comparison.

Clinical death experiences also relate to a similar realm of celestial travel, perhaps comparable to Mr. Spock being "beamed up" to the Starship Enterprise. But there is a difference between the realm of astral travel and the realm of clinical death. In the latter, either heaven or hell may be encountered in a soul-shaking sequence of events that changes the primordial being. In the mystical astral travel, one's destination is unknown, and is at the whim of the spirit guide or the drug involved. It is unreliable for replication of the next trip, whether good or bad.

In summary, OBEs can be induced by most anything: accidents, fever, toxicity, self-induced hypnosis, acute fright, or an impending disaster. Perhaps you have already experienced one firsthand. Fortunately, not all OBEs are NDEs, and not all NDEs are OBEs. An example is the story of a crazy pilot.

Late one evening, a middle-aged pilot was watching a solid blanket of clouds pass beneath him, the Aztec's shadow outrunning the last of the sun, Huntsville lying somewhere ahead and Chattanooga beyond that.

The plane jostled a little bit when the pilot changed fuel tanks.

"The DME indicates Huntsville is twenty-five knots off the nose. We can put down there if you like," the pilot said to the hospital administrator, who was acting as copilot.

At that very moment, while the old Aztec lumbered in the chop, the starboard engine decided to quit. Immediate hard left rudder and pulling left wing low didn't help much at that high altitude, and the plane drifted rapidly down into the nasty snowstorm below.

As the Aztec fell through the clouds, sudden night brought down a curtain, and the confinement of the cockpit became a jostling closet. All at once the windshield smashed over with blinding rime ice, narrowing the closet, claustrophobia seizing the guts.

The pilot struggled desperately to keep the wings level, looking for the outboard lights, the instrument panel dancing in the pink haze. Cold with perspiration fright and mumbling prayers, the pilot tried to raise Huntsville for emergency headings.

Then the strangest thing happened. Somehow the pilot seemed to be jostled out of the plane, his body falling precipitously. Startled bewilderment and acute fear fell away and all became quiet. He was suspended in time. He looked up at the banking plane to see the administrator wide-eyed with terror, and the pilot next to him vigorously wrestling with the controls.

"Doesn't that dumb pilot see the problem?" the time-suspended pilot thought. "Switch the fuel tanks again," he yelled up. "Your motor's out of gas!"

Strangely, the pilot at the controls seemed to hear him and switched the tanks. The dead engine abruptly roared to life, almost turning the plane upside down in the process. "No wonder the jerk almost turned over," the floating pilot said. "Still had full throttle and pushing full rudder."

Anxious to help the poor imbecile, the displaced pilot willed himself back into the cockpit and forcefully took over the controls. The re-embodied pilot leveled the Aztec and discovered that the fuel to the starboard engine had not been completely switched to the "on" position.

The plane soon lifted out of the storm, bursting through gray remnants into the welcoming twilight above. Soon thereafter the ice blew off and a new course was directed by flight control and an instrument flight plan was established.

I derived some memorable conclusions from that hair-raising experience.

I'd fly through rainstorms maybe, snowstorms never.

Friendly with God? You bet I was.

Astral travel? Out-of-the-body? Altered states of consciousness? I would call it that. I also know you don't need drugs to fly. Simply get scared out of your socks and you can get out of your body without any need of drugs or the touch of death's embrace.

ALTERED STATES OF CONSCIOUSNESS

In a personal way, through extreme fright, I had found that any altered state of consciousness can induce an OBE, the temporary escape to seek "enlightenment." Resuscitation or clinical death is not necessary. Any form of hypnosis, whether self-induced or induced by someone else, or by chemicals, vibrations, sounds, electrical stimuli, or most anything else, opens the tunnel where the light can be seen. It is not always glorious. It can be hell. OBEs without fright can be obtained by deep meditation, yoga exercises, incantations, mantral recitations, or other favorite mystical quirks—anything altering the brain's mechanism of functional perceptions.

According to neurophysiologists, all subconscious emotions and past memories arise in the limbic system and hippocampus areas of the brain, structures buried deep in the temporal lobes and lateral to the ventricles (cavities which collect cerebrospinal fluid). Electrical stimulation of these areas can produce some remarkable pictures in the mind, as can constriction of blood flow or deprivation of oxygen and nutrients to the brain tissue. Any of these mechanisms, however, lack any replication of the sequence which characterizes the resuscitation experience.

As mentioned, Schoonmaker found that blood oxygen levels measured at the time of cardiac arrests and near-death experiences were still sufficient for normal brain function. Melvin Morse also found no oxygen level difference between patients with and without near-death experiences.[8] Also as mentioned, patients on drugs are the least likely to have experiences of this type. Regarding random visualizations during temporal lobe "seizures," epilepsy is not a common condition in near-death experiencers.

Neither are brain waves confined to one side of the brain over the other, as claimed by some psychic investigators. Alpha brain waves in general become dominant as sleep approaches and it is at this level of near-sleep that the mind can best be invaded and captured by any force. It seems the ideal time for experimentation with OBEs, necromancy, scrying, hypnosis, or spirit possession—the time when the mind is unprotected, the time when neurons can best be manipulated by a force. It is the twilight zone, the time of culpability, the time when foreign influences can be wonderfully exciting. It is the alpha looking glass of the mind, the window to the soul. The end point is claimed by some to be the Omega, but Jehovah states that both the Alpha and Omega belong to him.

These altered states of consciousness are nothing new. A glimpse of glory has been inducible for centuries, the history of drugs as an example. However, Freud liked to describe the dream-OBEs as the "royal road to the unconscious." Freud, in fact, made dreams fascinating, using them to reveal unexpected diagnoses. And dreams are still used today for diagnostic assistance. For instance, as the very first symptom of oncoming

Alzheimer's disease, the ability to experience dreams may completely vanish. Diseases of blindness may yield their first warning by decolorizing the patient's normally colorized dreams.

Oliver Sacks, a neuropsychiatrist in a large hospital in the Bronx, also believes that dreams can actually forecast specific illnesses. One woman dreamed that she was paralyzed, mesmerized, and turned to stone. The next morning she awakened frozen, catatonic, and unable to move. This was the first finding of an acute encephalitis, a viral infection of the brain.

Another of Dr. Sacks's patients, forming the basis of the feature film *Awakenings,* first noticed the onset of his Parkinsonism by symptoms which appeared in his dreams long before they became manifest in his body. It started with an OBE played out in slow motion. The patient saw himself racing forward and unable to stop. He became stiff and slow, and his motions awkward, frozen in time. Dopamine tablets, a remarkable suppressant of the disease, caused a response of vivid, brilliant colors appearing in his dreams and this presaged a miraculous "resurrection" of his immobilized body.[9]

Concerning spirit counseling in the altered state, one can never be sure who is knocking at the door until one opens the door. If it's not a pleasant visitor, or one that pretends to be pleasant, chaos may occur. That's when one experimenter tried to call the hot line of the Emergency Psychic Counseling Services in Los Angeles. Instead of factual help concerning demonic encounters, the victim was ironically told, "Welcome to the club!"—before the phone was hung up.

How do you go and break free into the lofty astral planes beyond the earth? A common technique is something like this: seclude yourself, concentrate completely, utterly relax, center yourself, pull down the door, and call out the specific mantra for the spirit guide you have invited. Of course, they may not be the counselors you desired. Similar to the fruit bowl, you're pulling one out of the grab bag. His name may be foreign to you or not of your liking, because you are opening the door of your soul to a stranger, a privilege you would not extend to a stranger knocking on the door of your home. You've invited an unidentified being into the most private part of your life where he is at liberty to rob your house, perhaps rape your soul.

Reading of Carl Jung's "collective unconscious," Johanna Michaelsen was stimulated to become a graduate of a mind-altering course which she said was called Silva Mind Control, perhaps related to the ones now called "centers for problem solving." Johanna took no chances in arranging for her spirit counselor. She selected "Jesus" as her Jungian Christian archetype for her spirit guide. Sure enough, the spirit called "Jesus" appeared when summoned. It was only later that she discovered this spirit called "Jesus" was not the real Jesus. He was only an imitation.

One can never be sure who is knocking at the door until one opens the door.

Johanna initially began with the Alpha level of concentration. Then she practiced advanced work in Applied ESP, another type of altered state. She would first find a comfortable place on the floor, progressively relax and devoid her mind of all thought and all control. She became very sleepy as she counted down to the Alpha level of brain activity. In the Alpha state she would reach up and pull down an imagined door and call the special mantra to summon "Jesus" or at other times "Sarah." These were the two spirit guides Johanna had been assigned. All students had both a male and female spirit counselor. This is how Johanna describes her first contact encounter with the spirit guide called "Jesus":

> As the door came down, the room was filled with a radiant light that emanated from the figure standing behind it. . . . Shimmering brown hair parted in the middle, a high forehead, dark skin; eyes brown, deep, and gentle. There! It was Jesus! The door went down now of its own accord, revealing the rest of the figure which was robed in a long white linen garment. He was glowing with a holy radiance and smiling softly. I stood, then fell at his feet.[10]

During one of her routine programming days Johanna was told to enter her mental laboratory, to count down, and greet her emerging counselors. The same hypnogogic metronome (commonly used with a piano) played in the background as before, but this time her two spirit figures appeared simultaneously. As she watched, the beautiful-appearing figures of both Sarah and Jesus rapidly changed into horrible faces which reminded her of "growling werewolves."

"They just stood there watching me . . . [and as I approached the faces changed again]. . . . The face of Jesus flashed on— shining and loving—then in a flash, the werewolf reappeared. The same was happening with Sarah."[11]

Johanna was led to believe that this was merely a test of her faith. Regardless of how frightening they might appear, the figures explained, she must not think of them as evil. She must instead "learn to trust and accept them regardless of the discrepant images they might present."

Johanna continued to accept this faulty explanation even after her friend Kim, who had also selected another "Jesus" as her spirit guide, quickly recanted her own practices when she recognized that this "Jesus" was the "face of Satan" pressing upon her.

Johanna tried to escape but couldn't. She had already become intertwined and captured by the forces she now served. A long time later, thanks to the intervention of strong Christian friends, she said the real Jesus entered her life, and this enabled her to escape her captors.

OBEs IN THE HISTORY OF FREUD AND JUNG

As we mentioned previously, it was Freud and Jung who popularized glimpses of glory and the methods of obtaining them. At the turn of the century, hypnosis was Freud's invention to expose and analyze childhood difficulties and present them as the most likely cause of one's current adult difficulties. Should any case of hypnosis prove difficult, a little cocaine would be added. Thanks to Freud's popularization of its medical use, cocaine, along with alcohol and opiates, became "the third scourge of humanity" and a means of reaching from glory into depravity, as with Dr. Jekyll and Mr. Hyde. The scourge was originally unleashed by Freud on the medical profession in the year 1884.

Freud was a physician imparted with a remarkably morbid fear of death, but this was merely one of his multiple phobias. He couldn't attend funerals because he was deathly afraid of a corpse. He was also adamant that there was "no God" and that "no religious experiences existed" except in the illusions of the mind. It was his protege, Carl Jung, as we shall see, who would enlighten him on this subject.

Although Freud claimed to be a materialist, he nevertheless obtained his real-life material from the spirit world of hypnosis and altered states of consciousness. This has become the present foundation for the New Age of Reason and the new faith of intellectuals who reject any concept of accountability other than man's own control of mankind. It was Carl Gustav Jung who later refined modern psychology with the concept of mental archetypes.

Carl Jung, Freud's "adopted son" and pupil, became the successor and founder of both the "New Age Consciousness" and "modern psychology" (psychology defined as the study of the mind or psyche—that is, the study of abstract thought as opposed to the electrical and physiological phenomena of the brain). Although both were medical doctors, Freud and Jung remained worlds apart in what they interpreted as the "truth" as they were extracted from studies of the mind and those "truths" extracted from the spirit or the soul.

While Freud was deathly afraid of death, Jung was the exact opposite. Carl Jung loved the dead. He loved the spirit world. He loved the archetypes of the mind. Using the *Tibetan Book of the Dead* as his bible, Jung would actually go and preach to the dead. Carrying the book under his arm, he would board the train with the corpse and serve as a companion while en route to the funeral location, preaching on the way.

As did Freud, Jung specialized in both dream analysis and psychoanalysis. But it was Jung who believed in the limitless potential of the unconscious, the knowledge shared and contained by all individuals, complex knowledge, a glory which could be "tapped into" with a variety of meditation, hypnosis, or forms of channeling. Jung called this the "collective unconscious" where each individual is part of the cosmos, offering a vast source of infinite and glorious knowledge which merely needed to be jump started through self-realization of one's own inherent divinity. Thus, the individual himself offers the means of tapping into the whole universe to see the glory of it all, to know that all is one and all is god, and to know we are one with the universe.

This is, of course, the ancient Hindu Vedas reborn, where everybody is part of everything—where the rock, the wind, the earth, and the universe are your brothers. And your brother is your brother—unless he is your brother Cain and decides to kill you. But that, too, would be all right, since there is neither right nor wrong in the universe. This is part of New Age psychology.

This idea is a reincarnation modification by our modern intellectuals where everybody can become God—that is, except Jesus, of course. They maintain that Jesus was only another prophet and no more a part of God than you or I.

More recently, however, the New Age gospel has thoughtfully bypassed the need of reincarnation by introducing the new concept of the "Omega Point," based entirely on the homogeneously positive or glorious near-death experiences which show a direct passage into a heaven-for-all with no karma.

Carl Jung, on the other hand, favored the cause of reincarnation and studied the mind for the potential existence of past lives. He insisted there were hidden, incredible stores of knowledge in areas of the mind which were beyond Freud's reach, areas which went beyond mere intrauterine and childhood experiences; areas which extended far back before life in the womb into previous lives. Lives which destined your present personality. Lives which molded the psyche and influenced the soul. This exposure of past-lives experience through self-hypnosis supposedly proved reincarnation; but they may, in some cases, represent actual spirit "possession," according to expert reincarnationist Ian Stevenson.

The main *forte* of Jung's endeavors, however, went far beyond the living and involved methods for contacting the dead. Jung used this necromancy to contact the limitless spirit world. Jung also went on spiritual trips himself. One of his favorite trips was to contact his dead grandfather who would, after the proper rituals, materialize out of a large portrait hanging on the living room wall. The grandfather would step down out of the picture and in a glorious reunion, both he and Carl would stroll arm-in-arm into the garden to talk out difficult problems.

While Carl Jung worshipped his grandfather, his relationship with his dead father was the opposite. Jung's father had been a hell's-fire preacher. But one night, in September of 1922, it seemed that Carl's father materialized from the dead to seek Jung's advice concerning the father's own marital problems. Carl commented that they "walked into the library to discuss it." Carl began to wonder why his dead father would seek marital advice when his wife, Carl's mother, was still living. To solve the problem, Carl put his fabulous "dream analysis" to work (which is still used today):

> My parents' marriage was not a happy one. . . . My dream was a forecast of my mother's death [which in fact occurred a short time later], for here was my father who, after an absence of twenty-six years, wished to ask a psychologist about the newest insights and information on marital problems since he would soon have to resume this relationship again [when they would rejoin each other in the spirit world].[12]

Both Carl Jung and Sigmund Freud were burdened with their own aberrations, phobias, and neuroses, which continue to taint today's psychology, resulting in a disunity of over 250 diversified schools of thought, none of them fulfilling the required reproducibility to make psychology a science. Undaunted, Jung nevertheless fondled the occult as if it were indeed a science, entitling one of his books *Psychology and the Occult*, employing the occult as the foundation for the so-called "science" of psychology as it is known today.

But the foundation remains as shaky as the relationship between its founding fathers. Jung and Freud could not even agree to disagree, adding to the reasons for the hundreds of existing schools presenting opposing therapies, each codifying their own formulas.

When they met in 1909, Jung told Freud that he could prove the existence of the spiritual world and of psychic religious experiences, the very things Freud insisted were only "illusions." As part of the proof, Jung told Freud he would "make a 'shot' come out of the bookcase" that stood nearby in his study. Sure enough, a booming explosion came out which caused Freud, the master guru of all psychology, to faint dead away. This exemplified the phobias and neuroses which Freud and Jung foisted upon the rest of us as the "science" of psychology.

The next time they met, in 1912, worse things occurred. Jung's persistent talk of corpses proved to be Freud's nemesis, and the mentor, Freud, fainted once again.[13] As a result, Freud accused Jung of harboring an unconscious death wish against him, which Jung came to believe was true when, in a dream, Jung killed

"Siegfried," the Germanic hero. On the basis of dream interpretation, Jung interpreted this "Siegfried" to be "Sig Freud," or Sigmund Freud. Because of the morbid fear that he would indeed kill Sigmund Freud, Jung teetered on the brink of what he called "total psychotic breakdown" for the next six years. These are the near-psychotic fathers of modern psychiatry and psychology! Almost all New Age seminars today, when you look at their programs, include lectures on Freudian and, especially, Jungian psychology.

During this time of near psychosis the "holy spirit" appeared to Jung in the form of a dove and a host of spirit entities materialized. The leader of these spirits was called "Philemon," and it was Philemon who became Jung's close friend and mentor. It was "Philemon-the-demon," as some prefer to call him, who supervised and inspired the writing of the *Seven Sermons to the Dead*. Jung described the situation like this:

> The whole house was . . . crammed full of spirits. They were packed deep right up to the door, and the air was so thick I could hardly breathe. . . . Then it began to flow out of me, and in the course of three evenings the thing *[Septem Sermones ad Mortuos]* was written.
>
> [Then his soul departed into the world of the "unconscious," where] . . . the unconscious corresponds to the mystical land of the dead. . . . If, therefore, one has a fantasy of the soul vanishing, this means that it has withdrawn into the unconscious . . . [and] soon after the disappearance of my soul the "dead" appeared to me and the result was the *Septem Sermones.*
>
> [And as a result there were some unusual effects noted.] In the midst of this period when I was so preoccupied with the images of the unconscious, I came to the decision to withdraw from the university, where I had lectured for eight years. . . . I felt I could no longer keep up with the world of the intellect. . . . The material brought to light from the unconscious had, almost literally, struck me dumb.
>
> [Previous to that, Jung had consciously arrived at a startling conclusion.] It is of course ironical that I, a psychiatrist, should at almost every step of my experiment have run into

the same psychic material which is *the stuff of psychosis and found in the insane.*[14] (Emphasis mine)

At the same time Jung claimed "the contents of psychic experiences are real [and] . . . I tried to demonstrate this in my scientific work." While he particularly emphasized "that the goal of psychic development is the self," Jung psychologized his work into the scientific language of today, as if it were some sort of science in spite of the fact that there was no analytical thread of consistency.

To fulfill the dream of all philosophers, mystics, and theologians, Jung toured the world in search of the mystic holy grail called "the truth." He absorbed Hinduism from the East and the "I Ching" from the Orient. In fact, the Orient seemed to fascinate Jung, hexagrams appearing when reed sticks were thrown from each hand, the designs answering proposed questions as predictably as did the Ouija board and other psychic games which Jung used to invoke the occult.

The great Jung, the master, used many other methods to evoke the occult. In 1911 he wrote: "My evenings are taken up very largely with astrology. I make horoscopic calculations in order to find a clue to the core of psychological truth. Some remarkable things have turned up which will certainly appear incredible to you."[15]

These incredible things repeatedly involved amazing occultic powers. There was one important flaw, however. He recognized that the occultic powers were never 100 percent correct. Often they were wrong. They could never approach the biblical prophets who were either 100 percent correct or were otherwise stoned to death. Isn't it strange, for instance, that Ezra, Nehemiah, Jeremiah, Ezekiel, and Daniel never had to apologize for being wrong?

Whence came the powers observed by Jung? Jung said that Philemon was one of the first figures he had encountered during his descent to the "underworld." Jung noted specifically that Philemon had "horns and wings," and was "lame in one foot." This was the spirit entity who gave Jung his spiritual enlightenment to start modern psychology. This "wise old man," Jung recalled, reminded him of Goethe's *Faust,* the figure who arrogantly killed two other characters in the book called Philemon and Baucis. Perhaps in this way, the Philemon complex became personally transferred to Jung when, after a prolonged illness, Philemon's physical lameness was transmitted to Jung himself.[16]

Thus began the original concept of "psychosomatic transfer," the psychiatrist becoming the patient. In the case of Jung and Philemon, one was as spiritually ill as the other, a result of tampering with the spirit world.

SPIRIT COUNSELING AND OBEs

Need inner healing? Need problems solved? Need to know the future? How would you like an astral trip without drugs? It can be done through counseling with spirits through Jungian psychology, but I would not advise it. You will find details available in any of the seminars held at the annual Humanistic Psychology Association meetings or in the magazines of the New Age bookstores, such as *Shaman's Drum.* But you should cloak yourself with plenty of godly protection beforehand.

Experiments with spirits have potentially horrendous risks: the risk of possession by the entity or force you have contacted, the risk of relinquishing control of your mental faculties, the risk of possession by the reincarnating spirit of the previously dead—the risk of things which God has called an "abomination" (Deut. 18:12).

Could these risks be part of the "dark side of the force," portrayed in *Star Wars?* Faith in these forces is popular and apparently continues to influence Mark Hamill, alias Luke Skywalker. At least, that was the implication I had when he and I appeared, along with other guests, on a TV talk show in Los Angeles. He was promoting *Star Wars* and I was small potatoes promoting a rather obscure book called *Beyond Death's Door.*

I suppose Hamill was right when he suggested that the "bright and dark side" of the force were merely different sides of the same force. Naturally, I wondered if the bright side could represent Lucifer and the dark side could represent Satan—two sides of the same force, a different face appearing on each side of the coin.

Of course, the two forces in theological thinking are traditionally acknowledged as God and Lucifer, diametric opposites, worlds apart, fighting for the souls of mankind, thus representing

completely separate entities, and not the suggested single force
with interchangeable faces noted in *Star Wars*.

I noticed that in many books of faith the coined phrase "god of
forces" almost always portrayed evil. These evil gods included
Satan, Shiva, Kali, Pan, Baal, and a host of others, and they were
also known as "the gods of destruction."

Of all these gods, only one God, Jehovah, the God of the Bible,
vows to destroy all of these other false gods in end times (Jer.
10:11). In addition, all the techniques to reach those gods—hypnosis, astral travel, ESP, clairvoyance, divination, shamanism,
scrying, and witchcraft—will also be destroyed.

Meanwhile, these techniques to reach these gods or forces are
deadly potent and offer potential powers so enormous and so
fantastic that it would seem difficult to resist the temptation when
so many others are participating.

At first it seems unfair that God would forbid even a small
peek into this counterfeit glory, a trivial contact with mediums,
charmers, fortune-tellers, astrologers, horoscopes, channelers, or
psychics. Even self-induction of OBEs and NDEs might seem
benign. But such dabbling is dangerous and forbidden. It invokes
and calls upon forces directly opposed to God—forces which
have already been cast out of heaven (Lev. 20:9, 27; Deut. 13:1–5,
18:10–12).

To obfuscate their purpose, the ancient names of these occultic
practices have been purposefully changed to more euphemistic
terms. Fortune-tellers are now known as "futurists," and demon
possession is politely called "channeling," "automatic writing," or
"astral travel." Evil forces still play the old-fashioned games with
Ouija boards, I Ching sticks, and Tarot cards. While scrying has
replaced the old crystal ball and mirrors, crystal charms still serve
as antennae to communicate with the ancient masters. "Meditation" replaces the term "self hypnosis" while yoga exercises and
mantras continue to introduce many inquisitive people to new
spirit entities sent by the god of forces, the god of destruction, the
interchangeable dark side of Satan who can light the tunnel for
some as the bright side of Lucifer.

8

COSMIC
CONSCIOUSNESS

It was on a cold wintry night when I met Bob Kovalesky (not his real name). A ghostly wind cried out as it swept in from Lake Ontario, shaking black trees, penetrating the bone, and pushing me along the flagged path toward the big Georgian house. I knocked, and a large-framed figure loomed in the porch lights. He had a square face and hazel-blue eyes that darted fitfully with paranoid glances. He motioned me in without a word, closing the door against the wind. I followed him into a plush living room.

Bob was dressed too warmly—white shirt with long sleeves, perspiration under the arms, wrinkled grey pants, worn-out house shoes. The room was overheated, but Bob Kovalesky was cold and trembling, fear troubling the eyes—the haunted look of a man about seventy instead of the man of forty years old.

Shaking his head, Bob eased himself wearily onto the sofa and said, "I was thinking of blowing my brains out."

I sat next to him and slipped an arm over his shoulder. "That bad?"

"Yes, that bad!" he said and looked toward the window where the wind rattled the shutters. A couple of deep breaths later he motioned toward the table at the window. "The gun is in there," he sighed. "It was very difficult waiting here for you to come."

"Well, I'm here," I said, pouring myself scalding coffee from the plastic pot Bob had offered. "Better fill me in where you left off in Toronto this afternoon."

Music from the FM radio appeared, and I produced a pen and pad and began to take notes. Bob Kovalesky was brusk and powerfully made. He represented the template of Toronto's leading industrial executives. He had the formula for success. He had found methods to climb the pinnacle, formulas to eliminate competitive businesses. The technique, he said, was simple mind control—to control them before they controlled you.

The story started in his youth. A childhood of hardships. He was so poor that he was determined never to be poor again. When he discovered that the average person uses only 15 percent of the brain's capacity, Bob wanted to improve his lowly status by developing the vast resources of the unused brain.

He began with the Planned Happiness Institute where they taught him how to enter a self-hypnotic trance and mentally formulate objects, then manipulate them into usefulness. To improve the power of hypnosis he added Transcendental Meditation through the "Science of Being" group. There he was taught to control other people's minds by imposing his own thoughts. As it began to work, Bob became more successful in business. The Bible of his childhood had warned against things like hypnosis and he searched until he found the part about "Casting down imaginations and every high thing that exalteth itself against the knowledge of God" (2 Cor. 10:5 KJV). It didn't matter, Bob concluded, because the hypnotic techniques were working. That's what counts, he told himself—what works—and not the source of the power. Origin made no difference.

Over the years Bob added astrology, the ancient metaphysical game of the Babylonians. Soon he became skilled in drawing his own horoscopes and used them to forecast and direct his own business decisions.

One thing bothered Bob. It was evident that astrology was not always accurate—never able to withstand the scientific tests of reliability and reproducibility.

Discouraged by the inconsistency, Bob added yoga, communication systems that came in various packages. Hatha yoga, he found, promised the participant would become vibrant and irresistible, mastering in love, peace, and joy. So he employed a private guru. At first yoga exercises seemed boring, but one day the secret mantral incantations made him shake and tremble as a glimpse of ghostly incarnate beings were brought forth. After reassuring him, the spirits outlined some powerful techniques to wield over his business competitors and to conquer almost anyone else he chose.

As time went on, however, some of these entities persisted and wouldn't disappear, as had been their custom. For no reason, they started to become unfriendly and began to control his thoughts and actions when it used to be the other way around. His mantral recitations, used to facilitate his yoga exercises, no longer called up his spirit guide but conjured up beings he had never heard of, beings he had never requested. Yoga incantations and transcendental meditations were supposed to be benign things.

Unhappy with these events, Bob turned to other fields of parapsychology, and it wasn't long before his life became filled with the occult and supernatural. He smoked too much, drank too much, accomplished little, and his marriage was faltering.

While in the lotus position of advanced yoga one evening, he heard a voice drifting down from the rafters. He thought he had heard it before, but this time it seemed to say, "Kill her, kill her, kill her!" By now Bob was convinced that a demon was ordering him to kill his wife. Casting thought waves, the demon made it clear that Bob's wife was an interference, that she did not "belong." Bob finally realized that this voice represented the source of all of his acquired power.

Bob said, "I was no longer in control of myself. I was under the control of the voice. I became afraid to go to bed at night. I turned the lights on before I could sleep and needed more and more booze before I could close my eyes."

I got up, walked to the table, and took the gun from Bob. "You won't be needing this," I said, placing the gun in my pocket. I smiled and said, "See your business partner in the morning. I know him. I think he can help you."

The next day, his business partner sensed the spiritual possession of Bob and openly asked if he knew Jesus. "I thought he was crazy," Bob said, "but then I knew that he knew. For no apparent reason I started crying uncontrollably. It was that simple. It was the moment that I accepted Jesus!

"After asking Jesus into my life I suddenly felt free of the deadly grasp of the spirits that controlled my life. So free in my spirit that when I went home that evening my wife thought I had joined another cult. After that it was like getting remarried. Greatest thing in my life." To Bob, a near glimpse of glory.

What's really out there? What lurks in the dark corners of eternity? In these corners Bob discovered the domain of two distinct forces—good and evil—each contesting with untold powers. But again, the evil force presented the confusing bright side and the dark side was seldom seen—until the night the spirits unexpectedly turned on him.

Opposing this force of split personality, Bob discovered the force of God and his angels, presenting only a single face. The apostle Paul summarized it well in Ephesians 6:12–13:

> For we are not fighting against people made of flesh and blood, but against persons without bodies—the evil rulers of the unseen world, those mighty satanic beings and great evil princes of darkness who rule this world; and against the huge numbers of wicked spirits in the spirit world.
>
> So use every piece of God's armor to resist the enemy whenever he attacks, and when it is all over, you will still be standing up (TLB).

NEW AGE CONSCIOUSNESS

Ever since the philosophy of New Age Consciousness was introduced by Sigmund Freud through drugs and hypnosis, then solidified by Carl Gustav Jung through archetypal images, the new investigative sciences have revived and expanded this base. They are reaching back into the ancient practices of sorcery and shamanism (witchcraft) and remolding them for modern society by camouflaging the names with appealing appellations like spirit counseling, scrying, and psychic biofeedback. None of it is new. It is old. Eve consorted with the channeled serpent and heard voices thousands of years ago, as did Bob Kovalesky in our age. And it hasn't changed. On television and in research manuscripts, modern experts employ the same channeling for their information.

These paranormal methods have been sanctioned by the American Humanistic Association (AHA), a prestigious group founded by outstanding figures like Abraham Mazlow and Carl Rogers, and other disciples of Freud and Jung.

Attending the AHA's seminar section entitled "Jungian Psychology," I found Carl Jung was revered as a father-figure. Because his work was repeatedly quoted in the seminar, I researched Jung's life even more closely (some of which I have discussed in the previous chapter). I learned Jung was an astute fortune-teller as well as an accomplished medium, spiritist, and psychiatrist. For years he received images forecasting illnesses in his patients. This was long before Edgar Cayce made similar diagnoses in his famous trances as the "sleeping prophet." Jung's mysterious powers also permitted him to see death before it occurred. He not only foretold Freud's tragic death in 1914, but also forecast the death of his own attending physician in 1944, while being treated for a heart attack. At that time Jung himself had an out-of-the-body experience into cosmic consciousness:

> . . . [Jung] was floating high above the earth, embracing a glorious view from the snow-covered Himalayas through India, Ceylon, and the desert of Arabia to a corner of the Mediterranean.
> He knew he was leaving the earth.
> A short distance away a gigantic block of stone, like a meteorite, appeared. It was hollowed out into a rock temple. In lotus position a black Hindu was sitting on a stone bench to the right of the entrance. Jung felt that he was expected within . . . [and] within the temple, he would understand the meaning of his life. . . .
> [Later, from his sickbed] everything seemed artificial, a man-made prison, and for three weeks he protested against getting well. He had a grudge against his doctor who brought him back to life, but also worried about him because from the moment he saw him in his primal form he knew that very shortly he [his doctor] was going to die. And he did. On April 4, 1944, the doctor took to bed and soon after died of septicemia.[1]

The techniques for entering cosmic consciousness are many and include those already mentioned: hypnosis (either self-induced or Freudian), I Ching (a mystic game Jung enjoyed), cocaine (the game Freud preferred), mescaline (Aldous Huxley's game), LSD (Timothy Leary's favorite), seances (Cayce, Rogers,

Moody, Kubler-Ross), the game of spirit guides (the favorite of most New Agers), or the mystical Omega game (Kenneth Ring).

Cosmic traditions give great latitude of choice for the novice: TM, poltergeist, sorcery, divination, necromancy, yoga, telepathy, seances, voodoo, witchcraft, astrology, or any of the altered states of consciousness which produce spirit guides, counselors, advisors, or any other entities to take control of the mind. Brown Eyes was the nickname for our office nurse who was a novice and became caught up in the macabre.

BROWN EYES

Carefree and flamboyant, Brown Eyes was elated as we lifted off the runway. At three thousand feet she leaned forward. "How about some aerobatic maneuvers? Nothing much to see up here except clouds." She nudged the others, her soft brown eyes giving a wink.

Since the other nurses didn't seem to object, I pushed the right wing down and pulled the nose up, rolling the Aztec into a lazy eight then changing to a chandelle, sort of a dizzying combination. For a few minutes young Brown Eyes remained nonchalant, but then she seized the purse from the lap of the nurse next to her, opened it, and with a great heave, vomited it to overflowing. This made all of us a bit queasy, so we abandoned the aerobatics and found the airport.

It was a good laugh in the office the next day, but the joking ceased when Brown Eyes developed abdominal cramps. Fortunately for me, the cramps proved secondary to adhesions from a previous hysterectomy and had nothing to do with the flight. But it was worse than that. Spontaneous intestinal obstruction was the problem and corrective surgery was required.

Unfortunately, one complication followed another. First she vomited blood from an acute stress ulcer following the surgery, and this necessitated another operation to stop the bleeding. She did poorly. She developed further intestinal blockage, which required more surgery. This time unexpected areas of necrosis (tissue death) appeared in the bowel wall, and portions of dead bowel had to be removed.

Although Brown Eyes was in her late twenties, her body reacted like an old car. The fender fell off when the door was fixed, and when the fender was fixed, the motor fell apart. She was in shock, the blood pressure 60/40, the chest x-ray full of shadows that were either "shock lung" or "lung clots." They proved to be the latter. The clots, known as emboli, had dislodged into the main bloodstream from the operative injuries, darting swiftly until trapped in the lungs where small vessels acted like a sieve.

Instead of large clots, Brown Eyes's clots were small and numerous. She became very short of breath, coughing blood, developing deeper shock. Her physician, Dr. Thomas Mullady, arranged multiple consultations.

Several hours later, in a cold sweat, ghostly pale, pulse thready, her bright brown eyes began to dim. I knew at that moment we were going to lose her, and it broke my heart.

Before the ventilator was attached, she whispered something about a "coven." I thought she said "coughing," but she repeated the word as if it were a secret of some sort. I knew nothing about covens except those recorded in the Middle Ages. So I nodded as if I knew, but I didn't know until I began this researching and writing business. Later I asked several people if they recalled any mention of covens by Brown Eyes, but none of them had.

Still, something was there. Since I knew nothing of these things, I consulted Dr. John Weldon, a comparative theologian and an expert in the occult, a man who knew much about witchcraft and the mysteries.

John Weldon was in his office at the East Gate complex of the John Ankerberg TV headquarters, a rare walking library genius who selected his wardrobe to resemble a used bed, clothing wrinkled every which way, colors dull and mismatched.

He sat in a small chair wedged between the sloppy desk and homemade bookcases, huge tiers piled in endless rows, about to collapse. This was Weldon's own little realm in Ankerberg's marvelous enclave, one of several in the labyrinth of entombed workaholics.

Squinting up through uncombed strands of sandy hair, Weldon said, "Occultic power is not without a price. There have been some tragic complications in the kingdom of the occult." He paused to polish his spectacles on sheets of rumpled toilet paper. "Most people, for instance, don't know that the famous medium Arthur Ford ended up as a morphine addict and alcoholic. Or that Bishop Pike died tragically from his involvement in spiritism.

Or that medium Jane Roberts, using Seth as her all-knowing
spirit guide, died at the young age of fifty-five. Which meant, I
suspect, that either Seth was not all-knowing or that Seth chose
not to tell Jane of her impending death. Many other mediums
and channelers also became addicted to drugs or died mysteriously.

"Medium Edgar Cayce," Weldon continued recalling, "the silent prophet who channeled spirit voices, wasted to a mere sixty
pounds before he died. Some of his friends thought the strange
demise was related to too many psychic readings, suffering too
many psychic attacks, always encountering mysterious fires and
emotional torments."

What seemed to impress John Weldon as doubly tragic was
that these people who were mediums seemed unaware that their
associations were evil. They thought they were practicing something uplifting and promising. He said, "And if any one of them
attempted to escape from the practice of channeling or medium-
ship, some mysterious disease or affliction seemed to follow, frequently forcing them to return to their former occultic practices."
That's when I looked further into Ankerberg and Weldon's detailed manuscript on the subject.[2]

THE KUNDALINI

I've often wondered if Brown Eyes had been personally involved with the Kundalini, but I'll never really know. When she
was very sick she had pointed to the caduceus on my lapel and
whispered, "Kundalini," or something that sounded very much
like that. I didn't even know how to spell it at the time, but I ran
across the word again in recent research. Then I remembered the
history of Aesculapius, the mythical god of healing who used the
staff bearing a winged serpent. This modified staff eventually became the caduceus, the sign of medicine. Could this serpent on
the caduceus have anything to do with "the Kundalini?"

Dr. Tom Mullady (Brown Eyes's physician) didn't recall if she
had ever commented on the caduceus or showed any particular
interest in occultic things, nor did three of her old friends that I
asked. They did notice that she seemed vaguely mysterious in her
behavior when she became ill.

In the library I found only a few books on the subject. One of them was by a Hindu writer, Gopi Krishna, entitled simply, *Kundalini,* published in 1970 by Shambala Press out of Berkeley, California. Then I found another published by Anchor Books in 1979 called *Kundalini, Evolution and Enlightenment,* by John White, and another written by Hiroshi Motoyama entitled *Theories of the Chakras,* published in 1981 by Theosophical Publishing House.

In Sanskrit, Kundalini means "coiled up" like a snake and is supposed to be a latent form of bioenergy sleeping like a serpent at the bottom end of the human spine. With the proper formula, this energy is supposed to be activated, traveling up the spine from the tailbone through a special "channel" which anatomically, of course, does not even exist. But this Kundalini energy, traveling up the spine, sets off certain other energy centers called the "chakras." These chakral energy sites are said to be phenomenal. Like Ray Steven's song, I would think—about the squirrel that ran up the woman's skirt in the First Baptist Church of Pascagoula. It sounded electrifying.

These same chakral sites can also be "destabilizing" and "explosive." In fact, candidates are warned that this energy awakening is frequently "unpleasant and frightening."

Chakral sites are also the areas selected for use in acupuncture, said to serve as human transformers of the energy received from the vibrations of cosmic consciousness and the astral planes. The purported purpose of Kundalini energy is to achieve a glimpse of glory, to catapult the individual into a "higher state of consciousness."

But this energy is supposed to be both divine and divinizing, and is taken seriously by its devotees, and by Prof. Kenneth Ring, one of its investigators. It is supposed to serve as the limitless source for genius, psychic abilities, and especially for guiding humanity's evolution toward cosmic consciousness. The Kundalini hypothesis serves to open the Age of Consciousness, the "enlightenment." Man wanting to be God.

Of course, this hypothesis would place your brain at your rearend. A strange place to be sitting. But it is really the serpent and not the brain you're supposed to be sitting on, still a rather squirrely situation. Ironically, Buddha also sat on a serpent during a flood, but we shall present that later.

The specific yoga commands to activate the Kundalini are said to require a combination of postures *(asanas),* breath control *(pranayama),* and intense Hinduistic meditation upon the chakral centers.

Belief in Kundalini is no longer limited to superstitious people in foreign lands. Kundalini is surprisingly practiced in the United States by some of the entertainment elite. Descriptions can be found in books by Professor Kenneth Ring, a nonphysician psychologist at Connecticut University. Kundalini energy, remember, is supposed to propel the devotee in the direction of the new nirvanic heaven called "Omega Point."

This concept of "Omega," possibly cloned from the biblical description of Jehovah as the Alpha and Omega, the beginning and the end, was first coined long ago by Pierre Teilhard de Chardin, the free-thinking Jesuit priest and philosopher who completely redefined the gospel in his celebrated book *The Phenomenon of Man.* In it he conveniently paraphrases St. Paul to say "God shall be all in all," which is the pantheistic unity of man and all things. Teilhard frequently loses me in the details of the Omega, just as he often lost his French translator, Bernard Wall, and the book's foreworder, Sir Julian Huxley. For an example, look at the vagaries in this reference to the Omega:

> . . . a point through which we can nevertheless prognosticate the contact between thought, born of involution upon itself of the stuff of the universe, and the transcendent focus we call Omega, the principle which at one and the same time makes this involution irreversible and moves and collects it.[3]

The point of it all is the Omega message of universal unity and love, both in heaven and on earth. It is today's NDE cumulative philosophy of the beauty awaiting everyone in the next life.

Teilhard "aimed to bring Christianity up to date by founding it squarely upon the rock of evolution rather than upon certain events alleged to have occurred in Palestine nearly two thousand years ago," says researcher Phillip Johnson.[4]

Thus, in Teilhard's mind, the Omega Point was not the end of life, as the word might imply, but the beginning of life. By transposing and carefully massaging traditional biblical scriptures, he whipped them into a new force. Teilhard's Omega Point was not the point of man finding God, but of man finding himself, the birth of self-divinity. This idea enables the ancient Hindu nirvana to be updated to cosmic consciousness. It also denies the need for any living, external, personal, communicating God.

To repeat, the overwhelming good experiences of NDEs collected by Ring's delayed interview method were used as evidence to support Teilhard's Omega Point. The universal movement of humanity toward a heavenly point, regardless of beliefs, and no karma apparently required.

Formulating his own theories of life—why we are here and where we are going—Professor Ring has expanded upon Dr. Moody's original work with NDEs published in *Life after Life*. What Ring has done, however, is to go even further and glorify UFOs as an additional means of contacting the Omega Point (which I shall save for the last chapter).

In fact, quite a few of the NDE researchers have also wandered into the occult. For example, thanatologist/psychiatrist Dr. Kubler-Ross, author of the classic *Death and Dying,* was helpful to Kenneth Ring when he wrote *Heading Toward Omega*. Dr. Kubler-Ross now calls up her spirit guides Salem, Anka, and Willie to assist in her work, and has recorded their voices on audiotape.

However, the New Age movement is more deeply involved than that. Since "Jesus was only a man," say the New Age philosophers, we must have a new Christ for every new age or millenium in which we live. To find the next Christ, they also seek spirit guidance. They use cosmic consciousness to revive old pagan rituals that delve into the metaphysical, and frequently invoke the assistance of the Kundalini.

Just as NDEs enter cosmic awareness, says Prof. Ring, so can the Kundalini create a similar evolutionary leap without the necessity of near-death risks. If enlightened by the baptism of the force, the new convert should be able to comprehend the need for man to emerge through global transformation, into the newly evolved man who will be known as *Homo noeticus*. Professor Ring summarizes the relationship between Kundalini, the NDE, and the "new man" in the following manner:

> In full kundalini awakenings, what is experienced is significantly similar to what many NDErs report from their experiences. And more than that: The aftereffects of these deep kundalini awakenings seem to lead to individual transforma-

tions and personal world views essentially indistinguishable from those found in NDErs.

I propose that all these phenomena [NDEs] may be the outcome of a biological transformation of the human organism that is induced by the release of an energy long known to adepts [psychics] but only recently studied by scientists interested in transcendental experience. This energy is still called by its Sanskrit name, kundalini.[5]

Professor Ring now has a new twist: that NDEs may have nothing to do with death. "What occurs during an NDE has nothing inherently to do with death or with the transition into death."[6]

Nothing to do with death? That is precisely the point for separating near-death experiences from clinical death experiences, which enter the preliminary death process, a much more credible situation. In my opinion clinical death, our closest approach to study spiritual eternity, should be completely separated from all other NDEs, some of which do not result in any form of death.

So it all boils down to the old serpent, and today he is called the Kundalini. You recall when Brown Eyes was pointing to the serpents on the caduceus of my lapel, she seemed to have said "Kundalini." It caused me to investigate why this serpent (or the Kundalini) was so important to so many faiths as well as to so many people.

In the Bhagavad-Gita, one of the basic books of Hinduism, the Lord Krishna, the alleged seventh reincarnation of the god Vishnu, calls himself the "Prince of Demons," a title also used by Satan. But demons are nothing new to the Hindu because they are consistent with his beliefs. Since "all is one" to the Hindu, then Satan and God are also one, and so are all of his other gods. In another of the Hindu bibles, the Chandogya Upanishad, Krishna identifies himself both as "Visuki, Lord of the snakes" and as "Ananta, the holy serpent." Snakes in many faiths—do they have satanic symbolism?

Interestingly, Buddha, alias Siddhartha Gautama before he protested Hinduism and found the "right path," also used the snake as a symbol. Sitting on a snake, Buddha was miraculously saved from a terrible flood. This was in the sixth century B.C., sometime after he abandoned his wife and son to find the new life, thus enabling him to become the "enlightened one."

Thinking of Kundalini, I found that the history of snakes goes further. The gods Vishnu, Brahma, and Shiva, the holy trinity of Hinduism, are themselves associated with serpents. Shiva we have discussed. Brahma and Vishnu are shown together in one of Hinduism's most sacred paintings where they are supported on the coils of "Shesh" the serpent.

Shiva, the third god of the Hindu trinity, the one called "the god of destruction," specifically identified with the serpent by wearing the "Serpent King" (Bhuja-gendra) as a garland about his neck. Shiva is also known as "the god of forces" (possibly the same "god of forces" mentioned in Daniel 11:38?), and is the god most feared by the Hindu, the god placated and most popularized with the greatest following of worshippers. The same devotion is seen for the destructive gods in other faiths—popular because they are feared.

I recall Shiva's statue as it stood in the city square of Katmandu, dried blood from old sacrifices of animals at his feet—and conceivably even human sacrifices when dated back to the days when the city of London was no more than a hamlet. Early that morning in April 1990, I sensed a dull rumbling noise crescendoing from the direction of the Square. Before we knew it, my wife, Martha, and I had been caught up in the sudden surge between police ahead of us and rebelling protestors behind us. We were being swept down a side street toward the royal palace of King Birendra where a large group of military were barricaded. By day's end, some fifty people had been killed.

We hear so much these days about "the force." On this trip we learned firsthand about the "god of forces," also acclaimed as the "god of destruction." In the end times, the Judeo-Christian Bible specifically describes a god of forces: "The God of forces: and a god whom his fathers knew not" (Dan. 11:38 KJV). "The destroyer" is also described in Revelation 9:11: "Their king is the Prince of the bottomless pit whose name in Hebrew is Abaddon, and in Greek Apollyon (and in English, the Destroyer)" (TLB).

To obtain enlightenment, today's novice is still introduced to the "god of forces." The guru Maharishi Mahesh Yogi introduces his followers to the Lord Shiva as the "god of destruction." The Maharishi is also the one who uses Transcendental Meditation to introduce the Lord Shiva to children in the schools, at taxpayers' expense. The pseudoscientific name of "transpersonal psychology" has made meditation to foreign gods acceptable as a science, while traditional Christianity is now considered a religious offense.

Cosmic consciousness (the new Christ-consciousness) has now progressed to collegiate level. TM instructor Richard Scott frankly admits that any experience as a medium assists in utilizing both transcendental meditation and cosmic consciousness. Cosmic consciousness, when closely defined, he says, becomes another term for demon possession. He mentions how some of the cases become "terrified" and "completely out of control."[7] As we pointed out, a form of "possession" may explain some instances of reincarnation, according to expert Ian Stevenson.

Speaking of demon possession and the "god of forces," it is interesting that Kali, the wife of "Shiva the Destroyer," is also known as "Shakti," a word which also means "force." Many investigators believe this comes from the same mysterious force that "battles for the universe."

"Shakdti-pat" is yet another synonym for the force which super guru Baba Muktananda uses to baptize his followers. When a person receives this force, they "fall down in a trance," experiencing instantaneous "enlightenment," introducing them to their "infinite potential," and their "oneness with the universe." This is elsewhere called the "Lucifer initiation" by adherent David Sprangler.

Why this allegiance to Lucifer? Madame Helena Blavatsky, founder of the religion of Theosophy, openly states that "Satan, the Serpent of Genesis is the real creator and benefactor, the Father of Spiritual mankind . . . the ever loving messenger," with Jehovah as the cruel adversary.[8]

The importance of deifying Lucifer as the true god, was initiated by Theosophists more than half a century before it started flourishing in today's New Age beliefs. It has been continued during the intervening time by Annie Besant and Alice Bailey, and by Elizabeth Claire Prophet.[9]

Nor was Alice Bailey's blessing on the "Luciferic initiation of mankind" an isolated instance. A hundred years ago the top Masonic leader of the Scottish Rite of Freemasonry in Charleston, South Carolina predicted a global Luciferic initiation. Today David Spangler, a member of the NATO-based Planetary Initiative board of directors, says that Luciferic initiations will be facing many people in days ahead as they are initiated into the New Age.[10]

The benefits offered by this experience? The current slogan goes, "Anything you can conceive, you can achieve." When you finally realize that you yourself are god, you have accomplished the ultimate in self-realization. But then you are receiving the same message the serpent channeled to Eve. When you think about it, the initial cosmic consciousness occurred when Eve's "eyes were opened" by eating forbidden fruit from the tree of knowledge. Today, reaching for cosmic consciousness, we eat the fruit over and over again. TV talk shows ventriloquize the message, cleverly selling the "four lies" as the latest thing.

Is Christianity safe? Not if you look beyond the protective walls of your own church's sanctuary. Not for those churches who form private social clubs as if the rest of the world did not exist. Perhaps Christian salesmanship has faltered, and the Christian movement is gradually being replaced as we look only to ourselves and avoid the mandates of the Great Commission.

THE FOUR LIES

The four lies, Satan's unchanging promises, are so compacted that the depth of their meaning escapes casual inspection. It did for me. Because I missed their full meaning, I was forced to look again at Genesis 3, verses 4 and 5, and then numbered each lie within the text:

> But the serpent said to the woman, [1] "You will not die. For God knows that when you eat of it [2] your eyes will be opened, and [3] you will be like God, [4] knowing good and evil." (RSV).

These four simple assumptions were so astounding that I studied them individually.

1. *You will not die.*
(The basis of Reincarnation).

The first lie is obviously a lie because we all know that we will die. Cemeteries prove the fact. My clerical advisers say that we seminally inherited death as our birthright from Adam due to his rebellion. The Bible says the penalty of this disobedience (sin) is death. So we die physically and we die spiritually (separated from God). But there is a cure: Christ as our surrogate.

One very popular means to escape physical death is the hope of reincarnation—that you will not die, but "come back into flesh," as the word means. Round and round you go, reborn again and again, suffering the karma of previous misdeeds until you finally "get it right" and are absorbed into nirvana, where identity becomes lost forever.

What an ironic situation. The world, if reincarnation is true, should be getting better and better instead of worse and worse. We shouldn't need door locks or need burglar alarms. Disasters shouldn't require the National Guard to prevent looting, disorder, and anarchy. Wars should be rare events.

Under reincarnation the world's population should remain unchanged. Only one soul for one body as one person recycles from one body to another, entering the womb as the "third seed" for the next birth. On a one-to-one ratio, how could the population increase? As some deserving souls enter nirvana, the population should be *decreasing*. Instead, more persons are alive today than have ever existed in all of history before. In fact, the population doubles every twenty years.

Reincarnation has some real problems. For instance, what happens when the soul of one person has been possessed by another who is not yet dead? One soul split into two bodies? Reincarnation expert Ian Stevenson suggests that spirit "possession" may be part of reincarnation to explain this dichotomy. But "possession" is a word that opens the door to the possibility of a demon possessing the individual, and also suggests a source for recall of past lives.

Because karma is sometimes cruel, unmerciful, and unforgiving, some New Agers have chosen to replace karma and reincarnation with the revolutionary "Omega Point," where heaven has no entrance fee—no religion or beliefs are necessary —you "get it right" the first time around.

Many famous writers, politicians, and businessmen who are now dead believed in recycled lives. If these people now live in a new body, why don't they know it? And if they don't know it, what good does it do? How can they improve?

Among reincarnation advocates, now dead, are Carl Jung, Henry Ford, Thomas Jefferson, Henry Thoreau, Mark Twain,

George Ripley, and Henry Wadsworth Longfellow. But who are they now? A king or a pauper?

This "no-death" concept of reincarnation was supposedly confirmed in the late 1800s when Madam Helena Blavatsky received "Theosophy" from a channeling spirit entity at the foot of the Himalayas. She brought the concept to the new world in 1873, spawning the many spiritist churches and mind-science churches of today.

The official naming of the "New World Order" awaited one of Blavatsky's successors, Alice Bailey, perhaps the real founder of the New Age. The name "new world order" was subsequently used by the Nazis, and is now incorporated in the Aquarian Conspiracy paradigms of Marilyn Ferguson. Why President Bush used the name, I do not know.

2. *Your eyes will be opened.*
(The basis of Esotericism).

Eve was told she would not die if she ate from the Tree of Knowledge in Genesis 3:6:

> When the woman saw that the tree was good for food, that it was pleasant to the eyes, and a tree desirable to make one wise, she took of its fruit and ate. She also gave to her husband with her, and he ate.

Satan promised the fruit would lead to enlightenment and "her eyes would be opened." Thus, the faith of esotericism, which means that "If it feels good, do it!" Esoterics also claim to possess the "hidden knowledge" (from the tree of knowledge?) known only to the select few.

A century before Alexander the Great and a few decades after Socrates, Herodotus wrote about certain "mystery religions," which included the famous oracle at Delphi, used chiefly for healing and fortune-telling. One of these mystery religions involved the temple cult of Asclepius, the mythical Greek god of healing. Precise rooms or halls were used for the initiation rites, including the rituals of wearing a purple garment after ceremonial bathing. The initiate then proceeded to a central hall where they pledged ultimate secrecy before a sacred hearth, where small animals were sacrificed.

Centuries later, the Romans changed the name of the god to

Aesculapius and also changed the rituals. The apse of the temple now contained a crypt beneath, the initiate bathing in the dripping blood from a bull or a goat being sacrificed from the grated ceiling above. After the ceremony, the candidate exited the building to find warm springs for bathing. Open grounds for sleeping were all around, and the night was spent in meditation where dreams would supposedly reveal the ultimate of the mysteries and their "eyes would be opened."

The history is extensive. Since Hellenistic times similar "mysteries" have caught the attention of the Illuminati, the Third Eye, and many secret lodges and orders. It also caught the eye of Dr. Raymond Moody when he changed his retirement home into a Temple of Aesculapius.

3. *You will be like God.*
(The basis of Pantheism).

It is interesting that new age teaching is not "You shall be *like* gods" (as in the King James Version), but rather, "You shall be *as* God (Elohim)," which means that you personally have the attributes and qualifications of God. Since you are really a god, the famous saying would be true: "You can be anything you want to be." Chairman of the board? A millionaire? How about president? "Human" potential is now "God" potential.

Researcher Dave Hunt puts it another way: "If I am God, then why don't I know it? And if I know it, then why don't I act like it? And if I act like it, then why should I pay Shirley MacLaine $300 for weekend seminars to discover something I already know?"

Personally, I already know that I am not God because there is no way that I could invent a piece of stone or produce a blade of grass. And I certainly can't make a planet or a star. Why is man so stupid that he can't even make simple chlorophyll, the green stuff of vegetables and trees, the basic food of life? If we could only make chlorophyll, it is said, then a factory half the size of a football field would produce enough food to feed all the people on earth. No one would be hungry again. But we're too stupid to make chlorophyll.

Job asked God, "What is man that you think of him?" God's answer is given in Psalm 19:1 as well as Romans 1:19, "For the truth about God is known to them instinctively; God has put this knowledge in their hearts" (TLB). So we know we are not God because someone greater is God. Thus, instinctively, as if out of necessity, man calls upon God in desperate circumstances. Religion has nothing to do with it.

In my opinion, those who prefer to think of themselves as god are really not much better than rocks or trees, because "everything is God and God is everything." Satan's pantheism (meaning "many gods") fulfills his promise that "you will become as gods" —and that makes four billion gods on this planet.

4. *You will know good and evil.*
(The basis of Relativism).

Eating the fruit from the Tree of Knowledge supposedly gave us the hidden knowledge of good and evil. Make your own decisions regarding morality because everything is relative. This is *relativism.* Since nothing is right or wrong, the situation determines the morality of your choice. No need to consult God. Whatever seems right to you, do it. Even murder is relative. Like clones of Charles Manson, do your own thing. Morals don't count.

Carrying it further, since all is God, then evil must be God too! This idea gives a nod to the force with two faces—the dark and bright side, Satan and Lucifer—as opposed to Jehovah, the Alpha and Omega. Since there is no difference between good and evil, then evil does not exist. And, since evil does not exist, then sin also does not exist. And if sin does not exist, then salvation is not necessary. And if salvation is not necessary, then who needs God in the first place? The New Age logic.

These profound but simple lies of Satan are introducing multitudes to the New Age for the year 2000, also known as the Age of Humanism, the Age of Wisdom, the Age of Aquarius, the Age of Fulfillment. Regardless what one wishes to call it, Satan seems to be getting the upper hand for this age, almost a biblical prediction before Christ's arrival. The result is two opposing forces: the gospel of the Bible or the gospel of the Four Lies. Only one of these can be "the truth." Only one reveals who we are, why we are here, and where we are going.

BABYLON

Babylon, the cradle of civilization, was also the first "New World Order." This world order became the most magnificent power on earth, so independent that it rebelled against God. Not only the birthplace of mankind (the Garden of Eden was in that area), but it was also the birthplace of astrology and sorcery. At the zenith of its greatness, the people of Babylon were building a tower to memorialize the accomplishments of themselves. It was built to reach into the heavens.

Thus, Babylon was the first utopia and the first of humanistic religions—they believed only in mankind. The great "I AM" was man, not God. Like Sodom and Gomorrah that were to follow, God destroyed Babylon because of its self–indulgence, self–realization, and its rejection of God. God had said he would have no other gods before him. This included man as god.

> Now, then, hear this, you sensual one,
> Who dwells securely,
> Who says in your heart,
> "I am, and there is no one besides me.
> I shall not sit as a widow,
> Nor shall I know loss of children."
> But these two things shall come upon you suddenly in one day:
> Loss of children and widowhood.
> They shall come on you in full measure
> In spite of your many sorceries,
> In spite of the great power of your spells.
> And you felt secure in your wickedness and said,
> "No one sees me."
> Your wisdom and your knowledge, they have deluded you;
> For you have said in your heart,
> "I am, and there is no one besides me."
> But evil will come on you
> Which you will not know how to charm away;
> And disaster will fall on you
> For which you cannot atone,
> And destruction about which you do not know
> Will come on you suddenly.
>
> (Isaiah 47:8–11 NASB)

God warned the Babylonians that, "in spite of your many sorceries and the great power of your enchantments" the tower would be destroyed and the people scattered and the city never inhabited again. And so it came to pass. The fact that Babylon today lies in permanent ruin indicates which is the more powerful force, God or Satan, and which force will win in the end. If this is so, why do some elect to be on the losing end?

For instance, if astrology and horoscopes have unerring power, why didn't they protect Babylon, the people who invented these things, from total destruction? The birthplace of astrology was completely without power to save itself. Isaiah (48:13–14) had already predicted that all metaphysical powers would be useless against the forces of God, and that Babylon would be destroyed. In fact, God mocked them: "You have advisors by the ton—your astrologers and stargazers, who try to tell you what the future holds. But they are as useless as dried grass burning in the fire. They cannot even deliver themselves! You'll get no help from them at all" (Isaiah 47:13–14 TLB).

The final destruction of Babylon proved to be devastating. Years before it happened, the prophet Daniel also foretold the coming destruction of Babylon and went so far as to name the Persian emperor who would accomplish the desolation. His name would be Cyrus, Daniel said, and Daniel's information came from the heavenly force that makes no error. It was this inerrant force of God that directed Cyrus the Great to conquer Babylon in the year 536 B.C.

Separate from the book of Daniel and written at an entirely different time, Isaiah also detailed the wreckage of Babylon 150 years before the event occurred (Isaiah 45–47). This is the way it occurred: Two gates to the city of Babylon were carelessly left open. Through these gates the Persian scouts infiltrated the city and diverted the Euphrates River into an irrigation canal by means of the existing flood control system. This allowed the major part of the attacking Persian army to march into Babylon through a dried-up river bed, right under the city wall, into the middle of the city. Unopposed, the Persians conquered Babylon within a matter of hours.

In comparison, it took less time to conquer Babylon than the 100 hours it took General H. Norman Schwarzkopf's troops to conquer the forces of Sadam Hussein in Iraq, the very location of ancient Babylon.

Rather frighteningly, the Bible declares that Iran (ancient Persia) is still guarded and protected by the "Prince of Persia" (Dan.

10:13)—the same force which battled and delayed God's angels, Gabriel and Michael, for two full weeks before they overcame Satan's Prince of Persia and arrived to answer Daniel's prayers. The angels then told Daniel about the future of the world, forecasting tomorrow's news.

As part of the forecast, the Euphrates River will again be diverted near end times (Rev. 16:12) to allow the "Kings from the East" to invade Israel for the final battle of Armageddon. By speculation, "Desert Storm" could have been a warm-up for the big one, one adviser tells me. Who knows?

Meanwhile, Babylon of the future is prophesied to be resuscitated and to emerge in some form or another. In whatever form, it will revive the Old Age for the Final Age. The Final Age is described in Revelation as a woman clothed in purple and scarlet with a mystery name inscribed on her forehead: "BABYLON THE GREAT, THE MOTHER OF HARLOTS AND OF THE ABOMINATIONS OF THE EARTH" (Rev. 17:5).

Lutzer and DeVries summarize it this way: "Whereas Christianity says heaven is in the life to come, the New Age Movement says that heaven can't wait! It is pressing in upon us, simply waiting to be acknowledged and accepted. All around us there are signs that we are entering a new age of peace, where death does not exist and spiritual harmony rules. . . . We are saying farewell to the Piscean age (the era of Christianity) and welcoming the New Age of Aquarius."[11] The Age of Lucifer.

The battle is on. Countering the four spiritual laws of Satan's gospel are the Four Spiritual Laws of Bill Bright of Campus Crusade. These four are the Good News of the gospel:

1. God loves you and has a wonderful plan for your life.
2. Man is sinful and separated from God.
3. Jesus Christ is God's only provision for man's sin.
4. We must individually receive Jesus Christ as Savior and Lord.[12]

These four steps to salvation nicely counteract Satan's four laws for self-deification:

1. You shall not die.
2. Your eyes will be opened.

3. You will be like God.
4. You will know good and evil.

In summary, Satan's laws assume there is no death, no sin, no salvation, no morality, and that neither God nor Jesus Christ is necessary. God's laws are the exact opposite.

Assuming death is not oblivion, it means that each of us must make a choice to answer the vital question "Is it safe to die?" and to know which light awaits you at the end of the tunnel.

THE COVEN

What did all of this have to do with Brown Eyes, our office nurse? Well, the stories run parallel. The coven of witchcraft, if that's what it was, dates back before Babylon's sorcery, back to the Garden when Satan first announced the four laws. Witchcraft became the means to utilize these four laws, releasing real diabolical power. In the case of Brown Eyes it started innocently enough. Powers are within that only need awakening by contact with spirits.

I suppose the powers within might be compared to the power of electricity. It represents an inanimate force knowing neither good nor evil, but capable of either. A force that could be harnessed to do one's own bidding. The comparison of electricity with spiritual forces, however, contains one flaw. Electricity does not have a mind of its own. Electricity cannot think, direct, implicate, or possess. Spiritual forces can.

To harness spiritual power for personal use, which is the object of witchcraft, one must first obtain hidden knowledge through proper techniques—the right words and the right formulas. Instruction in these techniques is available today in universities through approved courses, or through any bookstore or video shop where witchcraft literature is sold.

Witchcraft techniques for many people seem benign enough: something like saying the Lord's Prayer backwards, or hanging the cross upside down, or even drinking the blood of animals. But possession can go far beyond that. It can involve ritual murders. For example, consider the people who took part in *Rosemary's Baby*. Charles Manson and his witches had invoked the "force" when Sharon Tate (wife of Roman Polanski, the director of *Rosemary's Baby*) and four others were ritually slain at the Tate mansion by Manson's group. There are also current ones that you and I could discuss over a cup of coffee.

While looking into witchcraft, I attended several satanist churches. The names varied. One was called the Church of the Tarot Cards, another the First Church of Satan, another the Church of Lucifer. One was directed by a former priest converted to a warlock. Strangely, some of the leaders believed neither in the existence of God nor of Satan, but only believed in benevolent Spirits to assist mankind.

Anton La Vey has said he believes in a force which he called the "godhead," an energy found in humans that serves as "a malleable source of action" for the magician or witch. While La Vey gives equal reverence to all names given to Satan—Lucifer, Kali, Lilith, Pan, Shiva, etc.—he said that the "force" was the important thing.

The techniques used to invoke witchcraft would vary. One gathering recited mantras and drew a pentagram on the floor that was centered on a single candle. A communion of bread and wine followed. Another church, a splinter group of the Church of Lucifer, was conducted by a renegade Jewish rabbi dressed in black robes. He dispensed blessings with an incense burner while a young girl of eighteen softly played the organ. Nothing "evil" appeared to be there.

I didn't see any covens. Most covens seem to be secret things, much like private clubs. Although witches were burned at the stake centuries ago, witches are now treated as honored attractions on talk shows. They are a hit. People are interested. These witches foretell the future or call up the dead. There are even TV classes to consult occultic sources concerning business power, sexual prowess, scrying, and channeling. The origin of these powers never seems to be questioned. As one talk show host said, "If it works, who cares?"

According to Ankerberg and Weldon, researchers of mysticism and the occult, many witches "have stated that they welcome the New Age movement; it not only reflects their views of the world, it also makes it easier for other people to accept witchcraft and to even become witches themselves." Popular guru Bhagwan Shree Rajneesh uses witchcraft, believing it constitutes "one of the greatest possibilities of human growth."[13]

In summary, it was evident that Brown Eyes, before she died, had desperately wanted to tell someone about the coven, the witchcraft, the Kundalini, and the "force." But no one seemed to listen. We attributed it to delirium.

One day I asked a church member if she had heard anything about witches or witchcraft in the area. She seemed quite irate that I could even ask such a question. "Surely you don't believe in that stuff, do you?" she said. "That stuff is strictly from the Middle Ages—something for kids and hobgoblins at Halloween. I keep away from trash like that—and so should you!"

As I was to discover later, this woman was the mother of Brown Eyes.

THE
ARRIVAL
OF THE
NEW AGE

THE FORCE

"Feel the force, Luke. You must feel the force around you. It is in you, the land, and the ship. It is because you did not believe that you have failed," said Yoda, as he showed Luke how to telepathically use the force to raise the spaceship out of the planet's underground swamp. Luke Skywalker was dumbfounded. How could he control the force? The ghost of Obi-wan, risen from the dead, had already warned Luke to wait until he had mastered the technique of controlling the force. Later, Darth Vader also emphasized the point when he said to Luke: "You've only begun to discover your power. If only you had known the power of the Dark Side. . . . Join me, and together we can rule the galaxy."

I heard these quotes while on a TV talk show in Los Angeles discussing *The Empire Strikes Back.* Mark Hamill (Luke Skywalker) seemed convinced that the "force" was something to consider in all problems. After all, TM concentration had allowed Luke to communicate his need for rescue to Princess Leia as he dangled from the lower end of the Death Star. The rescue occurred near the end of the picture as Leia and Luke bid farewell, engaging the ship into hyperdrive, using the now famous benediction, "May the force be with you."

And that benediction is the wish of many converts of *Star Wars* and its sequels, bringing early light for the new age.

Sitting next to a real celebrity like Mark Hamill, the TV cameras had elevated me to momentary stardom. Except that no one seemed particularly interested in my segment of the talk show—death being such a dull subject.

Being on the same television program revealed what some of the notables think about the force, its energy, and the meaning of it all. Two guests wore crystals, glitters, or charms about their necks.

"The crystals are your teachers," one of them pointed out in the Green Room before the show. "The crystal is a simple means of contacting the force to obtain psychic abilities. Good for healing too. The crystals, like antennae, pick up the good vibes from the astral layers of the galaxies."

Can healing miracles come from vibrations or forces? Of the two possible forces out there, where do the miracles come from? But none of the experts wearing crystals seemed concerned about that. "If it works, don't knock it," one of them said. "This Jesus force of our grandparents is just an antiquated concept."

To make it more appealing, the forces portrayed in *Star Wars* appear to be the "light" side and the "dark" side of the *same* energy. However, my theological consultants say that Lucifer is the light side and Satan the dark side, but both still represent the *same force*, the force which is opposed to God.

The background of the "force" is interesting because a lot of people have become ardent believers. George Lucas, who masterminded *Star Wars,* was a pupil of Joseph Campbell, who proclaimed that "Heaven and Hell and all the gods are within each of us." One sovereign God of the universe was unthinkable. It was a pervading force, an energy. Joseph Campbell was also a devotee of Carl Jung, who stressed the importance of the self. Jung's collective unconscious, you will recall, expanded Freud's concept of the individual mind into something that was part of the universe. It was god within, not God without. The "self" was part and parcel of the universe, part of the energies controlled by the force. The force that was to energize the New Age.

To obtain this state of infinite expansion, different modi operandi can be used, including of course, yoga, meditation, drugs, hypnosis, or spirits. Crystals and scrying can also be used to call up the power of the force. I remember that Superman called upon his fictitious powers from the cave of crystals "far away in the North" (perhaps mimicking the phrase used to locate heaven in Isaiah 14:13). At any rate, without crystals Superman wasn't very super.

Crystals can also be used to awaken the secret Kundalini forces within. However, the experts covertly warn that any of these powers are not innocuous. Complications can occur. "You may experience a separation of the physical and psychic selves and the abilities to use one or the other," said Uma Silbey in *The Complete Crystal Guidebook.* She states that these states of higher consciousness may "intertwine with your own" and, she warns, "sometimes when this happens you may feel as if you are really 'going crazy.'" At other times, at more propitious moments, one energy force may hopefully assist another to evolve its own psychic potentials:

> As the kundalini rises, different powers tend to develop. These can help you in your crystal work. . . . These powers tend to be those of clairaudience, psychic healing abilities, astral projection.[1]

The force is not always invisible energy. Spirit guides, or counselors, may appear in person with the proper summoning techniques, the proper mantra, meditation, ritual, or "tuning" device. "Tuning" devices include vibrations, crystals, amulets, or certain "woods," such as Ouija boards, I Ching, or Tarot symbols. Of course, the whole process is easier using the knowledge from the right guru, the right psychedelic drugs, or the right spirit counselors.

Shirley MacLaine's spirit guide is an Indian lady named "the Mayan," who insists she came from a distant star system called the Pleiades, a favorite area for psychic claims. MacLaine's spirit guide spoke the following channeled message for Shirley through Kevin Ryerson and Shirley's artist companion, David: "In order to get the fruit of the tree you have to go out on a limb." Such is the way that *Out on a Limb* became the title of her book.

The recurrent biblical defacement by occultic mimicry brings to question the title of the book: Did Eve have to go out on a limb to reach the forbidden fruit?

In the popular TV miniseries, Shirley and David start the sequence at Malibu beach. As they turn to face the Pacific Ocean, David encourages reticent Shirley, "Come on—yell it out—don't be chicken. Say it convincingly—'I am God.'"

With her arms outstretched to the ocean, Shirley's conviction repeatedly mounts as she yells out, "I am God, I am God, I am God." At the end of the mesmerizing chant Shirley feels "liberated" and "overjoyed."

Now for the next scene. Time to visit the ancient Andes in Peru, the source of the mystic folklore of the Mayan Indian. There in the mountains David and Shirley "find" themselves— and also find themselves in a mutual bath in the wilderness, a warm pool against the night, a natural spring carved out of rock.

"Have you ever left your body?" David bluntly asks as he prepares to use the force to induce an out-of-the-body experience. "Well, I have myself, scores of times," he says. "It's really no big deal. Just relax. Trust the process. Let go." He nods approvingly. "Go on, let go."

At that moment, surrounded by the bubbling water, an incredible feeling comes over Shirley MacLaine. She feels an amazing "oneness" with all things, an experience of "universal reality." A surge of energy appears, perhaps an energy resembling the Kundalini phenomenon, because she describes "electricity" running through her. Then suddenly her spirit separates and Shirley finds herself looking down at her body lying in the pool.

In a twinkling, the magnificent develops from the mundane, demonstrating that an out-of-the-body experience can occur without near-death.

Taking the Land Rover for the next scene, Shirley becomes lost in the mountains, which can become very cold at night even in the summer. The "Mayan" had to be summoned to use the force of telepathy to find Shirley. By telepathy, the Mayan guides David to the site in a Harrison Ford type of rescue.

Reunited, Shirley and David accelerate the Rover along a treacherously narrow mountain road with precipitous drop-offs on alternate sides. At this crucial point David decides to reveal the true power of the force to Shirley. As they race along, David raises his hands from the steering wheel and permits the invisible Mayan spirit to drive the truck. The truck miraculously drives itself along and Shirley becomes hysterical, knowing that a nonphysical hierarchy does indeed exist, coaxing people to surrender themselves to the force.[2]

Was there a "higher power" who chose Shirley MacLaine to be a New Age teacher, a teacher who was to influence millions? The parade passed largely unnoticed by the laissez-faire part of the Christian community; an important trend for the future was developing under our noses.

Contacting a superconsciousness also intrigued author Tal Brooke to ingest a great amount of LSD in capsule form. He was convinced that superconsciousness was indeed life's greatest jewel and finding it is the real reason we are here.

Brooke's baptism, the enlightenment of drugs combined with a guiding guru, simulated the New Age baptism which claims to incorporate all known religions—except Christianity, of course.

Brooke did not dismiss this new force as impotent or imaginary. It was quite real, and the force helped Tal and his guru, Sai Baba, perform many miracles, including the healing of alleged cancers that had been declared incurable by Western physicians.

Just like Tal, Johanna Michaelsen used the force in Mexico. She performed miracles and healings under "Pachita" and the spirit guides channeled through her. Both Tal and Johanna separately thought they were helping mankind. They were convinced they were following true prophets until the Holy Spirit intervened some time later, pointing out Christ's warning about false prophets:

> At that time if anyone says to you, "Look, here is the Christ!" or, "There he is!" do not believe it. For false Christs and false prophets will appear and perform great signs and miracles to deceive even the elect—if that were possible. See, I have told you ahead of time.
>
> (Matt 24:24–25 NIV)

So it doesn't seem to matter which way one prefers to look at the force—Lucifer the bright side or Satan the dark side. It remains the same force, the force contesting against God, the force that is the master of deception. So powerful will the force become that, as the time approaches for Christ's return, even the most faithful will be deceived, still feeling secure, still following the crowd:

The world will be at ease—banquets and parties and weddings—just as it was in Noah's time before the sudden coming of the flood; people wouldn't believe what was going to happen until the flood actually arrived and took them all away. So shall my coming be.

(Matt. 24:37–39 TLB)

FOUNDERS OF THE NEW AGE

Members of the New Age Movement, numerous and in all walks of life, are not at all timid about whose banner they carry. Many of them outwardly boast of Lucifer, some actually preferring to follow Satan as the dark side.

One staunch Lucifer advocate is David Spangler. Previously with the Findhorn Foundation in Scotland, subsequently sitting on the Board of Directors of Planetary Citizens, he has been teaching political science at the University of Wisconsin. Spangler is also contributing editor to *New Age Magazine.* In the book entitled *Reflections on the Christ,* Spangler wrote openly about Lucifer with glowing approval:

Lucifer works within each of us to bring us to wholeness, and as we move into a new age, which is the age of man's wholeness, each of us in some way is brought to that point which I term the *Luciferic initiation,* the particular doorway through which the individual must pass if he is to come fully into the presence of his light and his wholeness.

Lucifer comes to give us the final gift of wholeness. If we accept it, then he is free and we are free. *That is the Luciferic initiation. It is one that many people now, and in the days ahead, will be facing, for it is an initiation into the New Age.*[3] (Emphasis mine)

Thus the leaders have admitted that Lucifer is the real Force which underlies and initiates the New Age movement, the movement which includes many thousands of organizations networking throughout the globe with the intent of bringing about a New World Order (President Bush was apparently not aware of this meaning when he used the term). This order is allegedly meant for good, but actually represents a disguised plot which the leaders call a purposeful "conspiracy": A whole new world order of politics, religion, holistic health, and economic change which completely writes God out of the picture to deify Lucifer instead. It is another light, another glory.

Some important names come to the surface in this planetary initiative of the New Age, called the Planetary Citizens. According to author and lawyer Constance Cumbey, the organization members have included Brooke Newell (Vice President of the Chase Manhattan Bank), Gerhard Elston (Amnesty International), Helen Kramer (International Association of Machinists), Peter Caddy (founder of Findhorn), Norman Cousins (of the World Council of Wise Persons), Aurelio Peccei (founder of the Club of Rome), and the Lucis Trust.[4]

The name "Lucis Trust" is intriguing. Incorporated as the Lucifer Publishing Company in 1922, it continues to publish from the United Nations Plaza in a tax-exempt status. The name "Lucis" appears to be a combination of "Lucifer" and "Isis" (the Egyptian sun-goddess). The company's important publications include the books and meditations of Alice Bailey, one of the great pioneers in the New Age movement.

Alice was interestingly employed in a fish cannery in California, but left when she began receiving startling messages from the Tibetan Masters, which had previously inspired Blavatsky's American Theosophical Society. The society was originally formed in 1875 by Helena Blavatsky, who, between her several European love affairs in high society, chewed hashish to enhance her telepathic abilities.

Alice was the one who officially coined the term "New World Order" to describe the New Age movement.[5] She intended the term to mean a planetary control system: a government whose function was to conform any "obstinate religious groups" (Jews, Muslims, Christians) to the new system, as well as to permanently control global food, money, and all environmental supplies. This definition of the New World Order has apparently not changed. Its purpose: to capture and unify all nations and peoples with no political boundaries involved.

Marilyn Ferguson continues the traditions of Bailey, her predecessor, and Blavatsky before that. Ferguson frankly describes the movement as a "conspiracy" to "transform thought." It is important to note that one of its main underlying purposes is to break your orthodox religion and mine:

. . . a change in the way human beings see themselves in relationship to each other and to the divine. During "great awakenings" there is a shift from a religion mediated by authorities to one of direct spiritual experience. Not unexpectedly, some religious groups see the emergent spiritual tradition as a fearful threat to the Judeo-Christian tradition.[6]

"There are legions of conspirators," Ferguson says. "They are in corporations, universities and hospitals," and this powerful coalition of conspirators blames the rise of New Age spirituality on the laissez-faire timidity and cloistered silence of the Christian church in America today:

Eastern metaphysics and the New Consciousness, on the other hand, derive their popularity in part from the fact that they directly challenge the oppressive assumptions of technocratic Western mentality. They have not been afraid to charge our rationalist, materialist, mercantile culture with depleting the quality of human life. . . . Leaders of these movements have stepped into the vacancy created by the church's prophetic silence.[7]

The Christian is told to discern the source of any enlightenment by using the Bible. The non-Christian, however, attempts to "shift brain function" to perceive enlightenments. This, they say, can be done in various ways. The great Aldous Huxley used drugs as his "permanent routes to enlightenment," but Ferguson prefers other spiritual disciplines to enlightenment, including Zen Buddhism, yoga, Christian mysticism, transcendental meditation, Sufism (a Muslim mysticism), and the Kabbalah (a radical Jewish sect).

Ferguson illustrates the road to enlightenment by interviewing Fritjof Capra, a physicist-scientist and close follower of the cause. As Capra sat by the ocean late one summer afternoon watching the waves, feeling the rhythm of his breathing, he suddenly experienced the whole environment as a "cosmic dance," and a "living experience":

I "saw" cascades of energy coming down from outer space, in which particles were created and destroyed in rhythmic pulses; I "saw" the atoms of the elements and those of my body participating in this cosmic dance of energy; I felt its rhythm and I "heard" its sound and at that moment I *knew* this was the Dance of Shiva.[8]

That's right, the dance of Shiva, the "god of forces," "the god of destruction." The "spiritual awakening" was also there and the "baptism" of the New Age offered a new way to obtain a peek at the glory of Omega.

What is the overall plan? What is the purpose for this invisible and leaderless network of science and politics? The plan for the cosmic consciousness that the enlightened must acquire? There is a well-defined plan, which the authors candidly call a conspiracy. Following Luciferic initiations for the selected ones, the plan is to force a gradual redistribution of the world's resources, the establishment of a world food authority, a world credit card system, a universal tax, and, of course, a one-world government commanded by either a one-world army or a global police force. A biblical prediction? My theological experts say it is.

The "plan" is to develop a new humanistic utopia. Celebration of the accomplishments of man is nothing new, it has been repeated throughout history, couched for each age in new terminology. The thread of a plan has been carefully preserved by the Ascended Masters using various esoteric societies such as the Illuminati, the all-seeing eye (also contained in the capstone of the pyramid imprinted on the back of the U.S. dollar bill), and the Theosophical Society. Long before the present ecumenical movement conceived a similar idea for all religions, Madame Helena Blavatsky called for the "unity of all religions." She dubbed this the great "Esoteric Philosophy":

> Esoteric Philosophy reconciles all nations, strips every one of its outward human garments, and shows the root of each to be identical with that of every other great religion. It proves the necessity of a Divine Absolute Principle in Nature. It denies Deity no more than it does the sun. Esoteric Philosophy has never rejected God in Nature, nor Deity as the absolute and abstract. *It only refuses to accept any of the gods of the so-called monotheistic religions, gods created by man in his own image and likeness. A blasphemous and sorry caricature of the ever unknowable.*[9] (Emphasis mine)

This was the same Madame Blavatsky who introduced Mahatma Gandhi to the value and importance of his native Hinduism when he was a young student in London. It was also Madame Blavatsky who composed *Isis Unveiled* and *The Secret Doctrine* under the inspired direction of the same "masters," receiving revelations through a demon–manipulated process called automatic writing.

The history of the expanded "plan" and its conspiracy for the New Age goes on. After Helena Blavatsky's death, the organization continued under Annie Besant (who also happened to be the mistress of Bernard Shaw), until Annie's unsuccessful attempt in 1929 to reveal the antichrist in the form of a man named Krishnamurti. When the attempt failed, the reins of Theosophy went to the former wife of an Episcopal rector by the name of—guess who?—Alice Ann Bailey.

Mrs. Bailey, also under spirit direction, published her many works through the previously mentioned Lucis Publishing Company (formerly the Lucifer Publishing Company), which she helped establish. Then she helped build the foundational doctrines for the New Age movement through its present outlets, the Arcane School, the Triangles, the World Servers, and the World Goodwill.

To extend the thought of known movement of antichrist forces, Alice Bailey was inspired to name the upcoming year 2000 the "Age of Aquarius." Her secret thoughts and directions are openly contained in her doctrinal statements:

> Christ came to bring an end to the Jewish dispensation which should have climaxed and passed away as a religion with the movement of the sun out of Aries into Pisces. He, therefore, presented Himself to them as their Messiah, manifesting through the Jewish race. In the rejection of Christ as the Messiah, the Jewish race has remained symbolically and practically in the sign Aries, the Scapegoat; they have to pass —again speaking symbolically—into the sign, Pisces, the Fishes, and recognize their Messiah when He comes again in the sign Aquarius.[10]

And who will be the celebrated new messiah for the next millennium? One of the New Age prophets, Benjamin Creme—an influential Englishman who is supported by politicians, ministers, doctors, UN officials, and members of Congress—announced that "The Christ is Now Here" in the leading newspapers of several nations in April of 1982. Fortunately, the new Christ did not appear that summer as predicted on worldwide television. Their next hope, apparently, is that he will appear somewhere near the year 2000.

In the modus operandi of the plan, a new Christ appears every one thousand years by astrological calculations. For the present millennium his name may be "Lord Maitreya," to be known by Christians as the Christ (second coming), to the Jews as the Messiah (first coming), the Buddhists as the Fifth Buddha, the Moslims as the Imam Mahdi, and the Hindus as the Krishna. Everybody will recognize him as their god, thus placating all faiths with the universal belief.

These sound like strange and far-out doctrinal systems inside the Bible Belt where I reside, but people will be surprised to find that outside of the belt these doctrines are popular and already accepted. Much of this "new" system is enthusiastically supported by the media, believed by scientists, and endorsed by intellectuals. Placing a twist on the traditional faiths, the new doctrine effectively dilutes and replaces the biblical principles upon which our country was founded.

Spectacular as lightning (in contrast to any Maitreya), the true Christ will appear as "fire in the heavens" for everyone to see. However, before the false Christ appears, the Apostle Paul foretells a great "falling away" of many Christians, which may already be occurring:

> Now we beseech you, brethren, by the coming of our Lord Jesus Christ, and by our gathering together unto him,
>
> That ye be not soon shaken in mind, or be troubled, neither by spirit, nor by word, nor by letter as from us, as that the day of Christ is at hand.
>
> Let no man deceive you by any means: for that day shall not come, except there come a falling away [apostasy] first, and that man of sin be revealed, the son of perdition.
>
> (2 Thes. 2:1–3 KJV)

How this apostasy, or "falling away" from the faith of our fathers would occur and how the antichrist would appear has also been outlined in the Scriptures:

Who is a liar but he that denieth that Jesus is the Christ? He is antichrist [the substitute Christ], that denieth the Father and the Son.

(1 John 2:22 KJV)

And every spirit that does not confess that Jesus Christ has come in the flesh is not of God. And this is the spirit of the Antichrist, which you have heard was coming, and is now already in the world.

(1 John 4:3)

Who is this spirit, the one already in the world who will send this Christ for the New Age? The answer is suggested in the compiled writings of Benjamin Creme, David Spangler, Alice Bailey, and Helena Blavatsky. They say the "God," known as the Sanat Kumara (an obviously scrambled name for Satan), will send the new Christ for the New Age. Sanat, Satan, or Lucifer. Lucifer, the glorious angel of light, the Ancient of Days, the Initiator, the Destroyer, the Omega. In the chain of command there are many other kumaras under the Sanat Kumara. And below the kumaras are many masters, the least of all being "the Master Jesus."[11]

In this way, when the New World religion will have a new Christ, the old Christ—Jesus—will be relegated to the bottom of the ladder, only reporting to those above him.

With uncanny foresight, Paul forewarned of "another Jesus," as if he already knew the false Christ was coming:

But I fear, lest by any means, as the serpent beguiled Eve through his subtilty, so your minds should be corrupted from the simplicity that is in Christ.

For if he that cometh preacheth another Jesus, whom we have not preached, or if ye receive another spirit, which ye have not received, or another gospel, which ye have not accepted [do not believe it].

(2 Cor. 11:3–4 KJV)

According to Marilyn McGuire, Executive Director of the New Age Publishing and Retailing Alliance, there are some 2,500 occult bookstores in the United States and over 3,000 publishers of occult books and journals. Sales in New Age books alone are estimated at $1 billion a year. The entertainment industry has rapidly accepted the New Age gospel, including such entertainers as Helen Reddy, Marsha Mason, Lisa Bonet, Tina Turner, and musician Paul Horn.[12]

In her acceptance speech for the 1987 Emmy award, Sharon Gless, of the TV series "Cagney and Lacey," attributed her success to "Lazaris," while Linda Evans of "Dynasty" fame and Joyce DeWitt of "Three's Company" each followed the spirit of "Mafu" as channeled through another person.[13]

But it goes beyond entertainment. New Agers want to reinterpret and blend all fields of knowledge to harmonize with New Age beliefs, including physics, psychology, biology, religion, politics, and sociology. Mystical experiences have persuaded them this is needed to reveal the "true" interpretation of these disciplines and to help educate people to be converted to New Age thinking.[14]

From the New Age point of view, education of the present generation is capitulated as a loss because of the "Christian tradition" that has already been "inbred" into common people like you and me. To start a transition of colossal magnitude, they concede that the next generation is the place to go. And the place to start, of course, is the school.

THE NEW EDUCATIONAL SYSTEM

We know more of our children's nighttime exposure at home than we know about their daytime exposure at school. We really don't know what's going on at school. Unfortunately, the plan is already in place and may be presenting a New Age glimpse of hell, with amorality and violence developing for the next generation.

In the elementary and early grades a strong trend toward humanistic education has already been established, gradually displacing traditional values since the Bible was effectively removed from schools. Without parents' awareness, moral values in schools have subtly changed to occultic indoctrinations, says Eric Buehrer, an officer in the educative system and vice-president of Citizens for Excellence in Education.

"Global Education" is the name Buehrer gives to the new system. Beneath this exciting innovation lies a Pandora's Box. Many educators believe the ultimate goal of the new system is to modify values and undermine the concept of right and wrong. They believe its purpose is to destroy the basic concepts of patriotism, nationalism, capitalism, and the fundamental concepts of God, both in the family and in society.

Many of us are not aware of this war being waged for the control of our children's minds and souls.

What is this conspiracy that has introduced radical global education into the classroom of your child? It started long before Marilyn Ferguson published the famous *Aquarian Conspiracy* in 1980. Education is a basic part of the plan to be fully implemented by the year 2000, a plan to purposefully exclude the old guard of the present adult generation, and to involve the youth who have not been contaminated with our "antiquated" ideas. Away from home children can be more readily molded into the thoughts of the New World Order.

"The deliberate use of consciousness-expanding techniques in education is new in mass schooling," observes Marilyn Ferguson. Since her original publication, a decade of change in education has occurred, permitting new thought to replace the biblical tradition of the founders of our educational system. This change will involve every grade, Marilyn Ferguson says, and will mark the awakening of the New Age: "Because of its power for social healing and awakening, they [New Age educators] conspire to bring the philosophy [of the New Age] into the classroom in every grade."[15]

Because of the vital importance of these educational changes, which is an educational conspiracy to involve thousands, a survey to study its extensiveness was conducted. Of the New Agers surveyed, Marilyn Ferguson found that:

> More were involved in education than in any other single category of work. They were teachers, administrators, policy makers, educational psychologists. . . . Subtle forces are at work, factors you are not likely to see in banner headlines. For example, tens of thousands of classroom teachers, edu-

cational consultants and psychologists, counselors, administrators, researchers, and faculty members in colleges of education have been among the millions engaged in personal transformation [exposing individuals to the mysteries of the godhood originating within man].[16]

Many of us are not aware of this war being waged for the control of our children's minds and souls. In Seattle schools some teachers equated "global education" as a synonym for "atheistic communistic humanism." The bill to support the new educational system was defeated, but some parents have since become apathetic and the future voting stance has softened.

Meanwhile, the hidden battle goes on. Donald N. Morris of UNICEF supported the global concept of atheist philosopher Bertrand Russell to "teach the folly of divisions among all races, nations, and creeds" in any and all schools. Racial history, individual patriotism, and beliefs should be removed, Russell says, to support the current creeds of the multitudes of educators of the new thought of the New Age. The purpose should be one world educational system, one world monetary system, one world religion, and one world government with no national borders. This is the future utopia of mankind, effectively removing everything God did at Babel while attempting to restore the very civilization God had condemned and destroyed.[17]

Thus, Robert Muller, previous undersecretary of the United Nations Economic and Social Council, believes all children should specifically be taught karma and Hinduism "as one of the most accurate religions" in terms of modern astrophysics and science. In other words, Muller wants to replace Christianity with something that he personally prefers—New Age Hinduism. By claiming karma to be a "science," the dogma of any religious connotations can be concealed, similar to the way yoga as a "science" replaces prayer in public schools.

At home, during evening hours, the traditional family responsibility of teaching moral and religious values is substituted by the four to six hours of television children are allowed to watch, promoting or approving violence, crime, pornography, and drugs. TV has degraded generations of traditional values because parents have defaulted their responsibility as teachers, exposing glimpses of hell as mundane events.

Dr. Beverly Galyean was a consultant in Los Angeles public schools for a program called "confluent education." In her book *Language from Within,* she suggests that all children in all grades, including kindergarten, be led into "guided fantasies." Since then, the teaching method has had widespread influence in the National Educational Association. This "guided fantasy" is the type of trip your child may be experiencing today in your school without your knowledge:

> Close your eyes and relax, I will lead you in a guided fantasy. Imagine . . . a very beautiful valley. . . . Ahead of you is a mountain. . . . You have magic powers so climbing is easy . . . at the top . . . look into the sun and as you do the face of a very wise person slowly appears. You ask, . . . "What must I do to find happiness in my life right now?" The person answers. . . . Listen to this person speaking. . . . You may . . . engage in a conversation. When you feel finished with your conversation, come back to us here in the room. Write an account of what was spoken between you and the wise person.[18]

The "wise person" turns out to be a spirit guide. The Bible is out while mass hypnosis is in. In this case hypnosis has changed its name to "guided imagery," and spirit guides become "imaginary guides." These entities are not to be called "spirits, ghosts, or even demons," the children are told, because they are "friendly" guides.

"Although many parents may be unaware that their children are being involved, when children's groups are questioned about friendly guides or spirit helpers, many of the children will raise their hands that they have played these games or participated in meditations," says Kathleen Hayes, an author, journalist, and elementary teacher in Denver.[19]

The alleged purpose of having these games with imaginary guides is to increase children's academic achievement. They say it is to build confidence and self-esteem. What it does, however, is to introduce the child to forces and spirits which are directly antagonistic to God. It teaches them to find their own spirits for help. Spirits of the dead are often used "because the dead would possess great stores of information we all must have."

This is creating a problem. "It is a sad commentary on society," says educator Eric Buehrer, "when we feel we have reached the desperate point of having to hypnotize young people into good behavior and healthy attitudes. I hardly think that parents send their children to school to undergo such treatment."[20]

Hypnotic suggestions progress with the higher elementary grades. For example, with the window blinds open and the lights turned off, children are instructed to sit up straight with eyes closed. The teacher then reads a three-page script describing a guided journey to Hawaii (one of the favorite places). When they mentally arrive on the beach, the children are told to look up at a beautiful rainbow. As they concentrate upon the rainbow, they will find peace and calm as each color is focused upon individually, every color evoking an emotion. As the child grows with the habit into later life, the emotions are no longer tranquil but become dangerous, often resembling the disturbing chakra energies that can lead to emotional disorders. While in this hypnotic state, the children must repeat to themselves, "I like myself; I am happy; I am in perfect health; I have full control of myself."

After this rainbow exercise, says educator William Hewitt, the next lesson encourages them to build a workshop in their imagination, a private place where they can go anytime they wish and invite any helper they need, whether the helper is dead or alive.

> In this session you will meet your two advisors. . . . Now press the control button [on the chair of your mind] to open the door into your workshop. Now mentally say, "I welcome my male advisor into my workshop. Please enter and sit in your chair." . . . Greet your male advisor. Ask him his name. Study his appearance. Thank him for coming. . . . Now, mentally say, "I welcome my female advisor into my workshop."[21]

Then they are to ask their helpers what they should do in this life, what goal they should seek to achieve and how to improve themselves and solve problems. To improve efficiency in learning, some professional Learning Centers are available through TV guides or local newspapers in most every city. They guarantee to improve your child's skills and aptitudes, but they don't mention the involvement of spirit guides. Parents may not be aware of the hidden agenda.

"Think of the generation of children," states educator Eric

Buehrer, "who will grow to adulthood relying on demonic counsel for their decision-making process. These children will be our
future judges, legislators, mayors, governors, and presidents. It is
incumbent upon all people, including parents who home-school
or send their children to private school, to work to change this
dangerous trend in public education."[22]

"Public schools are not safe havens," he says, speaking for
other educators, "and now private schools are beginning to be
involved." Replacing Christianity are the concepts of yoga, meditation, imagery, and altered states of consciousness. Control of
the mind becomes easier when rendered neutral by hypnosis or
any of the altered states. It is during this neutral time that the
brain's electronic computer board becomes easily accessible for
"others" to reprogram. Like opening the door for a thief to come
in and steal your mind. And you don't even know the person.

Christian schools are no longer immune simply because they
are "Christian." Many traditional churches are permitting new
programs of "visualization techniques" and "positive thinking"
within their teaching. Programs offer updated courses for creating miracles for one's self. If adults are using spiritual imagination for self-improvement, why not the children?

At the heart of hypnosis and all altered states of consciousness
is imagination. The Bible specifically presents imaginings as dangerous and evil. Imagination was first mentioned in Genesis 6:5.
"And God saw that the wickedness of man was great in the earth,
and that every imagination of the thoughts of his heart was only
evil continually" (KJV). Later, Jeremiah states that the heart of
man is "exceedingly evil." And Paul says we should be "casting
down imaginations" (2 Cor. 10:5 KJV).

If any spirit is not from God, it has to be from Satan. And if it
is from Satan, then the spirit, no matter how pleasant and friendly
the force may appear, has to be demonic. Many of the spirit
"helpers" called up for your child are spirits from the dead, either
historic figures or noted members of the individual's deceased
family. Saul was beheaded for calling up Solomon from the dead.
"Familiar spirits," the Bible calls them. An "abomination," God
calls them.

> There shalt not be found among you any one that . . .
> useth divination [fortune-tellers, palm readers, soothsayers],

or an observer of times [psychics, mediums, astrologers, past-lives therapists], or an enchanter [one who uses hypnosis or casts spells], or a witch [followers of Darkness or Satan],

Or a charmer [one who uses Ouija boards, Tarot cards, I Ching, pendulums, automatic writing, good luck charms, crystals, talisman], or a consulter with familiar spirits [spirit guides, yoga, ESP, mind control and psychic phenomena], or a wizard [sorcerers, occultic magicians], or a necromancer [one who uses seances or one who calls up the dead].

For all that do these things are an abomination unto the LORD.

(Deut. 18:10–12 KJV)

Imaging spirits, the clerics of the cloth tell me, is equivalent to mental idolatry; and idolatry is not only a "detestable" thing (1 Peter 4:3 NIV), but "works of the flesh" (Gal. 5:19) which brings the "wrath of God" (Col. 3:6).

Imaging other gods or creating an idol through visualization is forbidden in many passages: "Thou shalt not bow down to their gods, nor serve them . . . but thou shalt utterly overthrow them, and quite break down their images" (Ex. 23:24 KJV). "Thou shalt have no other gods before me" (Ex. 20:3 KJV), and "I will set my face against anyone who consults mediums and wizards instead of me" (Lev. 20:6 TLB) or "Lest ye corrupt yourselves" by making a statue of God or attempting to create an idol in any form (Deut. 4:16 KJV).

NEW TECHNIQUES OF TEACHING

Now don't swing to the other extreme. Imagination is a good and normal part of every person's life, especially children. It only becomes dangerous when it involves the spirit world or spirit guides. It is also a problem for those who grow into adulthood and continue to create fantasy worlds within their lives. Continued or chronic imaginations, therefore, are the substance of psychoses and the sick mind. It introduces a situation where the mystic or shaman can replace the need for Christ in everyday problems. The spiritual potential for psychotic development is in the perverse thoughts implanted in developing minds by videos and books. Far from innocuous, occult researcher Dave Hunt puts the underlying problem this way:

Our eyes are turned from Christ to ourselves. Instead of being transformed into His image by the Spirit of God, we now seek to transform ourselves by the power of visualization into the new self-image we have fantasized. Visualization and other occult techniques for activating powerful forces have been practiced secretly and consistently for thousands of years. Today they are out in the open as part of the New Age movement and are widely accepted even by sincere Christians who are not aware of the origins or dangers involved. . . .

Once again the danger is in confusing our own conjured-up dreams of success with God's will for our lives, developing techniques for fulfilling our desires, and confusing an imaginative process that we initiate for *inspiration* that God alone can give.[23]

Lust, envy, greed, and other evil things also involve mental visualization or mental idolatry, and these things are forbidden. The Scripture instructs us to meditate upon the *word* and not upon pictures—to intensely contemplate as though *eating* the Word (Jer. 15:16)—never trying to *visualize* God nor materializing from the mind the things we hope for. "There is not one verse in all of Scripture," says Dave Hunt, "that associates imagination or visualization with meditation." In fact, the Bible tells us we should be "casting down imaginations and every high thing that exalteth itself against the knowledge of God" (2 Cor. 10:5 KJV).

And yet many churches are integrating psychology with Christianity to produce altered techniques for prayer and healing which are nowhere to be found in the Bible. These techniques include "inner healing," which was started by Agnes Sanford shortly after World War II and expanded into the writings of such Christian leaders as Robert Wise, Paul Yonggi Cho, and Dennis and Rita Bennett. Phrases such as "Christian visualization," "the role of visualization and imagination in prayers," "prayers using imagery," and "meditational prayers that use symbols, images, and visualization" can be found in these writings. From a Southern Baptist seminary, Morton Kelsey advocates the use of ESP, Ouija boards, and communication with the dead.[24]

Although now deceased, Agnes Sanford, under the strong

conceptual influences of Swiss psychiatrist Carl Gustav Jung, introduced both "inner healing" and the new techniques for "visualization" into the church. It was her close friend Morton Kelsey who promoted within the church those theories which Jung had received from his spirit guide, Philemon, whose mysterious history we discussed in chapter seven. It was Jung's "archetypal images" and "active imagination" that Kelsey employed to enter the spirit world.

> There are many ways to enter the strange, beautiful—and sometimes terrifying—territory of the inner world. The methods mentioned here are well-tried ways of using imagination for religious purposes.
> Only through the use of images in our meditation can we actually open the door to the inner world and walk through it to experience the riches available in spiritual reality.[25]

While one foremost TV evangelist believes "positive imaging is the first step" to the goal of success (note the primary goal is success, not other ideals), his compatriot, Norman Vincent Peale, using the meditation technique suggested by Marilyn Helleberg, concentrated upon a gleaming "white mist" or "life force" to breathe in the very sense of vital energy. "God is energy," Peale says. "As you breathe God in [the white mist], as you visualize His energy, you will be reenergized!"[26]

There is a great difference between *receiving* visions and dreams from God and *developing* or *projecting* them ourselves. God's prophets carefully state that God's words came to them after the Lord *willed* it. They never used a ritual or technique to control God. Jeremiah repeatedly says "The word of the Lord came to me," but on one occasion it took three weeks before the word "came"—not "voilà," at the instantaneous will of man. When the word "came to him," it came through *God's* time, not man's. The phrase "came to him" is also recorded nearly fifty times in Ezekiel. Biblical prophets were not inspired to write the Scriptures through self-initiated techniques for contacting God, but "as they were moved by the Holy Spirit" (2 Peter 1:21).

This is contrary to the current visualization and occultic techniques squeezed from new biblical interpretations by modern prophets of "success motivation," says Dave Hunt. Jeremiah warns of the arrival of such prophets:

Thus saith the LORD of hosts, Hearken not unto the words of the prophets . . . they speak a vision of their own heart, and not out of the mouth of the LORD. . . .

They say unto every one that walketh after the imagination of his own heart, No evil shall come upon you. . . .

They are prophets of the deceit of their own heart; Which think to cause my people to forget my name by their dreams. . . .

Ye have perverted the words of the living God.
(Jeremiah 23:16, 17, 26–27, 36 KJV)

These practices are in direct conflict with Scripture, my ministerial specialists inform me, which emphasizes meditation upon God's truth, not upon any feelings or fantasies or conjured images of any sort.

Some of these warnings may not reach the next generation, since biblical traditions are no longer being taught in the home nor are they allowed in schools. Our children represent the first generation which prefers imagery to reading—vis-à-vis television —outselling and outperforming reading in any form. Educator Jacques Ellul looks at it this way:

Our generation has largely given up on language as the primary means of communication, preferring images instead. Whether it is television, computer graphics, or the psychological technique of visualization, images are primary while language and dialogue are eclipsed.

Language is the medium with which we ask and answer the question of truth. With language we are able to formulate our ethics and make judgments.

While the spoken word promotes reasoning, interaction and careful thinking, the image promotes conformity and mass manipulation.

When imagery becomes primary, our very humanity is threatened.[27]

Another reason for educational demise was summarized by Andy Rooney on TV's "60 Minutes": "We don't need better techniques, better schools or better teachers. What we need is better parents."

A TRIP TO HELL RESULTING

Thus, without parental guidance, both television and the media now offer amorality and the macabre, with a trip to hell resulting. Here is a media example that was absorbed into television:

> He begged them not to kill her, he said, looking up at his wife from the floor, and then they kicked him in the head again. The chair was pulled away and her body started swinging freely from the chandelier, tied by her long gray hair, uncoiled from the large bun she wore in the fashion of her mother. He remembered the quiet music still on the radio as they stabbed her again and again with each returning motion of her body's pendulum.[28]

The story goes on that "they took the money as an afterthought, but that's not all they really wanted, and the old man died a few days later, a beaten hulk. He was past eighty."

When one of these men was later caught in the act of another crime, the judge complained that "it became a problem where to put the prisoner" to await the usual protracted trials of justice. The jail systems were "so strained," he said.

As America's roots change from the concept of God to no-God, as moral values bend to permit televised binges on make-believe gore and programs that encourage "safe" sex, opinions vary as to the destiny and outcome of this promised "New Age," the so-called age of knowledge and reason.

A poll conducted by the Gallup Organization in mid-March of 1991 showed that 40 percent of people think movie violence is a "very great" cause of real-life violence, and an additional 28 percent thought it a "considerable" cause. Only 11 percent thought it had little to do with it.[29]

In *Die Hard 2,* the audience leans forward to enjoy Bruce Willis rolling continuously in slow motion across the floor blowing away several mercenaries in one swift motion. Arnold Schwarzenegger, in *Terminator 2,* attempts an even more massive extermination of the unwanted. The director, James Cameron, explains "there is a fine line between action which is good, and violence which is bad. Now, basically, action and violence are the same thing. The question is a matter of style, a matter of degree, a matter of the kind of moral stance taken by the film."[30]

The bright side of the force and the dark side. Who can tell the difference? The New Age of Reason says there is no difference, that good and evil do not exist. You don't have to care who they're "gunning down" as long as it's not you or your friends, or who they're mutilating as long as it's not your family, nor who they're raping if it's not your daughter.

These films, videos, and tapes that teach moral freedom are grossing millions. Few can wait for the next horror in a Stephen King book. In music they can't wait for the next replay of MTVs hit song about a teen incest victim pumping a bullet into her daddy's brain. Or the Getto Boys' "Mind of a Lunatic," with copyrighted lyrics that say that when the girl begged for her life they thoughtfully gave her a flower while gently slitting her throat, holding close her bleeding body until she stopped shaking, raping the corpse after she bled to death.

"What are we doing to ourselves?" one distraught father asked, looking for a reason for his daughter's senseless murder a month before. "Is this crazy world the result of the politic of the New Age, the new force of things? How are we to know good from evil any more? Without direction, a sunrise appears the same as a sunset. It is when the sun is overhead that these evil people see no direction and claim that day is night and night is day—that evil is good and good is evil."

Ashley Johnson, age five, was playing hopscotch at a birthday party in Los Angeles when a bullet hit her in the back and blew through her chest. She cried for a while, coughed up some blood, and died.

"Dear Jesus, what's happened to us?" says Calvin Shears, a street preacher who helps the families of these dead and crippled kids. "What have we let happen to our children?"

Reporter Richard Price of *USA Today* (Nov. 6, 1991) gave this description:

> This is a nightmare. Children are being butchered at an astonishing rate here, and the force behind it is an insane, horrible game that has exploded across the face of the nation, not just here—teen-agers playing with guns. In greater Los Angeles alone, as many as 100,000 kids are running around shooting at each other.
>
> These are kids killing kids. They believe that what they're

doing is right, they are completely out of control, and they are growing stronger every year. The violence is unparalleled in U.S. history. The 1990 total here, a record: more than 600 dead and 5,000 wounded.

And they are on a record pace again this year. Every single day in this city, an average of two people are killed and 16 injured in gang violence.

"It's horrible. It's horrifying," says Brenda Allmond, trauma coordinator at Martin Luther King Hospital, which last year handled victims of 1,300 gun shots, 272 stabbings and 400 assaults—85 percent of them gang-related.[31]

Violence and crime have already identified the coming millennium, despite the humanists' fervent belief that man's heart is "basically good." Murder has increased 25 percent since 1985, including 24,000 homicides in 1991, says the Senate Judiciary Committee. In fact, an increase in sales of burglar alarms, protective fencing, and weapons have made them a better investment than the stock market.

From the FBI Uniform Crime Report the following daily crimes will occur in the U.S. alone: 59 murders, 262 rapes, 1,584 robberies, 2,607 assaults, 4,287 car thefts, and 8,680 burglaries.[32]

There was a flaw in the Jeffrey Dahmer case. Dahmer had admitted to seventeen grisly dismemberment murders in Wisconsin and Ohio. Two months before his arrest, three policemen had visited Dahmer's apartment, and on May 27, 1991, they returned a fourteen-year-old-boy wandering on a nearby street, nude, drugged, and bleeding, to Dahmer's apartment where they thought he belonged. This boy was among eleven dismembered bodies that were later found in Dahmer's apartment.[33]

A few days before, Richard Ramirez, the "Night Stalker," was sentenced to death for a string of sex slayings in southern California. His sex fulfillment was apparently allowed to continue in jail. Eight to ten female fans per week, some of them strangers, were allowed half-hour visitation rights for his convenience. Some of the visitors noticed a pentagram scrawled on the knee of his red prison outfit. Ramirez had been known to leave similar satanic symbols etched at the scenes of his crimes, sometimes forcing his victims to swear to Satan while they were being assaulted by murder, rape, or sodomy.[34]

In the same month that thirty-four-year-old Texan Donald Leroy Evans, who had slain sixty people in seventeen states, claimed
to be America's worst serial killer, Mr. and Mrs. Joe Hughes of
Chattanooga became the fifth house on their block to be burglar-
ized. In the same front page, Chattanooga's city councilman William Cotton wanted junior high and high school students
searched for weapons and the school buildings patrolled by uni-
formed police to insure safety. Also in that month, the Associated
Press reported that increased violence had spread to involve
sports officials. "Kill the umpire" actually became more than a
slogan. One referee now keeps a gun in his car. Another referee
works under a false name and says he backs his car into the
parking space so he can make a fast getaway.[35]

So much for the evolving human potential and its New Age
advocates. The humanists maintain that reincarnation, their favorite game, is continually improving mankind and that mankind
is good. This is contrast to the prophet Jeremiah who insists that
the human heart is "exceedingly wicked." Proof of evil is now
becoming evident in the elderly.

Seventy-year-old Margaret Embrey was brought to the emergency room at Ben Taub General Hospital in Houston covered
with bedsores, all infested by maggots, bones peeking through at
the base. She looked like a victim of Auschwitz, having lost forty
pounds in six months, dehydrated, and malnourished.

Like child abuse, elder abuse has become a growing national
problem affecting 5 percent (1.5 million) of the elderly population. But Texas was one of the earlier states to pass a law convicting elder neglect, with a $10,000 fine and five years to life in
prison—a criminal offense with which Mrs. Embrey's grand-
daughter and her husband have been charged.[36]

Other cases of elder neglect occur because nursing homes are
overcrowded or understaffed. JoAnn (not her real name) placed
her eighty-four-year-old grandmother in a nursing home because
of a massive stroke, still with a clear mind. "The bed was wet all
the time . . . after she messed the bed, it would be hours before
somebody appeared. . . . She had to eat with her hands. One
day they had spaghetti for lunch. I came in and here she was with
spaghetti still hanging out of the left side of her mouth . . . and
lunch had been over for nearly an hour." As a result of neglect,
JoAnn took her grandmother back home.[37]

There are also hospital admitting problems. As we reviewed ambulance runs as members of the Regional Emergency Medical Council for Southeastern Tennessee, I asked Dr. Jim Creel, one of several emergency room physicians there, why we were seeing a rash of the "Granny Dumping" syndrome, where families, tiring of granny's bedsores and messy diapers at home, were dumping granny at the hospital entrance and then "bolting," leaving no identification or even a how-do-you-do.

Jim made a gesture of disgust. "I would say the families are either broke or overwhelmed or just worn out. They can't tolerate more than a few months of round-the-clock care. Since Medicare doesn't pay for custodial care, the relatives soon get the bright idea of dropping granny off at the emergency room entrance, honking their horn until the door opens, and then getting out of there. It's called the 'taillight' sign. Next, we're faced with the dilemma of trying to find out who they are, especially when they don't even know themselves. But once they're in, then it's the hospital's responsibility. Even after we patch them up, its a hard thing to find a nursing home that wants them."

In the new medicine for the New Age, why not experiment with the elderly and make them useful? Robin Hood in reverse? Why not use their bodies as spare parts for more productive people? But when do good experiments become bad? And what are the controls? Alzheimer's patients, for instance, with bad minds but good bodies, could be used to produce much needed immune complexes at huge profits for the experimenter, and just forget the demented experimentee. For example, resistant viruses or cancer cells could be injected into these human guinea pigs to grow antibodies in their serum, and the antibodies for the serum serially injected back into the donor to suppress the particular disease with which that person might be dying. Thus the original donor gets a touch of glory while the nursing home patient survives for more money-making experiments, no longer a financial burden to anyone and the Medicare system becomes subsidized.

For the elderly that can't be useful to the Aquarian Conspiracy, a reincarnated Joseph Mengele could solve Medicare's problem of supporting the 25 million Americans now over the age of sixty-five (12 percent of the population). The number will quadruple in the next ten years. That means the retired "useless eaters" (as

Mengele and Hitler called them) will soon outnumber the working force that feeds them.

To ease the Medicare burden, there is another sinister proposal: a surprise birthday party for those over seventy that would include a pleasant poison in the birthday cake. But that would get rid of some good people too. At age seventy some are young while other people are old at age forty. In fact, man's creative energy is sometimes better beyond age seventy, as evidenced in the lives of Winston Churchill, Bertrand Russell, George Bernard Shaw, Sophocles, Leo Tolstoy, and Benjamin Franklin. At the end of his life Franklin said, "Had I gone at seventy, it would have cut off twelve of the most active years of my life," which included representing the United States in France and helping to draft the U.S. Constitution.

Nor is depletion to be limited to the elderly any longer. To purify humanity, those who are lame, halt, and blind would be next. The Darwinian hypothesis for survival of the fittest would be enforced by man.

Meanwhile, the mentally insane could be the first body-part donors, offering useless people the opportunity to supply wealthy recipients relief from their unfortunate degeneration of body parts. You may recall the mention of the Montes de Oca Mental Health Institute in the city of Lujan just outside of Buenos Aires. Some of the missing 1400 mental inmates who were said to have "escaped" were later found as corpses with missing body parts. The body of one sixteen-year-old boy was found dumped in a well with his eyes missing. Other corpses showed that their body's blood had been drained into laboratory storage banks for future use. Hospital director Dr. Florencio Sanchez and eleven others were arrested. "We expect to find more irregularities as the investigation continues," said Ricardo Sarmigento, spokesman of the Argentine Health Ministry.[38]

What is the answer to the violence, drugs, and abusiveness abetted by the new educational system, by the media, and by television? Do you think censoring these systems would be effective? I would personally vote "yes." And there are still other potentials:

"It's the Jesus Factor," said Keith Beckworth, a tall, lean, athletic-looking man staying at Teen Challenge. "The Jesus Factor is the force that makes the difference. Without this force, none of us would make it. But with him, we're all making it. Once you know the difference and find the real force you can't get enough. It's not just a glimpse of glory from something like drugs or sex. It stays with you. It's like a new life. You want more."

Keith had been confined in a straitjacket because of Angel Dust for the first two months of his six-month stay in Bellevue Mental Hospital in New York.

"One day I was selling crack," Keith said. "I was outside of my turf on the other side of the Bronx."

"What about the other gangs?"

"Money is money."

"What happened?"

"Well, I left my younger brother in the car while I went in the store to buy some cigarettes. I heard this awful blast, but by the time I got to the car, whoever was there had gone. My brother's face was gone, too, and his brains were splattered over the steering wheel."

"I'm sorry," I said quietly. "Is that why you got out of drugs?"

He shook his head. "Don't you see? My brother gave his life in my place. I was the one who was meant to get that blast. But he took it for me."

"That made the change?"

He nodded. "It made me realize that what they're saying in Teen Challenge is true. Jesus was the one who took my place when the death was meant for me. He was like my kid brother, don't you see that?"

THE
ABODE
OF
GLORY

"Oh, what's the difference, when you're dead, you're dead!" Pete said, popping another cookie into his mouth. "Now you're here and full of life." He paused, pointing a cookie at the dead man. "And guess what? You're out of it!"

I looked up, pushing the cadence on the dead man, hoping the flatline would respond in some miraculous way. The man's bloody shirt was sprinkled with cookie crumbs, and I tucked it up out of the way. Pete seemed unperturbed.

"Give it up, old buddy—I am," Pete said, discarding the ambu-bag and turning off the oxygen. He put the cookies down and called the answering service for messages. Cradling the receiver, he commented with a smile, "You can almost see his immortal soul hovering above us already, waiting for the right moment to zip through a tunnel of light to find the happy hunting grounds." Pete was giving me another elbow-in-the-ribs sort of thing. He said, "Or maybe he's on his way to this hell you talk about. But you're wearing yourself out either way. He's been a straight line for five minutes. He'll only be an imbecile if you wake him up now."

Mary, the nurse, who seldom said anything, was discarding the bloody sheets, and cutting off the shirt with scissors. "Don't you have any respect at all, doctor?" she said, scrubbing the dead body so vigorously that the corpse almost looked alive. "The man sleeps in death now. This is not the time for coarse humor!"

Sputtering cookie crumbs, Pete chided, "He sleeps in death?" Pointing again with the cookie Pete said, "He won't care how long he's been sleeping—two seconds or two thousand years—if he ever does come out of it. So what's the difference? When you're dead, you're dead! So who cares?"

While Mary serviced the corpse, Pete and I moved down the hall to talk to the family. I said to Pete, "Mary has special respect for the dead man's soul—so why the confrontation?"

There was not a flicker of concern in Pete's face. He was a free-thinking agnostic, I could see that, but the expression changed to one of wonder just the same.

"All right, if he's not sleeping I admit there are several possibilities for the old boy's spirit—if there is such a thing. The spirit might be wandering somewhere in space." He wiped his hands on his shirt and gestured. "On the other hand, he could still be here in the room, his spirit getting all shriveled up into a single cell like the reincarnationists say, floating around and waiting to fertilize a womb to start the next reincarnation. Otherwise," he said, placing a hand on my shoulder, "it could be the way you look at it. He could right now be having a sporting good time of it—in heaven or in hell."

He deposited the cookie box into the container outside the family waiting room. "As for me, old buddy, I like it the way it is. I like to think that when you're dead, you're dead. Kaput. Oblivion. Atheism not only gives me freedom, but gives me a whole lot of time to think about it."

Thus, Pete's two belief possibilities involved an after-life existence in one of two worlds: as well as either the microcosm of the cell, the world of the third seed, or the macrocosm of the universe where the astral planes might be located. Because these beliefs were quite secularly common—but unseen by Christian communities—I spent several hours shuffling through books and huddling with experts. Here are some of the findings for each world:

THE MACROCOSM

One night as I was peering through the telescope at the university's night observatory, the astrophysics professor was telling the class that there are so many suns in our galaxy—stars limited to our Milky Way—that there are at least thirty suns for every person living here on earth. He further pointed out that there are billions of other galaxies, many of them bigger than our own Milky Way. A limitless number.

"If you have trouble believing that," he said, pushing his spectacles further up on his nose, a dim light reflecting from his bald spot, "then you're just not informed. These facts are all confirmed by various spectrograph, radar, radio and space probe laboratories."

"Scientifically you must have faith," he said. "To believe, you must think beyond yourselves. There is at least one black hole in our own Milky Way, more in other Milky Ways—black stars that have such immense gravitational force that they draw in their own light, making them difficult to detect. They have a force of gravity so strong that they are progressively sucking up other stars like a vacuum cleaner, growing in size and mass until they will someday explode and shake our heavens. Do you believe that?"

Pacing about in the dark file at the telescope, he answered himself. "Yes," he said, "we are supposed to have great faith. The same faith most astronomers have in the 'Big Bang' theory, where the source of the original matter to make the explosion remains unknown. But by reasoning, if any of this was created, then who created the creator? And if it wasn't, where did the original mass come from in the first place?"

Satisfied with his challenge, the white-frocked astronomer smiled and spread his hands. "It takes no more faith to believe the evolution bit than the creation bit, because they both seem utterly ridiculous. How could something come out of nothing, either by an intelligence or by chance?"

This was important to me. It meant God or no God. The possibility of living again or being dead forever. Whether you were made for a purpose or evolved by meaningless chance, it follows that creation or evolution must determine what happens to you when you die. Either God made us or we made ourselves. It takes faith either way, either a philosophy or a religion.

The following week the professor had us imagine that we were on a space ship orbiting a black hole. The space ship would accelerate faster and faster as it approached the black star. With the increasing speed, time would become slower and slower until it

was completely lost as it exceeded the speed of light. Never another tick of the clock. Impossible to grow old. The fountain of
youth. Neither time nor the occupants would grow old. They
would have entered eternity without death, and found a permanent glimpse of glory without dying.

This world of infinity, the eternity proposed by science, is also
the realm of spiritual existence. It could be the eternity proposed
by all the bibles of all religions. The place of heaven and hell. Not
merely a glimpse of glory or a glimpse of hell, but an eternal
dwelling.

Perhaps there are other bridges to eternity besides death,
speed, and time. Since eternity and infinity have become bywords
of science, Einstein's relativity is now more relative. More scientists are spirit-minded, but many seek information through the
mysteries of spirit guides rather than the traditions of religion. As
a primary probe, the metaphysical is beginning to replace the
telescope.

Our astrophysics teacher mentioned the possibility of some
sort of heaven existing in the time warp of space. Isaiah 14:13
suggested an area somewhere in the North. But if John 14:2 is
true—that Christ is now there preparing a place for believers—
then how would we ever get there? Just to reach Andromeda, our
nearest galaxy, would take over two million years at the unimaginable speed of light, which is the equivalent of six trillion miles a
year, or 186,000 miles per second. Of course, at this speed, no
noticeable time would elapse during the two million year trip to
Andromeda—but how much further would it be to reach the
proposed heaven in "the far North?"

The trip might seem impossible, even at the speed of light. But
what about using the speed of thought? Thought represents the
instantaneous speed reported by those who have recovered from
clinical death, those who have traveled beyond death's door and
have returned to tell us about it.

Such thought speed may have already been biblically described.
Philip, in Acts 8:40, after baptizing the eunuch in one place,
found himself suddenly in Azotus, a city far up the coast. Thought
transfer? Is nothing impossible with God?

Perhaps no more impossible than the creation of the universe
itself, so immense that its size is beyond the wildest imagination.
Absolutely incomprehensible. Boundless and constantly moving,

the universe continues to display events of awesome violence. Stars explode with unimaginable fury and whole galaxies are ripped apart. Swirling magnetic fields whip particles through space at greater speeds than those achieved by our most powerful accelerators. Stupendous powers bounded only by the constraints of physical laws. But the controlling laws are there. Laws and secret formulas which the Carl Sagans of today continually try to unravel.

Consider the formula which allows stars to burn for eons of time—burning hydrogen in thermonuclear form—the most common single ingredient of all the billions of stars like our own sun. The furnaces of all the suns in all the universe have been stoked and fired in the same way, using tremendous gravity to hold and implode the fusion, preventing the furnace from being blown away. At least most of the time. Exceeding the formula in either direction, some stars explode, some implode.

In 1905, through the deceptively simple equation of $E = MC^2$, Albert Einstein explained the theory of relativity. In the formula E stands for energy, M for mass, and C for the speed of light in a vacuum. The key is that the speed of light, multiplied by itself, is such a large figure that even the minutest amount of mass is converted to a fantastically enormous amount of energy. It is because the loss of substance and size is so infinitesimally small that the sun can keep burning huge amounts of energy for countless eons without any noticeable reduction in either size or heat generation.

Meanwhile, our own little solar system is moving onward at 150 miles per second. But moving from where to where? Moving outward from some original exploding mass? But where did the original mass come from?

In search for answers, NASA's Cosmic Background Explorer satellite, launched in 1989, made a microwave map of the heavens to find vast cloud layers of minute matter in interstellar space which they think represents residual matter from the "Big Bang," which may have occurred 15 billion years ago. "This is a picture of creation," says physicist Alan Kogut of NASA's Goddard Space Center in Greenbelt, Maryland. "They have found the holy grail of cosmology," says Michael Turner, University of Chicago physicist. "If you're religious, it's like looking at God," says astrophysicist George Smoot, of Berkeley Laboratory and University of California (*USA Today,* April 24, 1992).

Bibles do not tell us how God made the universe—whether he made the stars individually or scattered them from a central point —the galaxies traveling away toward an infinite periphery, and leaving interstellar dust along the way. The background spectrographic colors of this dust were so old when photographed by the explorer satellite that the Doppler effect was shifted from the conventional color spectrum, and required the use of liquid helium to visualize that part of the spectrum before the space probe could obtain a satisfactory picture.

Regardless of the specifics of how the universe was formed, the Judeo-Christian Bible is quite specific that God so loved the world that he carefully molded and fashioned it with all things needed for living habitation, personally creating man from the dust thereof.

But some scientists are so fearful that creation did occur—that some form of accountability could therefore exist—that they search for help from UFOs or hope for extraterrestrial life to question and weaken religious fundamentalism. By trying to find intelligent life in other worlds, they endeavor to prove one of two things: that God either loved many other worlds besides our own, or that evolution is true and God is false.

In 1984 Carl Sagan persuaded Steven Spielberg, the creator of *E.T.* (the imaginary extraterrestrial simulated into a realistic projection), to fund and sponsor a SETI (Search for Extraterrestrial Intelligence) project at Harvard to the tune of $100,000. Since then NASA further secured the program with $100 million (*Newsweek,* October 12, 1992).

Using Hercules as a sample of a near-by galaxy, Sharon Begley of *Newsweek* said it would require 50,000 years to detect any intelligent response to a radio signal sent from earth. Since no one can wait that long, it was then decided to detect any radio signals already existent and previously sent by any intelligent life in space from ages ago. To avoid cosmic clutter and stellar noises, the clearer microwave part of the radio spectrum was selected as a listening medium.

On October 12, 1992, the 500th anniversary of the old world's finding the new, NASA launched its own age of discovery by activating the 1000-foot-diameter radio telescope suspended over a chasm in the Puerto Rican jungle and another in the Mojave Desert.[1]

Of the 400 billion stars in our Milky Way, nearly 10 percent of them, or 40 billion, are like our sun in age and composition and could be life-giving to any planets orbiting them, according to Sharon Begley's interviews with the experts.

"With apparently billions of opportunities for life to arise in our galaxy, it would be astounding if we turned out to be the sole example of intelligent life," said astronomer Paul Horowitz of Harvard University when interviewed by *Newsweek.* "The galaxy may be teeming with life and technology." And our Milky Way galaxy is only one of an estimated 100 billion in the universe.

Could God have loved other worlds also? Are scientists seeking a preliminary glimpse of glory before death brings the answer to each of them? And what would be the response of theologians if intelligent life were found elsewhere?

In 1895 Charles Darwin had to rush the publication of *Origin of Species* when he learned that competitor Alfred Russell Wallace was about to publish a similar theory. Prematurely accepting Darwin's theory as fact, scientists have since been scrambling to find substantiating evidence—especially the missing fossil links—possibly for fear of releasing the premise of religious fundamentalists and thus losing monetary grants.

Because the theory of common ancestry is an unprovable hypothesis, scientists have, as a result, turned Darwinism into their own religion. It has become an indispensable ideology for prejudicial protection against religious fundamentalism, which they consider a threat to scientific freedom, a threat to evolution as a "science" accepted in public schools, as well as a threat to continued support by monetary research grants.

Since Darwinism is a hypothesis of deduction rather than something subject to empirical demonstration, the immense gaps in phyla, classes, and orders recently had to be supported by the new hypothesis of "punctuated equilibrium," proposed by scientists Gould and Eldridge to save Darwinism from extinction. This was the magic wand to explain the scattered, unsequential development of unrelated new species, as noted by Phillip Johnson, teaching at the University of California at Berkeley.[2]

Darwin was himself disturbed about his theory as well. It has been said that on his deathbed Darwin questioned his own evolutionary hypothesis and sought to discover the Biblical creator instead (see chapter 6).

With this controversy in mind, I journeyed 600 miles off the coast of Ecuador to the same Galapagos Islands that had intrigued Darwin, looking at the famous blue-footed boobies, the huge turtles, the marsupials, and other wildlife. As a lay person, of course, I couldn't see any visible evidence of transitional forms that would link one animal group with another. No really strange creatures that have been suggested in the literature.

Nevertheless, in elementary school literature, the texts pictorially explain to our children that things of the sea had put on feathers and learned to fly. What they don't mention is that during the animal's transition of developing wings, they would be completely defenseless with neither arms to help run nor wings to fly, and therefore all would die helpless by Darwin's law of survival of the fittest.

Furthermore, the children's texts imply that man appeared sometime after the ape. Perhaps when the ape learned to shave. Of course, this is a joke, but not much better than the logic approved by school boards as "science" or "fact" when they are no more than conjecture, a faith, and therefore another religion. Evolution requires as much faith as does creation, both representing philosophies or religions, and neither of them is a science.

If God could make little green apples, much less the complexities of man, then making the complexities of the universe should be no problem. If one is conceded, the other is admitted, since even the microcosm of simple man is so marvelously complex that it rivals the macrocosm of the universe. Although the universe is so large and the human cell so small, the intricacies and precisions of each are so astounding that the concept of evolution from nothing may be more ludicrous than that of creation. Both seem ludicrous on the face of it, but there are no other alternatives.

THE MICROCOSM

Since the logic of most reincarnation faiths involves the rebirth of one person into another through the previous person's residual "third seed," traversing the womb to co-opt and enter a new birth, we should carefully investigate the realm of the microcosm where that "third seed" supposedly exists and functions.

If you think this universe, the macrocosm, blows your mind, then come with me on a journey into the infinitely small world of the human cell, the microcosm. In this world of the microcosm we will not explore the complete cell, but only the small center part called the nucleus, a structure barely visible under the ordinary microscope. It is an area no larger than the dot of a pencil.

Hidden within this nucleus is still another glimpse of glory: the world containing the vital messages of life itself. This immense amount of information is incredibly compacted into twenty-three pairs of small chromosomes. These chromosomes are threads of protein that just sit there looking at each other, communicating with one another through many smaller protein particles called genes. The genes match up in constant communication and give messages on an astounding assembly line for reproduction and repair. There are an incredible number of genes—100,000 of them—crammed into each individual chromosome, all cells together containing three billion subunits of information hooked into specialized DNA components of the protein.

The "human genome" represents all the information found in one human being. While there are twenty-three pairs of chromosomes in each of our cells, the total number of cells in one human body is a staggering ten to the fourteenth power. All this information fundamentally controls and regulates the development of the whole human being from a single cell.

The intricacy is magnificent and incredible. Merely deciphering the possible 100,000 genetic combinations would require a fantastic computational analyses. For instance, it would take the largest Cray supercomputer almost a year just to calculate the various possibilities of these genetic combinations.

To alleviate much of the technical difficulty, however, Leroy Hood, M.D., Ph.D., Professor of Biology and Director of the Cancer Center at the California Institute of Technology, has helped develop a revolutionary "superchip" to run a three dimensional computer. This specialized superchip can do in three-and-a-half seconds what it would take a standard work station computer eleven long days to complete!

Now it becomes conceivable to arrange a computation of the human genome. However, it will take just a few more years to complete the task, because the amount of genetic encoding in one human being is absolutely staggering. For example, the identification of all the genes in one individual person would require an encyclopedia of 500 volumes, each volume containing 1,000 pages, and each page containing 1,000 words. Such an "Encyclopedia of Life" would be so immense that it would stretch two-thirds the length of a football field.[3] A glimpse of glory from the creator? Or from chance?

If I were a lawyer, which I am not, I would rest my case at this point, because there is no logical way that such precise and overwhelming data could evolve from the chaos of chance.

As if that were not enough, there are still other worlds within the cell. Messenger systems of the hormones, the enzymes, the synapses. The fibers emanating from one human brain alone, for instance, are so long, if put together, they would stretch to the moon and back, and we haven't even begun to understand the intricacies and functions or even the meanings of all these fibers.

The leaps and bounds of progress in the last decade are unbelievable. Take genes, for example. Back in the early 1970s it took a Nobel scientist and twenty-five colleagues a long five years to make just one gene. Now this task can be done in a single afternoon. What it would take one person a year to do can now be done in just a single day because of a new method of color-coding automation of DNA protein sequences. Twelve thousand of these protein base pairs can now be accomplished in one day.

Delving into the very mysteries of life, scientists are trying to orchestrate the precise molecular music needed to turn on the specific batteries of genes to differentially produce such things as a hair cell or a muscle cell or a brain cell. Just how far we will be allowed to go is not evident. Ecologically we destroy ourselves as we continue to invent potentially lethal things (genetic manipulations and atomic bombs), perhaps testing the tolerance of God himself who destroyed nations like Babylon when they reached too far.

Studying chromosomes through the years, watching them pair and embrace and love, mating in the dance of life, twisting and turning, splicing, rearranging and communicating, man has discovered his own means of imitation and intervention in this precise and exquisite pageantry of divine chromosomal choreography. As we approach the birth and rebirth of our cells, will we inevitably reach into our own devastation? Or will God intervene before the end?

It is intriguing what man has managed to manipulate in this exciting field. In the area the size of a fly speck, we have developed ingenious probes and chemistries by utilizing the new cutting and joining enzymes, rearranging the intranuclear chromosomal substances to produce enzymes called antinucleases and ligases. With these novel enzyme toys, genetic engineering has opened a vast new pharmaceutical industry using recombinant DNA techniques—much like cutting paper dolls and dressing them in different clothes, able to change the clothes at will.

Already synthesized are proteins, which, when injected into the patient, stimulate red cell production to correct anemia. Other proteins are injected to stimulate white cell production to fight infections, and clot-dissolving proteins are injected to dissolve clots of early heart attacks at their onset. Many of us have already received some of these shots. Synthesized proteins are saving lives today.

Now under construction are very special proteins that will recognize specific cancers, potentially recognizing and killing every cancer cell containing that particular configuration. This specificity would prevent the wanton destruction of normal tissues, something present techniques of x-ray and chemotherapy treatments cannot avoid. It is this unavoidable tissue destruction that causes the dreaded side effects in the treatment of cancer patients—such as nausea, vomiting, and hair loss. Sometimes the treatment is worse than the disease.

Besides obliterating cancer, there are other fantastic genetic-manipulation possibilities, including the development of antibodies to destroy the AIDS virus and many other infectious diseases.

Consider the huge agricultural field. Genetic manipulations could allow giant, disease-resistant vegetables to grow. Stock animals could be transformed into a new generation. Faster race horses, enormous cattle, even huge pigs could result from new growth hormones and enzymes.

Industrial and biological uses would also be boundless. The problem of oil spills, for instance, could be attacked by attaching a petroleum-digesting enzyme to simple bacteria. Then, by infecting bales of hay with these same bacteria and throwing these bales into vast oil spills, the bacteria would rapidly consume the oil, but die of starvation when the task was completed. This is one example of the multimillion-dollar industries that await genetic engineering. Beyond this are other limitless horizons.

Many birth defects could also be preventable. If there is an evident error in the precise genetic pageantry of our ancestry, this might be corrected. The newborn child could have a cellular chemistry survey performed and the discovered defects possibly corrected or circumvented—perhaps even prevented if diagnosed before birth.

Heredity in the future could be rather precisely mapped in textbook form. Imagine your doctor consulting this encyclopedia to classify genetic defects. Let's say he looks up Volume XII, Chapter 8, Paragraph 45, to discover the genetic combination responsible for some birth defect in the cardiovascular system—a hole in the heart, for example—and from this information he could determine what other defects could be associated, how to test them, and how to treat them.

Of course, if diagnosed before birth, the information would also afford the mother an option for disposal of the unwanted, an elected abortion for a known specific defect, something to further perturb the entrails of ethics and morals and give a taste of who is responsible—family, physician, lawyer, or astrologer.

Thus the cosmos within, the microcosm, this glimpse of glory into the minuscules of inner space, implies not only the question "Is it safe to die?" but also, "Is it safe to live?"

The criminal is also at risk for genetic discovery. He may find that it is not safe to live, or even safe to make a living, because the arm of genetics is much longer than the arm of the law. A murderer, for instance, can be precisely traced by DNA "fingerprinting," much more accurate than conventional fingerprinting. Traces of blood, or semen, or samples of hair or of any cells left at the scene of the crime, can lead to the culprit's identification. Scientists can pick the suspect out of a crowd with such uncanny accuracy that the odds are a million to one in their favor.

DNA fingerprinting was first invented in 1985 by the British biologist Alec Jeffreys, age thirty or so, at the University of Leicester. Two years later the technique became commonly used in crime laboratories around the world.

At that time, the murder and rape of two fifteen-year-old girls remained unsolved. Police tracked down the true criminal by requesting blood sampling of all the men in the neighborhood. Police attention was drawn to one of them, Colin Pitchfork, when he asked a friend to give blood in his stead. Pitchfork was arrested, and his blood sample exactly matched the semen stains found on the victims.[4]

Since we inherit half of our DNA from our fathers and half from our mothers, parentage is another area easily identified. A drop of blood from a man and a boy can determine, with 99.999 percent accuracy, if the man is the true father of the boy.

And now, with the unfolding of the Genome Encyclopedia, scientists will soon be able to pinpoint the gene for such things as eye color, for example, and tell not only the criminal's eye color but other distinctive features as well.

Thus genetics can be used for good or evil, much like atomic energy could be used for an atomic bomb or as power to light your home. In this way, the perennial problem surfaces: does it represent the evil side of good or the good side of evil?

So all is not good in the potential of the genome. A specific race, for instance, could conceivably be eliminated. A virus could be manipulated and attached to the racially identified cells to genetically seek out, infect, and destroy the male sperm of that race. This virus could be covertly introduced into the local water or food supply and permanently sterilize members of that selected race, ending the next generation.

On the negative side, today's genetic information would have provided Hitler or Dr. Joseph Mengele, the physician in charge of experimentation, a dream world in which to play exciting games with Asians and Africans, and other specific races—but probably not the Jews and gypsies and those without specific racial identification. But other genetic toys could replace the inconvenience of bullets, gas, starvation, and the like.

The complexity of the human cell, this world within the dot of a pencil, is so staggering that evolution of human life by chance, when you take time to think about it, seems incomprehensible. Much like a modern metropolis without an architect or a majestic masterpiece without a painter.

Similarly, it takes great faith to imagine the universe as a product of chance. Of course, these thoughts are pivotal to the subject "Is it safe to die?" unless you already know where you are going, how you got here, and who's in charge.

What is "the truth" sought forever by the great sages of history? God has put knowledge of "the truth"—the riddle of the existence of things—in their hearts. Jesus who made all things said "I am the Truth," and God placed the truth in our hearts:

> Since earliest times men have seen the earth and sky and all God made, and have known of his existence and great eternal power. So they will have no excuse.
>
> (Rom. 1:20 TLB)

> The heavens are telling the glory of God; they are a marvelous display of his craftsmanship. Day and night they keep on telling about God. Without a sound or word, silent in the skies, their message reaches out to all the world.
>
> (Ps. 19:1–4 TLB)

A preview of heaven through clinical death may give a clue as to which was true: evolution or creation, but only biological death will give the answer.

"Give me one irrefutable proof of God," demanded Frederick the Great of his minister, the Duke d'Argens.

"The Jew," replied the minister quite simply. "The proof, your majesty, is the Jew."

PLANNING FOR TOMORROW

Concerning Pete, the doctor who died, it was the old problem of using the Bible to prove the Bible—when a separate source is really needed to prove the logic. But before he died, Pete had been looking. Something was there. In his research of the afterlife, something had moved inside him. A finger was touching his soul when he had found these two worlds in the afterlife, and it disturbed him.

The macrocosm of the universe's astral planes did not rest well with Pete, and he was just as uncomfortable with the microcosm concept of a hidden third germ cell carrying reincarnation from one life into another.

Pete was upset with both of these "new thought" concepts of the afterlife. The "astral planes of Nirvana," he thought, were a wastebasket to dump everything beyond human perception.

Pete said that rebirth through a residual germ cell was equally ridiculous. He could not visualize a dead person's soul shriveled into the nucleus of one cell and then carried by the winds to fertilize a womb. It would be like a dandelion seed—some far-fetched notion of westernized Hinduism.

Fertilization under the microscope, Pete had pointed out, always involved two cells, never three. How did the postulated third cell find its way up the womb instead of up the nose or up the ear? Pete insisted that no human reproductive cell could survive when exposed to air. Without moisture, germ cells immediately die—unless germ cells should limit their flying to rainy nights for some reason. But not even pollen can fly on rainy nights.

Pete was still fascinated by the problem. "Most scientists believe we will learn more about biology and medicine in the next twenty years than we have learned in the last two thousand years."

"Fantastic!" I replied, walking next to him down the hall.

"Not so fantastic," he said. Pete's face seemed shadowed in thought. "The macrocosm outside and the microcosm inside—if there is a God, how much further will we be permitted to go? Is there a limit to knowledge? How close we can come to the truth —to God?"

"Who knows," I said. "Daniel was told to keep his book shut— that it would not be understood until end times—'When travel and education shall be vastly increased.' "

I felt an unreasonable foreboding when Pete departed that afternoon in a heavy mixture of rain and snow for the hundred-mile drive to Atlanta to Emory University Hospital.

As I discovered later, radar had spotted him a few miles south of Marietta. He was exceeding the speed limit by a mere ten miles per hour, they said. Upset about the trivial difference, Pete had insisted on seeing the police chief. At the station, he was told he would have to go all the way back to Marietta to appear in court. Pete became furious, clutched his chest, and fell dead. CPR was ineffectual. Pete died of a massive heart attack.

As I look back on it all, Pete's purpose in life was to make money, dress well, and "have fun." Pete reasoned "God's not going anywhere, so I can deal with Him later."

Both of us wanted the best of both worlds. We were both like that. But one day I felt a small breeze brush against me while reading the book of Matthew. It was Jesus talking:

Therefore I tell you, do not worry about your life, what you will eat or drink; or about your body, what you will wear. Is not life more important than food, and the body more important than clothes? Look at the birds of the air; they do not sow or reap or store away in barns, and yet your heavenly Father feeds them. Are you not much more valuable than they? Who of you by worrying can add a single hour to his life?

And why do you worry about clothes? See how the lilies of the field grow. They do not labor or spin. Yet I tell you that not even Solomon in all his splendor was dressed like one of these. If that is how God clothes the grass of the field, which is here today and tomorrow is thrown into the fire, will he not much more clothe you, O you of little faith? So do not worry, saying, "What shall we eat?" or "What shall we drink?" or "What shall we wear?" For the pagans run after all these things, and your heavenly Father knows that you need them. But seek first his kingdom and his righteousness, and all these things will be given to you as well.

(Matt. 6:25–33 NIV)

He was talking directly to me. Like Pete, I had been seeking "things," and it made me wonder what Pete might be doing right now.

THE
SEARCH
FOR
MEANING

HELL COMES FOR A VISIT

Before closing, we should mention still another source for close encounters with spirit beings which resemble NDEs and OBEs. It is the Unidentified Flying Object or "UFO." Both heavenly and hellish encounters have been described.

This added dimension, mentioned here at the end of the book, may or may not have a place in our travels, but I'll let you decide.

So far in the book, we have gone from the meditations of India to the Hinduism of Hollywood; from deathbed visions to altered states of consciousness; from drugs to astral travel; from positive thinking to creative imagination; from shamanism to the Judeo-Christian Bible; from NDEs to OBEs; from a search for heaven in the macrocosm to the microcosm. We've played games with crystals, hypnosis, seances, scrying, necromancy, and spirit guides, trying to determine if they were true or false.

But now we consider UFOs—what they mean and where they're from, and if they should be part of our study. What are they anyway? The most common belief is that UFOs represent incredibly advanced civilizations from outer space which are seeking to study, influence, and eventually contact humankind. Several million people now believe that UFOs are no longer misunderstood natural phenomena or deliberate hoaxes, but are real.

Some observers have even been "kidnapped" by the aliens. For hours on end at the Woodbridge Air Base in England, fifteen trained military personnel saw UFOs sending down beams of light, electronically distorting weapons, car radios, and engines.[1] Some UFOs have been seen and tracked on radar and photographed at a distance.[2]

UFOs are usually portrayed as entirely friendly spirit entities from outer space. Whether from other planets or from the spirit world, the issue to be determined is if their mission is good or evil. Since researchers find uniformly good or positive reports in all other mystical studies, are the mystical UFOs also as good as they seem? Or could they, like the NDEs and OBEs we have studied, also be representatives of evil forces? Stretching beyond infinity, are the UFOs coming from the same force? Or is it something different?

Using the same, identical paranormal phenomena gathered by other authors, we have tried to bring forth the hidden, negative experiences where hell-problems no longer remain a mystery. Our purpose is to reveal how hellish events do indeed exist in all fields of the paranormal, abolishing claims that these fields are all benevolent and good. I believe the UFO claims fit into this category as well.

The reason to add the subject of UFOs at this time is because of recent spiritualizing of UFOs by some well-known NDE researchers. They have developed the idea of joining the UFOs with NDEs to call them "extraordinary encounters" (EEs). Both groups "see the light" (the UFO observer sees the light approaching him, while the NDEr himself approaches the light), the potential for psychic after-effects developing in either.

In the new revelation of EEs, Kenneth Ring, one of the instigating fathers, evangelizes that "We are experiencing the first bursts of a new self-renewing power for the healing of the earth, with millennial energies that have been liberated through direct contact with the transcendental order.[3]

The new mind-set goes much deeper than that. Behind the transcendental order operates a 'planetary overmind,' or 'mind at large,' directing the psychospiritual preparation and evolution of mankind toward the direction of Omega. Ring does not name this 'overmind' as God, but I would doubt if he has ever considered the entity to be Satan. It is something that comes to mind.

Scientist Carl Sagan also investigates UFOs and has found cases of sexual molestation reported. Probable similar instances of alien abduction, Sagan thinks, were conceived in 1484 to be the activities of demons, causing Pope Innocent VIII to appoint an inquisition. The inquisitors thought the offspring of these demonic unions were eventually visited by devils to become witches. Sagan concludes, "the essential elements of the alien abduction story are there." Yet Sagan carefully avoids the mention of demonology as the cause. He concludes that UFOs are "of distinctly terrestrial origin."[4]

Professor Ring, on the other hand, is convinced that the encounters may "presage the *shamanizing of modern humanity*" (emphasis mine) (the word "shaman" is defined by Webster as "witch doctor"). Ring states these NDE and UFO spiritual contacts with a higher transcendental order are forcing us to think in a new way. He elaborates further that "UFOs are part of a *control* system, helping to regulate belief systems, culture, and even human evolution" (emphasis mine). Does this mean that Christianity is out? Maybe so, because Ring considers the extraterrestrials, or ETs, as agents of "deconstruction," which he defines as a "gradual but inexorable dismantling of the commonly held structures of thought and values, and that the combined NDEs and UFOs (the EEs) will bring about changes in both body and soul into the new man, *Homo noeticus* (perhaps akin to Nietzsche's Aryan race?)[5]

Who is this "guiding intelligence," this "mind at large" who can intervene in earthly affairs? Things affecting this world? The Bible says that Satan is the one in control of this earth, the one contesting for the control of souls. Satan is described as "the god of this world" (2 Cor. 4:4 KJV), "the ruler of this world" (John 16:11), "the deceiver of the nations" (Rev. 20:3), and that "the whole world is in the power of the evil one" (1 John 5:19 RSV).

In truth, I can vouch for the veracity of Kenneth Ring. While he and I have disagreed vigorously in previous debate, I personally know that he is brilliant, honest, and sincere. But he is also wrong. Very wrong. Negative, hellish experiences do indeed occur everywhere. They can even be seen in his own studies, the latest venture being the UFOs, which are the concepts presented in his

latest book, *The Omega Project,* which is endorsed by such notables as physicians Raymond Moody, Melvin Morse, and Larry
Dossey, and by Ph.D.s Fred Wolf and Andrew Greeley.

In keeping with the Freudian concept of childhood injuries and
the Jungian archetype of aliens as little creatures three to four
feet in height with big eyes and huge heads arriving in a brilliant
light with no tunnels, Kenneth Ring himself warns that UFOs can
sometimes be "frightening," and occasionally "compel extreme
emotions and elicit either an almost trancelike fascination or a
paralysis of terror."

"Some of these seem related to the kundalini syndrome," says
Ring, "whose energetic manifestations have already been linked
to NDEs, if not yet to UFO encounters . . . [which] may be
extremely destabilizing, both physically and psychologically . . .
[triggering] fears of impending madness."[6]

Another shocking negative problem is also obvious: humanoid
and alien coupling for the alleged purpose of birthing and
hybridinization to improve the alien race. There are several reported hints at this ungodly perversion.

One woman, who vividly recalls when she was abducted by an
alien craft when she was five years old, states the aliens placed
her on a table for examination "with much time spent around my
genitals." Another, also then at age five, recounted instruments
being "inserted vaginally and rectally" before she returned to her
own bed at home "screaming," then finding it difficult to sleep for
the next fifteen years. A man, recalling a UFO abduction at age
ten, said one of the aliens was a "dark green woman" who
manipulated him into sexual orgasm.

Adults seemed equally involved. A thirty-one-year-old college
graduate said her kidnapping aliens showed her "no compassion"
for experiments that were "dreadful, terrifying." At age thirty-six
a man claimed the aliens had two hands checking on his genitals.[7]

Do these sound like good, godly experiences? Or do these
sound like the alien spiritual entities could be demons out of
hell?

While there was also a positive side to some UFO experiences,
some may have been deceptive. Like some of the deceived
NDErs, perhaps, many UFOrs were "pleased" with the experience. One experiencer felt gifted with a new compassion: "My
compassion for other people . . . has led me to a greater peace

within myself." Still others felt an ecological calling to rescue the "murdered earth," receiving a call to "cosmic transformation."[8] But a transformation from what to what? A transformation from fundamentalist beliefs to the "new consciousness" where there is no God?

Many other prominent UFO researchers disagree. They say that UFOs are "far from good experiences." The dangers one finds in occult practices are the same as one encounters in contacts with UFOs: physical injury, severe mental damage, and perhaps demon possession. We will, at this point, review some of these negative UFO experiences, the ones denied—as they are in equivalent near-death experiences.

Dr. Jacques Vallee personally investigated some fifty cases of visual UFO contacts first hand, and "many of them involve secondary physical and medical effects, including twelve cases of fatal injuries in which the victim typically survived less than twenty-four hours."[9]

Psychologist Dr. David Jacobs notes: "Physically, the abduction experience can leave its victims with a wide range of aftereffects. Scars, eye problems, muscle pains, bruises, unusual vaginal and navel discharge, genital disorders, neurological problems . . . and so forth."[10] Other psychological consequences include sleep disturbances, fears, phobias, panic disorders, obsessions, bizarre "bleed-through" memories, out-of-body contacts with the "dead," and damage to psychosexual development in children.

As John Keel warns, "Dabbling with UFOs can be as dangerous as dabbling with black magic. . . . Paranoid schizophrenia, demonomania, and even suicide can result."[11]

Psychiatrist Dr. Berthold Schwartz has observed UFO-induced problems of "anxiety and panic reactions, confusion, mood and personality changes . . . wasting and burns."[12]

Dr. Bernard Finch observes that relatively close UFO encounters can result in headaches, dizziness, hallucinations, delusions, and amnesia.[13]

UFO researcher Charles Bowen states there is a risk of a "50-50 chance of something nasty happening."[14]

Brad Steiger warns, "UFOs have been responsible for murders, assaults, burnings . . . kidnappings . . . attacks on homes . . . and mysterious cremations."[15]

Jerome Clark refers to a number of hostile UFO encounters:

"They usually occur in secluded areas in the darkness, and the witnesses are often paralyzed, as was Maris de Wilde, injured like Flynn or Jesus Paz, killed as were Miguel Jose Viana and Manuel Pereria de Cruz or kidnapped like Rivlino Mafra da Silva."[16]

The renowned expert, Vallee, after his trip to Brazil to investigate firsthand a large number of sightings and contacts, realized that "the UFO problem was much more dangerous . . . than the literature of the field had indicated. . . . The medical injuries consecutive to UFO encounters [are] perhaps the most significant area of investigation for the future."[17]

In a different context, even Professor Ring admits that alien "possession" can occur:

> In my own view, many of the claims made by 'mental patients' that they are possessed by alien entities are best understood as representing a perfectly accurate assessment of what has happened to them. *It is time that we began taking the concept of possession seriously instead of dismissing it as a superstition or an hallucination.*[18] (Emphasis mine)

John Ankerberg and John Weldon conclude that "after twenty years of researching this field, involving tens of thousand of pages of information by hundreds of authors, we have yet to find a single indication that UFOs or UFO entities could be divine."[19]

The negative UFOs thus completely cripple and destabilize the Omega concept. In the last times, the Bible teaches, Satan will come upon the world with "all power and with pretended signs and wonders, and with all wicked deception," and that God will allow great signs in the sky (2 Thes. 2:9, 10; Luke 21:11). In this way, UFO sightings might be expected as our age draws to a close, since Satan controls such things because he is "the prince of the power of the air" (Eph. 2:2).

THE SEARCH FOR TRUTH

All seeking the glory of "the truth," movie stars go to India, black athletes become Muslims, and people like pathologist Fred Nichols become Buddhists. Others are still not sure what the truth could be, or if there is any truth to know, and it is this group who insist that "truth is relative."

On the Phil Donahue Show—or on almost any other talk show

—"opinions" are the things emphasized. The premise is that everyone has an opinion, and since everyone has a right to an opinion, then their opinion must be right for them; and granting that one opinion can be as good as another, then all opinions become valid.

Why are there so many opinions? Because there is no truth to know. Because the truth is relative. There is no standard of right and wrong. "Truth for you is whatever you want to believe," says Donahue. In this particular scenario the statement concerned parental instruction of moral values to their children. "No one knows anything for sure," agreed one mother on the panel, "so why should I impose my opinions upon my children? Neither do I feel that I have the right to dictate any individual religious system to my children. My children must seek their own reality."

"In other words, what's true for you may not be true for them?" asked Donahue.

"Exactly," replied the mother.

Horse manure, I said to myself. *What that mother is really saying is, "I have nothing to give my children—I have no legacy, no heritage, no principles, no rules of life. There is nothing I have truly learned in life."* At that point the mother paused for a while. "But it don't matter," she said, "because nothing is true." The residual implication is that we will never know anything about anything. Therefore, basic education is worth nothing, since there is nothing to know.

In the summarized words of author Frank Peretti, "There's no way for you to know if what I'm telling you is true unless you know what the truth is; and there's no way for you to know what the truth is unless there is a truth that you can know." Peretti maintains a completely contrary position: that truth is viable, truth is knowable, and truth is absolute.[20]

Where is the storehouse of truth? The humanists insist you will find the storehouse of wisdom within yourself. The Bible says that "If any of you lacks wisdom, let him ask of God . . . and it will be given to him" (James 1:5). Deception has to reside within one or the other of these two positions, so how are we to know?

There are some truths that seem absolute. Mathematics, for instance, is truth. Physics is truth. And science tries to be. Those who insist "there is no truth to know" may be favoring the infamous one who has "no truth in him—for he is a liar and the

father of lies" (John 8:44). But it is "spiritual" truth that most
people seek, because things seen are temporal while things unseen are usually eternal. Some of the biblical definitions of truth
are unequivocal. Jesus said, "I am the way, the truth, and the life.
No one comes to the Father except through Me." (John 14:6).
The truth that there is "no other way that man can be saved." As
I said before, this doesn't sound fair to me, but Jesus didn't, after
all, ask my opinion on the matter. "Because I tell you the truth
you believe me not," Jesus said. Therefore, I must either fully
accept or fully reject these statements. I have been given no other
choice. If I reject these statements I could well be following the
doctrine of demons mentioned in 1 Timothy 4:1: "Now the Spirit
expressly says that in latter times some will depart from the faith,
giving heed to deceiving spirits and doctrines of demons."

Along with Pilate, the one who judged Christ in biblical times,
comes Donahue and other modern TV hosts who still ask the
same question Pilate did: "What is truth?" But the answer to this
question they know instinctively:

For the truth about God is known to them instinctively;
God has put this knowledge in their hearts.

Since earliest times men have seen the earth and sky and
all God made, and have known of his existence and great
eternal power. So they will have no excuse [when they stand
before God at Judgment Day].

Yes, they knew about him all right, but they wouldn't admit it or worship him or even thank him for all his daily care.
And after a while they began to think up silly ideas of what
God was like and what he wanted them to do. The result was
that their foolish minds became dark and confused. Claiming
themselves to be wise without God, they became utter fools
instead. And then, instead of worshiping the glorious, ever-
living God, they took wood and stone and made idols for
themselves, carving them to look like mere birds and animals
and snakes and puny men.

So God let them go ahead into every sort of sex sin, and
do whatever they wanted to—yes, vile and sinful things with
each other's bodies. Instead of believing what they knew was
the truth about God, they deliberately chose to believe lies.

So they prayed to the things God made, but wouldn't obey the blessed God who made these things.

That is why God let go of them . . .

(Rom. 1:19–24 TLB)

Our ancestors were so convinced that they knew "the truth" that they had it incorporated as the fundamental platform of the Bill of Rights, and the Constitution of our government. The truth was the foundation rock upon which our country and all our educational systems were built. The truth was based upon the Christian religious principles of our forefathers, something our nation seems to have put aside.

According to the meticulous research of John Ankerberg, the intentions of our founding fathers were unmistakable.

George Washington, in his inaugural address as the first president said, "We should no less be persuaded that the propitious smile of heaven cannot be expected on a nation that disregards the eternal rules of order and right which heaven itself has ordained." Concluding his Thanksgiving Day address, he stated, "Of all the disposition that happens to lead to political prosperity, religion and morals are indispensable supports."[21]

Succeeding George Washington, John Adams wrote in 1775: "It is religion and morality alone which can establish the principles upon which freedom can securely stand. A patriot must be a religious man."[22]

Thomas Jefferson, our third president, wrote these words which remain engraved upon his memorial in Washington, D.C.: "God, who gave us life, gave us liberty. Can the liberties of a nation be secure when we remove the conviction that these liberties are the gift of God? Indeed, I tremble for my country when I reflect that God is just and His justice cannot sleep forever."[23]

During the Civil War Abraham Lincoln urged all Americans to participate in a national day of prayer: "We have been preserved these many years in peace and prosperity . . . we have grown in wealth and power as no other nation has ever grown. But we have forgotten God. We have forgotten the gracious hand which preserved us in peace . . . and we have vainly imagined that all these blessings were produced by some superior wisdom and virtue of our own. Intoxicated with unbroken success, we have become too self-sufficient to feel the necessity of redeeming and preserving grace. Too proud to pray to the God who made us. It behooves us then to humble ourselves before the offended power to confess our national sins and to pray for clemency and forgiveness."[24]

The Supreme Court, in its 1963 ruling to remove both prayer and the Bible from schools, apparently forgot the dictates made by their predecessors in 1892: "All our institutions must necessarily be based upon the embodied teachings of the Redeemer of mankind. It is impossible that it should be otherwise. In this sense our civilization and our institutions are emphatically Christian."[25]

Other presidents also embodied Christian principles. Woodrow Wilson said, "The Bible is the one supreme source of revelation of the meaning of life and the spiritual nature of man." Roosevelt commented: "No greater thing could come to our land today than a revival of the spirit of religion . . . a revival that would sweep through the homes of the nation . . . to their reassertion of their belief in God. I doubt if there is any problem, social, political or economic, that would not melt away before the fire of such a spiritual awakening."

The prelude to our nation's self-destruction? Progressing from the 1960s, or whenever we began losing the glimmer of our God, then our ethics, our morals, and our nation's strength seemed to crumble, closely following the same factors responsible for the Decline and Fall of the Roman Empire as recorded by Edward Gibbon in 1787:

1. Loss of dignity and sanctity of the home, and increased divorce rate (the old debate of then-vice-president Quayle vs. Murphy Brown),
2. higher taxes and spending of the public money (the welfare state),
3. the craze for pleasure and brutal sports (today's specialty of television),
4. the building of gigantic armaments when the real enemy was within (the national debt),
5. the decay of religion and the impotence of religious leaders (immorality and apostasy).

It took our nation only 200 years to near the point of disruption. It took the Roman Empire over twice as long. Who, then, will save us from ourselves? Ourselves?

The personal truth about ourselves? Many psychologists authoritatively state, "Your problem is that you really don't think of yourself highly enough—you must have a feeling of self-worth, self-esteem, and self-importance in order to overcome feelings of inadequacy." Since self-esteem is not a word found in the Bible, the secular word often implies looking into your "higher self," or perhaps seeking a spirit guide within to obtain self-appreciation.

Big corporations pay large amounts of money to conduct employee seminars in how to succeed, how to self-motivate, how to overcome insecurity, and how to beat the competition. "You can achieve anything you can conceive," they say. "You must look within yourself to tap into the power of cosmic consciousness."

Tap into the power within you? Develop self-esteem? These doctrines call on human potential and relegate God to antiquity. God is not necessary. Man is making God in man's image. "Tapping within the human potential to achieve all things," they say. This effectively denies Colossians 2:3 that "in Him [Christ] lie hidden all the mighty, untapped treasures of wisdom and knowledge"—and not in one's self.

Self-worth? Self-confidence? Self-sufficiency? Where are these things found in the Bible? Nowhere. Paul summarizes the problem well in 1 Corinthians 4:7: "What are you so puffed up about? What do you have that God hasn't given you? And if all you have is from God, why act as though you are so great, and as though you have accomplished something on your own?" (TLB). James 3:15 states that things pertaining to selfishness "are not God's kind of wisdom. Such things are earthly, unspiritual, inspired by the devil" (TLB). Finally, "when you realize your worthlessness before the Lord, he will lift you up, encourage you and help you" (James 4:10). If we elect not to do this, "you will be bragging about your own plans, and such self-confidence never pleases God" (James 4:16).

Many biblical passages warn about the dangers of self-esteem and self-accomplishment, in direct confrontation to the positive thinkers who emphasize self-importance and self-assurance as if they came directly out of the Scriptures. It assumes we can move mountains without involving the God who moves mountains.

"For the wisdom of this world is foolishness to God . . . God uses man's own brilliance to trap him; he stumbles over his own 'wisdom' and falls" (1 Cor. 3:19 TLB). And in 1 Corinthians 3:18, it is better to put aside your own intelligence "and be a fool, rather than let it hold you back from the true wisdom from above" (TLB).

Again, in Philippians 2:3: "Don't be selfish, don't live to make a good impression on others. Be humble, thinking of others as better than yourself" (TLB). It emphasizes that we are to be humble and to be like Christ: "And being found in human form he humbled himself and became obedient unto death (Phil 2:8 RSV). All our desires and needs should come through Christ. We are to rely on him "for I am gentle and lowly in heart, and, you will find rest for your souls" (Matt. 11:29 RSV).

And what did Christ tell us to do and how we should think of ourselves? Contrary to popular positive-thinking and "what's-in-it-for-me" theology for the New Age, Christ taught us to think less highly of ourselves than we do. In fact, we should deny ourselves:

> "Whosoever will come after me, let him deny himself, and take up his cross, and follow me. For whosoever will save his life shall lose it; but whosoever shall lose his life for my sake and the gospel's, the same shall save it. For what shall it profit a man, if he shall gain the whole world, and lose his own soul? Or what shall a man give in exchange for his soul? Whosoever therefore shall be ashamed of me and of my words in this adulterous and sinful generation; of him also shall the Son of man be ashamed, when he cometh in the glory of his Father with the holy angels."
>
> (Mark 8:34–38 KJV)

The comforting paradox is that I am somebody important after all—but through Christ and not through myself. "I can do all things through Christ who strengthens me" (Phil. 4:13). Gathering one's strength from Christ (and not from one's self), Christ said the potential is tremendous and extensive. "He that believeth on me, the works that I do shall he do also; and greater works than these shall he do" (John 14:12 KJV). The Holy Spirit within you gives you the limitless potential to accomplish tremendous things for good, but not within the individual's own human potential. It comes from God. I don't move mountains, Christ does (through faith). Self-worth? You bet. In Christ we are of extreme worth. In effect, Christ could have put it this way, "You alone were worthy enough for me to die for!"

THE FEAR OF DEATH

Everybody has fears of things unseen. Fear of things new and untried. Doubts are there. But believers who have experienced clinical death are no longer afraid. They have already glimpsed the glory. Paul, who had a personal experience with what might have been clinical death when he was stoned at Lystra, tells us that we should not we be afraid:

> Now we look forward with confidence to our heavenly bodies, realizing that every moment we spend in these earthly bodies is time spent away from our eternal home in heaven with Jesus. We know these things are true by believing, not by seeing. And we are not afraid, but are quite content to die, for then we will be at home with the Lord. So our aim is to please him always in everything we do, whether we are here in this body or away from this body and with him in heaven. For we must all stand before Christ to be judged and have our lives laid bare.
>
> (2 Cor. 5:6–10 TLB)

The Bible's implication is that death is a simple event where the individual simply leaves his earthly body. The individual is no longer confined by time and dimension, but is set free at last:

> For our earthly bodies, the ones we have now that can die, must be transformed into heavenly bodies that cannot perish but will live forever. When this happens, then at last this Scripture will come true—"Death is swallowed up in victory." O death, where then your victory? Where then your sting? For sin—the sting that causes death—will all be gone; and the law, which reveals our sins, will no longer be our judge. How we thank God for all of this! It is he who makes us victorious through Jesus Christ our Lord!
>
> (1 Cor. 15:53–57 TLB)

The eyes of despair can be seen in the insecure and in the unbelievers. Eyes with questions. Will it hurt? Is that the end of it all? Or is there life after death? Anything bad out there? Is it safe to die? Will it be Glory or Gehenna?

And what about the slow, agonizing deaths? What does it feel like hoping to die, waiting to die? Perhaps wanting to blow your brains out, but hesitant because you know it is wrong?

Want to help? These are the neglected patients. Nobody wants them. Nobody knows how to handle them. And they're everywhere. Look on the wards for the ravaged, the deplorable, the forlorn, the discarded. The people trashed by defeated doctors and helpless families. Some will be agitated from a deep depression.

Nothing like a little surgery to wake up the soul.

"Tell that doctor to stay out of my room," the patient told the nurse. "What does he know about cancer? How does he know how it feels? Told me he wanted to help, that he understood. Does he know that I've been burnt up with x-rays and reamed out with chemicals? What's he so knowledgeable about?"

"Perhaps he can help," she repeated quietly.

"What does he know about how I feel?" he challenged.

"Why don't you ask him? He has the same cancer you have. He's been through it. He knows what it feels like."

It's not always easy, this dealing with the dying. But if you can identify with them, then they can identify with you. The next day the patient let it all hang out and seemed to respond to that marvelous old remedy started two thousand years ago.

Look for trouble when you don't hear from a friend for a long time. Like lepers or social outcasts, they may be secreting themselves, forlorn and ashamed for people to see them. Don't wait for the obituary columns. Look them up in person. Listen to their questions, their anger, their frustrations.

Don't turn a deaf ear to an anguished cry. I did once. I had completely missed the diagnosis. I hadn't listened closely.

On her third or fourth hospital admission for recurrent lung failure from emphysema, the wife of Fire Chief Quinn looked extremely haggard. "I'm really tired of living like this. I have to struggle every moment just to breathe. The oxygen isn't helping anymore and the tube takes the skin off my nose."

The lung consultant glanced in my direction and shook his head. There was no cure for smoker's emphysema. Mike Quinn knew it too. I noted a look of frustration troubling his eyes.

"Let me take her home," Mike said, holding her closely.

"Does she have oxygen at home?" the consultant asked. I nodded.

That evening the chief rummaged about at home and found his old revolver. Five times the bullets went into his wife's head before he fired the final one into his own. The first five bullets, spent with age, proved to be duds, ricocheting off the bone of his wife's head but lodging just beneath the scalp. Although mentally deluded, she lived several months after that in a nursing home before she died.

For some unknown reason the sixth bullet proved to be active and Chief Quinn died immediately, never knowing that his wife was still alive.

There was a suicide pact there that I had failed to see. I had missed the diagnosis. Through similar experiences, more physicians are beginning to detect these problems before it is too late. We could have kept the chief's wife comfortable and free of misery with heavy medication.

Want a ministry? Here it is. Untouched. Neither the family nor the doctor is trained in dealing with the dying. They don't need a counselor, but a listener, a servant, a comforter. Advice and philosophy should not be imposed unless asked. With no one else present, ask them questions. Give them a chance to pour out their concerns and needs if they want to. Eventually they may seek your thoughts on the subject.

Disturbed family and friends often desert them at the most needed time. One girl said, "I can't stand to see mama like this." And as a result of denial of mama's death, she didn't get seen much. No one was there to hold her hand as she died. Some of the most memorable moments take place when death is occurring, and those with the courage to stay with mama never forget it. One never gets a guilt trip if they were there. If they weren't there, they hurt. They feel it.

You say you don't have license or training to do these things? Just being there is all it takes. An attitude. A concern. Should the patient ask, you may share the spiritual life that never dies, a life renewed in the Garden.

Should you abdicate the bedside duties, others are beginning to appear on the scene. Sometimes they are visitors or friends of other patients. They may want to console your loved one with a near-death experience of their own. They may want to introduce a new religion, the gospel of Omega, where heaven's gates are open to everybody who dies. No beliefs are unnecessary. "Just hold my hand," they say. "Soon we will see the light at the end of the tunnel. The light of unconditional love. Have faith. I will stay until the light comes to you."

Fantasy? No, it's happening! The religion of the NDEs is here. Notice if any of these evangelists are visiting your hospital. They feel that they are doing great things. They want to help.

Nothing like a little surgery to wake up the soul, to contemplate what life is all about. Most patients try to conceal their concerns about the possibility of death, but with oncoming surgery they face the moment of truth. Are you now in the hospital awaiting surgery? You're not sure if you will wake up from the anesthesia? What complication might occur? You're not ready for possibility of death, but you don't want to take any chances? You keep these problems to yourself, too "macho" to admit your doubts and fears. But you feel unsure. You need God. You need faith renewal. You need security. But no one will talk to you. So then you talk to God. We all do.

Afraid of death? Already, deep down inside, you know exactly where you're going. Take a really good look beyond your conscience into the window of your soul. No one wants the light of glory to ignite into the fires of hell. Since we're betting with our lives, we have to be right. No slip-ups allowed. But why wait until the brink of death's door? We may never have another chance.

CONQUERING DEATH

Engineer Fred Lupton, having survived half a dozen heart attacks, recalls being resuscitated from a couple of them, once by a young lady who happened to be waiting at the same bus stop in Washington, D.C. Fred was surprised that a scrape with death quickly illuminates the purpose of life. By training and ambition he had sought success and money as the goals. When catastrophe overtook him, these goals radically changed.

Fred asked me, "Do you know what you think about when your next breath may be your last? When you know you may not live another hour?" When I didn't answer, he said, "When your back is to the wall, the object of life is no longer money—the object, surprisingly enough, is *time.* Immediately the question becomes not how much *money* do I have left, but how much *time* do I have left. What you will do with each precious moment you have left." To explain his predicament, Fred cited this passage:

> Look here, you people who say, "Today or tomorrow we are going to such and such a town, stay there a year, and open up a profitable business." How do you know what is going to happen tomorrow? For the length of your lives is as uncertain as the morning fog—now you see it; soon it is gone. What you ought to say is, "If the Lord wants us to, we shall live and do this or that." Otherwise you will be bragging about your own plans, and such self-confidence never pleases God.
>
> Remember, too, that knowing what is right to do and then not doing it is sin.
>
> (James 4:13–17 TLB)

Fred Lupton has since survived a total heart transplant. A Presbyterian minister, as well as an engineer, Fred now insists that life should be planned ahead before calamity eliminates the opportunity of choice. In this way, Fred gives heart to a lot of dying people these days.

AN ENCOUNTER WITH GOD

It was shivering cold and icy that night I walked into the Milwaukee auditorium. My feet went up in the air and I was on my back in front a crowd of people at the entrance. They didn't laugh at first. Not until I got up, brushed myself off, and fell again. A smile fixed on my face, I padded on to the entranceway, pretending that nothing had happened.

Then, I scurried into the men's room to make repairs to my injured pride and my new suit, hoping they would not recognize my face when I emerged. When all was quiet I slipped past the people, some still looking for seats, to the backstage area.

I was the expert. I was the man from out of town with a suit-case, the guest speaker for the evening. Peeking out between the curtains I saw a capacity audience, and six volunteer ushers, one of them a Catholic priest in an old brown tweed suit sporting a clerical collar. When I was announced on stage I walked out pompously straight, head high, hiding the wince of pain. Soon I was into my speech, displaying slides on a large screen about everything from heart attacks, cholesterol, and death experiences to resuscitation encounters.

As the audience warmed to the subject, I forgot the ego trip on the ice. I had arrived. I was the star performer. My words were polished. Even the New Agers would have been proud of me. And I was proud of myself. Not much further, and I could have been god.

After many congratulations, as people began to thin out, the Catholic priest came forward. "Tremendous performance," Fa-ther Richard Korzenik said. "A most revealing lecture." Follow-ing more compliments, he invited me to his home.

It was about midnight when we entered his home, which con-sisted of merely one cramped room, a couple of chairs, and a cozy fireplace with bookcases all about. A small kitchen was closeted out of the far wall, all of this tiny arrangement housed in the rear of a small nursing home managed by the Camellus Order of the priesthood, of which he was a member.

Warming his hands at the small fireplace, the wise old priest surprised me when he said quietly, "Ever been in the presence of God?" Suddenly, everything was quiet. Swallowing scalding cof-fee from an old mug, the priest was peering over half-moon glasses, waiting for an answer.

I thought to myself, *now that was a dumb thing to ask. Why should I need to have an encounter with God? I was already a Christian, and a pretty good one at that. Certainly this should have been evident from my lectures.* So I finally said, "I don't know."

Following a fresh pot of coffee, a full hour went by, this man of the cloth mumbling Scriptures and praying with his eyes open, as if looking into eternity. Slowly, I was aware that the old priest had been quietly guiding me into a self-examination of some sort, as if he had been using a stethoscope and a mirror. Strangely, I did not resent this approach, because something was happening. The more I cooperated, it seemed the more I felt myself becoming smaller, infinitesimally smaller, as if an overwhelming force had entered the room, squeezing me into insignificance. A force where I was aware that I could not move, frozen for the instant, suspended in time. The awesomeness of this presence overcame me and I could not speak, and I continued to stare down at the Scriptures in my lap. I was trembling in ecstasy and fear. I could not manage to look elsewhere. This holy spirit was almost palpable. It was then I knew that I was in the presence of God. A holy moment. I felt that if I moved I would die.

This being or force responded to Scriptures. It pointed to the only Son of God. As it moved around me and upon me, I realized that it was holy and that I was nothing. Nothing at all. Self-esteem? Self-worth? They were gone. They could not possibly exist.

And then I could not stop crying. Uncontrollable crying. There was no room in me for me, for self. I knew I was unclean, abased, ashamed, in need of a bath. It was the exact opposite of the self-realization offered by forces opposing God. I was inadequate. When the varnish of vanity and self-righteousness had been removed, there was nothing left of this self-pride of mine, this self-assurance, this self-acclaim. In the presence of the Spirit of God I knew I was less than the chemicals I was made of. And yet he loved me. I knew full well that he loved me.

The most humbling experience of my life. It revealed to me *not who I am, but who he is.* The thought made my knees sink to the floor. I knew this was an experience with Jesus Christ. I knew I was finally in him and he in me.

I knew with confidence this was not an evil deception. It was the exact antithesis. Diametrically opposed. The whole affair revealed to me for the first time the complete falseness of all the humanistic religions. It revealed the underlying deception of the drug-induced trips of the mystics, the yoga enlightenment from the Far East, and the "I am" of self-realization. Two facts were clear: first, that *I am not God,* and second, that in the coffin I am worth nothing more than five dollars of basic constituents.

However, there is one magnificent and wonderful paradox of which I am assured. In the eyes of God (and not my own) *I am a person of extreme importance and of great worth.* The whole world does not have the worth of my own soul. So important am I that

God died specifically for me. To me, this is exciting—that I am indeed something very special to God. I am so special that God even knows the number of hairs on my head (Matt. 10:30). And because he made me, the family resemblance must be remarkably striking. The spitting image. As a child of God, I should actually shine forth, and let people see the family resemblance. As one of his children, God focuses down and sees me as a distinct person, separate from everyone else. And I will never lose this identity. This is the exact opposite to the new nirvana of Hollywood's Hinduism.

What about the "force" and those spirits defying righteousness? What about the touted "human potential," the diversionary goal of the revived New World Order, the order disguising Lucifer as the so-called "mind at large"? The Bible indicates that all these evil forces will (near end times) be allowed to conquer for a while until Christ returns to destroy them. Why is this allowed? I don't know. I've often wondered. There are so many things I don't know. And so many things I've wondered.

Some form of New World Order was conceived by Satan when he was deposed from heaven. It is still preserved by today's new faiths, possibly a prelude to the predicted reawakening of Babylon, using the same four promises: you will not die, you will be like gods, you will have all knowledge, and you will know what is good and evil. Looking for the utopia of another Babylon, we return to the religion of the Stone Age, paganly worshiping Mother Earth on one hand, while ecologically destroying it on the other.

TESTING THE SPIRITS

Of the eight to eleven million people who have had near-death experiences, most assumed that the glorious light at the end of the tunnel is both holy and good without testing the spirit or identifying the source. It's strange but the average person doesn't bother to investigate spiritual forgery. People will gratefully accept bogus spirits although they would be furious if someone tried to pass them bogus money. Probably the spiritual gullibility of man is why God specifically forbade man from contacting ghosts, guides, mediums, enchanters, or fortune-tellers (Deut. 18:10–12).

The popularity of spirit entities has returned. Most of the original NDE researchers and authors are now routinely calling up the dead and doing business with spirit entities. And they don't even know who these entities are. Anyone can be deceived in any experience unless the source of the spirit has been specifically identified or tested.

The test is simple enough. No matter how kind and considerate, evil spirits will invariably avoid or deny that Jesus Christ is the only Son of God. But seldom is the test administered, the victim overcome by glorious surroundings.

Why is it necessary to have a spiritual guidance system at all? Without them would we always be right and never deceived? Because spiritual gullibility is again popular, let's discuss it once more. Without rules, when you think about it, we would soon be in big trouble. It would be like a car without steering, a ship without a rudder, a pilot without a compass. If we were each permitted to make our own rules, anarchy would occur. Rules are needed to guide us on our journey, something to keep us safe when we cannot see. You say you don't believe in unseen things? You have no faith? Perhaps you already do. Let me illustrate with a story.

It was terribly black on that night we decided to fly some of the Ol' Miss basketball team home to Chattanooga following a game at Oxford. Martha, my wife, and Buddy, my son, were busy chasing stray pigs off the small runway for takeoff. It was a moonless night, the heavens blotted out by overcast. I jokingly asked the young men if anyone knew which was the way to Chattanooga. I should have known better. It was a stupid joke, because no one wanted to go anywhere after that. So I had to carefully explain such things as electronic guiding devices and the things that assure safe flying without seeing.

Because of lingering doubt, I had to go further. I pointed to the altimeter that indicated height, the DME that measured distance, the artificial horizon that showed level flight, the VOR that monitored direction by radio beam. I told them that an unseen flight control officer would also be monitoring and correcting us by radar to keep us on course. The compass and maps would be our mother, the instruments our father. Finally, a precision landing at Chattanooga would be guided through the cross hairs of an ILS system.

In the case of the spirit world, of course, the Bible becomes the Christian's guidance system and the Holy Spirit the control officer. This system keeps us informed and corrected until we reach our destination, the control officer guiding us through the proper door where it is safe, where glory becomes more than a glimpse, and the right path becomes the right runway.

In order to use the guidance system successfully, we cannot do our own thing or go our own way. Otherwise, we are utter fools. Biblical guidance rules, however, are safe and trustworthy because they have never needed modification or change for two thousand years. No re-editing or updating has ever been required.

Why test the spirits? Why must we have the right runway? Because God has promised that all these false gods and all false guiding systems will be destroyed (Jer. 10:11). This includes the guidance systems of such things as horoscopes, mirrors, crystal balls, Tarot cards, I Ching, fortune-tellers, shamans, mediums, and the like. Jeremiah specifically warns about horoscopes: "Don't act like people who make horoscopes and try to read their fate and future in the stars! . . . Their ways are futile and foolish" (Jer. 10:2 TLB). They will be cut down like a tree.

"We're heading toward Omega," say the leaders of a more updated guidance system. It sounds good. Based on things like NDEs, OBEs, and UFOs. And the message is beautiful: "All mankind is to live in love and harmony." Wonderful stuff, never negative. Since everyone gets a glimpse of glory, the near-death experiences only serve as "proof of human evolution and planetary transformation." Everyone gets to heaven. But should any be sent back, their mission is to remake the world, the world to become a new Babylonian utopia without God.

Omega is that glorious being of light at the end of the tunnel where there is no accountability, not even karma.

But when you think about it, Jehovah God is much more than Omega. He is both the Alpha and the Omega. But of a completely different definition. In four separate areas in the book of Revelation, Jehovah repeatedly tells us, "I am the Alpha and the Omega, the beginning and the end." Not "either" Alpha or Omega, but "both" Alpha and Omega at the same time, a meaning of astounding proportions: that God can walk simultaneously through time in either direction.

In summary, since each force claims to be the "light," one has to be false. Likewise, if each force claims to be the "Omega," they both can't be true. No matter how appealing, one has to be false.

Contesting so many renowned authors, I feel like a small voice on top of a far mountain, a voice lost in the great clamor of the opposing prophets nearby. If only I could call down fire from heaven like Elijah did on Mount Carmel, proving to 450 prophets of Baal the identity of the true God. If I could only use Elijah's words to the people, "How long are you going to waver between two opinions? If the Lord is God, follow him! But if Baal is God, then follow Him!" (1 Kings 18:21 RSV). But since I am not a prophet, my hopeful prayer is that God will in some way send down his fire to touch your soul and open your eyes to the truth.

"Choose this day whom you will serve," said Joshua (Josh. 24:15 RSV), while Matthew insisted, "No man can serve two masters: for either he will hate the one, and love the other; or else he will hold to the one and despise the other. Ye cannot serve God and mammon" (Matt. 6:24 KJV). Once again, those that follow the majority where the path is "wide" will eventually find their gods destroyed. They shall "vanish from the earth," says Jeremiah (Jer. 10:11 TLB).

Sooner or later, of course, all of us will find the truth. God has already promised that "every knee shall bow . . . and every tongue shall confess" to God (Rom. 14:11). God's simple message is "pay me now or pay me later." If that is fact, they why not confess him now while the Gospel is still good news? Later on the Gospel becomes bad news—when the opportunity is lost in death's appointed time. For a true glimpse of glory, make reservations now.

LIFE'S DOOR AND DEATH'S DOOR

Approaching death's door . . . will it be a glimpse of glory or a glimpse of hell? You're not sure?

We had almost flipped over during the takeoff from Atlanta's International Airport when the tower came in: *"Aztec Triple-one Yankee, why didn't you abort the takeoff?"*

I pulled the mike up. "This is *Triple-one Yankee.* We were off the ground when you called, the Eastern's wake in front of us and the Delta chasing behind. If we'd aborted, we'd have tied up the whole airport until you towed us off."

"When did you first notice the nosewheel was broken?"

"Hartsfield from *Yankee* . . . It broke near liftoff speed. She started shaking violently. When we lifted the nose off the runway, everything was smooth. That's when I called you. After that we were airborne."

"Six on board? We'll radio Chattanooga for fire trucks when you land. You may cartwheel. Take care. Now turn right on course, *Triple-one Yankee*. You are cleared direct from Hartsfield to Lovell Field."

No trouble steering in the air, but when landing made the rudder control change from tailfin to nosewheel, I knew the nosewheel would be flail. The Aztec could go sideways and flip. No guidance system at all. *The words "guidance system" again. Life seems full of this stuff.*

"Think we'll make it, doc?" It was my friend Glen Michaels in the copilot's seat, restlessly pulling at his collar.

I barely nodded. "Chattanooga's last instruction was to land on runway fourteen. Seldom used. Less messy that way. Leaves the main runway open. Look for fire trucks running along side. Last minute attitude and direction will be important. Must land nose up with full flaps. Main wheels have to touch at the slowest speed possible. I'll pull the stick back into my belly to keep the nosewheel from touching. Pray we don't flip and burn when she skids off the runway and goes crazy. Now tell everybody to tighten seat belts. It won't be long."

I think we all had an idea this might be the end of things, but I couldn't afford to feel nervous this time. But strange, at a time like this, perhaps like a deathbed, my thoughts floated through the wash from my past and I remembered the old priest at Milwaukee, Richard Korzenik. I could meet God once again. I knew with confidence where I would be.

"Can't you dump the gas beforehand?" Glen asked, nervously blowing his nose on yesterday's handkerchief.

"No way. Not in this plane. Look. There's old runway fourteen down there now, just beyond Missionary Ridge."

Much like the end of life, we would descend through an invisible tunnel, like an inverted ice-cream cone—time running out at the apex. The end of our journey could be the entrance to heaven or hell, the door where the truth hangs out.

As we approached at slow speed an invisible hand violently seized us, pulling the nose hard to starboard. Full left rudder, right wing down, and boosting the right engine kept her from blowing off the runway. Pulling the nose up, up, up, stalled her out, the main gear hitting as she sank. Slowly, the useless nosewheel finally touched ground and we went sailing over the grass. The firemen were there, anxious hoses in hand, apparently disappointed that we had not cartwheeled into the fires of hell. I apologized for that. And they towed us off.

A glimpse of glory? Close to it, I would guess. Made me wonder what glory would really look like—some patients had seen a city of golden streets and some had seen something like the Garden of Eden with beautiful surroundings. Some had seen both. Perhaps the reason I wondered was because I had been intrigued by the message in Genesis 3:22–24 that Eden had never been destroyed, merely hidden from the eyes of undeserving man:

> Then the LORD God said, "Behold, the man has become like one of Us, to know good and evil. And now, lest he put out his hand and take also of the tree of life, and eat, and live forever"—therefore the LORD God . . . drove out the man; and He placed cherubim at the east of the garden of Eden, and a flaming sword which turned every way, to guard the way to the tree of life.

The cherubim thus concealed the way to the tree of life so that man could not find it. Could it still be there? Would it still be possible to find our way to the tree of life? Or was this just a crazy notion? To me, the story of the prodigal son offers a clue.

You remember, the story was Jesus' parable of the rebelling son who took his inheritance and ran away to find the good life. When the money was wasted in revelry and good times, a famine swept the land and the son became desperately hungry. The only food or work he could find was feeding pigs. So scarce was food that he ate the pods that he fed the pigs. He was aware that he was no better off than the swine. Money, self-esteem, and self-importance disappeared.

Realizing a grave error, the son finally took responsibility and took up his own cross. He repented. He admitted he was wrong.

Self-esteem and self-glory were replaced by embarrassment and shame. He humbled himself and returned to his father to ask forgiveness. He said to himself: "I will get up and go to my father, and will say to him, 'Father, I have sinned against heaven, and in your sight; I am no longer worthy to be called your son; make me as one of your hired men.' "

"But while he was still a long way off," Jesus continued, "his father saw him, and felt compassion for him, and ran and embraced him, and kissed him."

It is a beautiful story. The father proceeded to have him bathed, clothed, a ring placed on his finger and a great welcoming party was prepared to introduce his refound son to a newfound life. " 'For this my son was dead and is alive again; he was lost and is found.' And they began to be merry" (Luke 15:24).

"Likewise, . . ." Jesus said, "there is joy in the presence of the angels of God over one sinner who repents" (v. 10) and this is the simple story of the Good News, and the Good News is simply finding the Tree of Life again. It has always been there. And Christ is the way. The entrance to the Garden. The everlasting life because he is the Tree of Life. That simple.

"Behold, I stand at the door and knock," Jesus says today. "If anyone hears My voice and opens the door, I will come in to him and dine with him, and he with Me" (Rev. 3:20). He specifically said he *would come in* if you open the door and invite him in where he can tell you what to do with your life. Take Jesus at his word. He cannot lie and you cannot lose. You've made him an offer he cannot refuse.

A final thought. Man has been the only creature made aware that he must die, and yet he refuses to believe it until the last moment when he's usually unprepared. So today is the day to be prepared. If you feel you want to open the door of your heart right now and invite Him in, just say this simple prayer with me:

Lord Jesus, I know that you are the only Son of God and I have been hiding from you. But now I come to you unclean and dirty, just as I am, but confessing and turning from my wrongdoing. You said if I would confess my sins that you would be faithful and righteous to forgive my sins and to cleanse me from all unrighteousness.

Lord Jesus, today I heard you knocking at the door of my

life. You promised you would come into my life if I opened the door. Now I open the door and dedicate my life to you. Show me what you want me to do. In Jesus' name, Amen.

If you said this prayer, you have just made the greatest decision of your life. Live or die, you cannot lose. Now you finally know the answer to the baffling question, is it safe to die? If you belong to Jesus Christ, you can bet your life on it!

APPENDIX:

Standard Method of Cardiopulmonary Resuscitation

First, you should enroll for a complete instruction course with your local Heart Association or Red Cross. The number will be listed in your telephone directory. Second, continue to rehearse your technique as you would your golf swing, since the need may arise at any time.

Step one, call or send for help (911, etc.).

Step two, shake and shout to determine consciousness. Patient should be on a firm surface. Observe if patient is breathing.

Step three, if victim is not breathing, tilt the victim's head upwards (chin toward the ceiling) to open the airway. Pinch off his nostrils with your fingers (to direct your breath into his lungs) and give two full breaths, mouth-to-mouth. His chest will rise if the airway is not obstructed.

Step four, feel for the neck pulse next to the Adam's apple. If no pulse, immediately simulate the heartbeat by compressing rhythmically downward over the lower breast bone with superimposed hands, elbows straight. Depress about two inches vertically at a smooth rate of about eighty compressions per minute. (Experimental modifications not yet recommended for routine use include interposed abdominal compressions, vest CPR, and compression/decompression mechanisms).

Step five, continue this cycle of events until help arrives, interrupting for two full breaths after every fifteen compressions.

Qualified help will intubate at once if not breathing (place access tube into windpipe), obtain IV access (lifelines for fluids started in the vein), electrically defibrillate if necessary, and initiate advanced cardiac life support routine.

NOTES

Preface
1. George Gallup initially estimated eight million near-death experiences in 1982 when he published *Adventures in Immortality* through McGraw-Hill in New York.

Chapter 2
1. Compare Deuteronomy 18:20–22, Leviticus 20:27, Jeremiah 28:15.

Chapter 3
1. *Life Magazine,* March 1992, 65.
2. *Life Magazine,* March 1992, 66.
3. *Beyond the Line,* Barton-Prinz Productions, Vancouver, B.C., 1992.
4. *Maclean's Newsmagazine,* 20 April 1992, 38.
5. *Life Magazine,* March 1992, 71.
6. *Life Magazine,* March 1992, 68; Diane Komp excerpt taken from the book, *A Window to Heaven* by Diane M. Komp, Ph.D. Copyright © 1992 by Diane Komp. Used by permission of Zondervan Publishing House, 28.
7. *Life Magazine,* March 1992.
8. *Maclean's Newsmagazine,* 20 April 1992, 37.
9. James Johnson and David Balsiger, *Beyond Defeat* (New York: Doubleday, 1978) as quoted in *Life Magazine,* March 1992, 70.

Chapter 4
1. *U.S. News and World Report,* November 1990.
2. *Newsweek,* 6 January 1992, 39.
3. *U.S. News and World Report,* 25 March 1991, 60.
4. *U.S. News and World Report,* 25 March 1991, 57.
5. Carl G. Johnson, *Hell, You Say?* (Newton: Timothy Books, 1974), ix.

6. Demetria Kalodimos, "A Glimpse of Glory," NBC-TV Nashville, Tennessee, September/October 1992.

7. Raymond A. Moody, *The Light Beyond: New Explorations by the Author of Life After Life* (New York: Bantam, 1989), 27.

8. Robert Kastenbaum, *Is There Life After Death?* (New York: Prentice Hall, 1984) 25, citing G. A. Garfield in Kastenbaum, ed., *Between Life and Death* (New York: Spring Publishers, 1979), 54–55.

9. S. B. Shaw, *The Dying Testimonies* (Noblesville: Newby Book Room, 1969), 49, 66, 119, 143, 214.

10. Marvin Ford, *On the Other Side* (Plainfield: Logos International, 1978), 93–94.

11. Jean-Baptiste Delacour, *Glimpses of the Beyond,* trans. E. B. Garside (New York: Delacorte Press, 1974), 22–25.

12. Stephen Board, "Light at the End of the Tunnel," *Eternity,* July 1977, 13–17.

13. Maurice Rawlings, *Beyond Death's Door* (Nashville: Thomas Nelson, 1978), 91–93.

14. Karlis Osis, and E. Haraldsson, *At the Hour of Death,* (New York: Avon Books, 1977), 90–91.

Chapter 5

1. John Ankerberg and John Weldon, *The Facts on Life after Death,* (Eugene: Harvest House Publishers, 1992), 34–35.

2. Gary R. Habermas, and J. P. Moreland, *Immortality: The Other Side of Death* (Nashville: Thomas Nelson Publishers, 1992), 157.

3. Habermas and Moreland, *Immortality*, 41.

4. John White, "What the Dying See," *Psychic,* September/October 1976, 40.

5. Karlis Osis, *Deathbed Observations by Physicians and Nurses* (Parapsychology Foundation, 1961), 30.

6. Basil Tyson, *UFOs: Satanic Terror* (Alberta: Horizon House Publishers, 1977), 101.

7. Robert Monroe, *Journeys Out of the Body,* (Garden City: Doubleday, Anchor Books), 138–39.

8. Lennie Kronisch, "Elisabeth Kubler-Ross: Messenger of Love," *Yoga Journal,* November/December 1976, 20.

9. Raymond Moody Jr., *Life After Life* (New York: Bantam, 1975), 140.

10. Raymond Moody Jr., *Reflections on Life After Life* (New York: Bantam, 1977), 18–19.

11. John Dart, "Heaven or Hell—Not the Burning Question It Used to Be," *Dallas Times Herald,* 2 September 1978, 17.

12. F. W. H. Myers, *Human Personality and Its Survival of Bodily Death* (Hyde Park: University Books, 1961), 212–217.

13. According to her daughter, Rebecca Love developed severe shock from cortisone given to treat an allergic rash. As consciousness faded, "everything turned black, and then I floated toward a wonderful, heavenly light." The description reminded Rebecca of her own mother's deathbed, whose face was said to glow, her eyes emitting a shining light, the scene so vivid to Jack, her errant son, that he experienced a life-turning conversion.

Chapter 6

1. Dina Ingber, "Visions of an Afterlife," *Science Digest,* vol. 89, no. 1, January/February 1981, 142.

2. Morse, *Closer to the Light,* 191–192.

3. Habermas and Moreland, *Immortality, the Other Side of Death,* 75.

4. Habermas and Moreland, *Immortality,* 94.

5. *U.S. News and World Report,* 25 March 1991, 57.

6. Albert Heim, "Uber den Tod durch Absturz," *Jb. Schweiz. Alpendub,* quoted in General Psychopathology, trans. Karl Jaspers (Manchester: University Press, 1963).

7. Kerby Anderson, *Life, Death and Beyond,* (Grand Rapids: Zondervan, 1980), 88.

8. K. Osis, and E. Haraldsson, *At the Hour of Death* (New York: Avon Books, 1977), 78.

9. Osis and Haraldsson, *At the Hour of Death,* 36–37.

10. S. B. Shaw, *The Dying Testimonies* (Noblesville: Newby Book Room, 1969), 204–205.

11. M. C. Pritchard, *Pebbles from the Brink* (Ottawa: Holiness Movement Print, 1913), 17.

12. Pritchard, *Pebbles,* 137.

13. Pritchard, *Pebbles,* 111.

14. Pritchard, *Pebbles,* 133.

15. John Myers, *Voices from the Edge of Eternity* (Old Tappan: Fleming Revell, 1968), 247–248.

16. Myers, *Voices,* 249.

17. Kenneth Ring, *Heading Toward Omega* (New York: William Morrow, 1984), 44.

18. Ring, *Heading Toward Omega*, 48.

19. Shaw, *Dying Testimonies* (Noblesville: Newby Book Room, 1969), 16.

20. Shaw, *Dying Testimonies*, 35–36.

21. Shaw, *Dying Testimonies*, 202.

22. Pritchard, *Pebbles*, 27.

23. Shaw, *Dying Testimonies*, 47–48.

24. Ring, *Heading Toward Omega*, 44–45.

25. Moody, *Reflections*, 46.

26. Moody, *Reflections*, 44.

27. P. M. H. Atwater, *Coming Back to Life*, (New York: Dodd, Mead & Company, 1988), 13.

28. Atwater, *Coming Back to Life*, 18–19.

29. Atwater, *Coming Back to Life*, 18.

30. Atwater, *Coming Back to Life*, 19.

31. Ring, *Heading Toward Omega*, 19.

32. *Los Angeles Times*, 4 October 1977.

33. *Los Angeles Times*, 28 September 1974.

Chapter 7

1. Tal Brooke, *When the World Will Be as One* (Eugene: Harvest House, 1989), 35.

2. Brooke, *When the World*, 33.

3. Brooke, *When the World*, 44–47.

4. Brooke, *When the World*, 48.

5. Michael Sabom, *Recollections of Death*, (New York: Harper and Row, 1982), 196–200.

6. Habermas and Moreland, *Immortality*, 124.

7. Brooke, *When the World*, 51.

8. Morse, *Closer to the Light*, 191.

9. Sacks, *M.D. Magazine*, February 1991.

10. Johanna Michaelsen, *The Beautiful Side of Evil* (Eugene: Harvest House, 1982), 74–75.

11. Michaelsen, *The Beautiful Side of Evil*, 77.

12. Carl G. Jung, *Memories, Dreams, Reflections* (New York: Vintage Books, 1965), 315.

13. Nandor Fodor, *Freud, Jung, and Occultism*, (New Hyde Park: University Books, 1971), 105.

14. Jung, *Memories,* 190–193.

15. Carl G. Jung, *Psychology and the Occult,* trans. R. F. C. Hull, (Princeton: Princeton University Press, 1977), ix.

16. Paul J. Stern, *C. G. Jung, The Haunted Prophet* (New York: Dell, 1976), 122–123.

Chapter 8

1. Fodor, *Freud, Jung, and Occultism,* 183–184.

2. John Ankerberg and John Weldon, *Cult Watch* (Eugene: Harvest House, 1991), 195–198.

3. Pierre Teilhard de Chardin, *The Phenomenon of Man* (New York: Harper and Brothers, 1959), 294, 306, 308.

4. Phillip Johnson, *Darwin on Trial* (Washington: Regnery Gateway, 1991), 129, 175.

5. Ring, *Heading Toward Omega,* 229, 231.

6. Ring, *Heading Toward Omega,* 226.

7. R. D. Scott, *Transcendental Misconceptions* (San Diego: Beta Books, 1978), 127–129.

8. Helena P. Blavatsky, *The Secret Doctrine,* vol. 3 (Los Angeles: Theosophy Co., 1925), 246.

9. Brooke, *When the World,* 175–177.

10. David Spangler, *Reflections on the Christ* (Scotland: Findhorn Community Press, 1978), 74.

11. Erwin Lutzer and John DeVries, *New Age* (Wheaton: Victor Books, 1989), 14–15.

12. Bill Bright, Tract from Campus Crusade for Christ International, 1965.

13. Ankerberg and Weldon, *Cult Watch,* 155.

Chapter 9

1. Uma Silbey, *The Complete Crystal Guidebook: A Practical Path to Personal Power, Self-Development and Healing Using Quartz Crystals* (New York: Bantam, 1987), 74.

2. Shirley MacLaine, "Out on a Limb," ABC-TV miniseries, January 1987.

3. David Spangler, *Reflections on the Christ,* 40, 44.

4. Constance Cumbey, *The Hidden Dangers of the Rainbow* (Shreveport: Huntington House, 1983), 139–141.

5. Alice A. Bailey, *The Externalization of the Hierarchy* (New York: Lucis Publishing Company, 1957), 190–191.

6. Marilyn Ferguson, *The Aquarian Conspiracy: Personal and Social Transformation in the 1980s* (Los Angeles: J. P. Tarcher, 1980), 369–370.

7. Ferguson, *The Aquarian Conspiracy*, 370.

8. Ferguson, *The Aquarian Conspiracy*, 374.

9. *The Golden Book of the Theosophical Society* (1925), 63–64.

10. Alice Bailey, *The Reappearance of the Christ* (New York: Lucis Publishing Company, 1948, 1976, 9th printing 1979), 81.

11. Cumbey, *Hidden Dangers,* 65–66.

12. Nina Easton, "Shirley MacLaine's Mysticism for the Masses," *The Los Angeles Times Magazine,* 6 September 1987, 8, 33.

13. Brooks Alexander, "Theology From the Twilight Zone," *Christianity Today,* 18 September 1987, 22.

14. Ankerberg and Weldon, *Cult Watch,* 135–136.

15. Ferguson, *The Aquarian Conspiracy,* 295, 288.

16. Ferguson, *The Aquarian Conspiracy,* 280–281.

17. Robert Muller, *New Genesis: Shaping A Global Spirituality* (Garden City: Image Books, 1984), 152.

18. Beverly Galyean, *Language from Within* (Longbeach: 1976), 91, as told by Dave Hunt in *Peace, Prosperity, and the Coming Holocaust* (Eugene: Harvest House, 1983), 78.

19. "New Age Plan for the 1990's," Audiotape by the Kathleen Hayes Ministries.

20. Eric Buehrer, *The New Age Masquerade,* (Brentwood: Wolgemuth and Hyatt, 1990), 96–97.

21. William Hewitt, *Beyond Hypnosis: A Program for Developing Your Psychic and Healing Power* (St. Paul: Llewellyn Publication, 1990), 154.

22. Buehrer, *New Age Masquerade,* 101.

23. Hunt, *Seduction of Christianity,* 200–201.

24. Hunt, *Seduction of Christianity,* 203, 205.

25. Morton Kelsey, *Transcend: A Guide to the Spiritual Quest* (New York: Crossroad, 1985), 23–32, 81, 136.

26. Norman Vincent Peale, "No More Stress or Tension," *Plus: The Magazine of Positive Thinking,* May 1986, 22–23.

27. Reed Jolley, "Language is the Medium," *Eternity Magazine,* May 1986, 43.

28. *Newsweek,* 11 April 1990.

29. *Newsweek,* 11 April 1990, 48.

30. *Newsweek,* 11 April 1990, 52.

31. *USA Today,* 6 November 1991.
32. *USA Today,* August 1991.
33. *USA Today,* 5 August 1991.
34. *USA Today,* 31 July 1991, 2A.
35. *Chattanooga News-Free Press,* 22 September 1991.
36. *Medical Economics,* 24 December 1990.
37. *Chattanooga News-Free Press,* 14 October 1991.
38. *Chatanooga News-Free Press*, 25 April 1992, 1073–1074.

Chapter 10
1. *Newsweek,* 12 October 1992.
2. Phillip Johnson, *Darwin on Trial,* (Washington: Regnery Gateway Publishers, 1991), 52 ff.
3. Leroy Hood, "The Human Genome Initiative." Opening Plenary Address given at the 40th Annual Meeting of the American College of Cardiology, Atlanta, 4 March 1991.
4. Earl Ubell, *Parade Magazine,* 31 March 1991.

Chapter 11
1. John Ankerberg, and John Weldon, *The Facts on UFO's* (Eugene: Harvest House, 1992), 5, 36.
2. Richard Haines, *Journal of Scientific Exploration,* vol. 1, no. 2, 1987.
3. Kenneth Ring, *The Omega Project,* (New York: William Morrow and Company, 1992), 236.
4. Carl Sagan, "What's Really Going On?" *Parade Magazine,* 7 March 1993, 6.
5. Ring, *Omega Project,* 239, 242–244, 236–237.
6. Ring, *Omega Project*, 51, 164.
7. Ring, *Omega Project*, 68, 72, 79, 84.
8. Ring, *Omega Project*, 177.
9. Jacques Vallee, *Confrontations: A Scientist's Search for Alien Contact* (New York: Ballantine, 1991), 15.
10. David M. Jacobs, "Abductions and the ET Hypothesis," *MUFON,* 1988 *International Symposium Proceedings: Abductions and the E.T. Hypothesis*, 87.
11. John A. Keel, *UFOs: Operation Trojan Horse* (New York: Putnam's, 1970), 220.
12. Berthold Schwartz, *Canadian UFO Report,* vol. 1, no. 8, Fall 1970.

13. Bernard Finch, "Beware the Saucers," *Flying Saucer Review,* vol. 12, no. 1, 5.

14. Charles Bowen, "Mail Bag," *Flying Saucer Review,* vol. 19, no. 5, 27.

15. Brad Steiger, *Flying Saucers Are Hostile* (New York: Award, 1976), 8.

16. Jerome Clark, "Why UFOs Are Hostile," *Flying Saucer Review,* vol. 13, no. 6, 19.

17. Vallee, *Confrontations,* 216–218.

18. Kenneth Ring, "A Transpersonal View of Consciousness: A Mapping of Farther Regions of Inner Space," *Journal of Transpersonal Psychology,* 1974, no. 2, 142–143, 150.

19. Ankerberg, and Weldon, *UFOs,* 43.

20. Frank Peretti, *Focus on the Family* Audiotapes by James Dobson.

21. John Ankerberg video tapes, "The Founding Fathers," Chattanooga, Tennessee, and Barton Wallbuilders, Inc., Aledo, Texas, September 1992.

22. John Ankerberg video tapes.

23. John Ankerberg video tapes.

24. John Ankerberg video tapes.

25. John Ankerberg video tapes.

ABOUT THE AUTHOR

Dr. Maurice Rawlings, specialist in cardiovascular diseases at the Diagnostic Center and the area hospitals of Chattanooga, graduated with honors from the George Washington University Medical School. He served in both the Army and the Navy and became chief of cardiology at the 97th General Hospital in Frankfurt, Germany. He then was promoted to personal physician at the Pentagon for the Joint Chiefs of Staff, which included Generals Marshall, Bradley, Patton, and Dwight Eisenhower before he became president of the United States.

In civilian life Dr. Rawlings was appointed to the National Teaching Faculty of the American Heart Association, specializing in teaching methods for the retrieval of patients from sudden death. He taught at various medical schools and hospitals and conducted courses for doctors and nurses in many countries. Dr. Rawlings is clinical assistant professor of medicine for the University of Tennessee at Chattanooga, a member of the International Committee on Cardiovascular Diseases, a past governor for the American College of Cardiology for the state of Tennessee, founder of the area's Regional Emergency Medical Services Council, faculty instructor for the Advanced Cardiac Life Support programs, and Fellow of the American College of Physicians, the College of Cardiology, and the College of Chest Physicians. In addition, he has authored three previous books and written several articles on heart disease for national medical journals.

Dr. Rawlings and his wife, Martha, are parents of five children and have eleven grandchildren. Dr. Rawlings is also a multi-engine instrument pilot, spends time on his north Georgia farm that encompasses a small lake, likes water skiing, and still teaches medicine but recently semi-retired "to smell the roses." Disappointed that "some of the roses don't smell so good," Dr. Rawlings has been looking for a means to make life's roses smell a lot better, and will try to share his findings with his readers.